Waste Prevention Policy and Behaviour

As prosperity levels rise, so too does the number of products and services being consumed. For policy makers in waste management facing a growing challenge, it is vital to understand the complex relationship between waste prevention policies and individual behaviour regarding waste generation. This book examines that interplay, taking a close look at the role of motivation, difficulties, values and constraints.

The first part of the book explores the theoretical framework, policy, barriers and facilitators for waste prevention behaviour. The second part presents in-depth case studies from three cities (São Paulo, Sheffield and Tokyo) examining the contextual factors, behavioural variations among them and the role of motivation and constraints in their populations. The book provides a detailed picture of how waste prevention policies enter the private, domestic sphere, offering insights for generating behavioural change at the household level and thus moving larger communities towards sustainable waste management.

The book will be of interest to students and researchers in the areas of environmental policy, management, sociology, psychology, geography, technology and waste studies.

Ana Paula Bortoleto is an Assistant Professor at the Faculty of Civil Engineering at the State University of Campinas, Brazil.

T0393977

Routledge Studies in Waste Management and Policy

Waste Prevention Policy and Behaviour
New approaches to reducing waste generation and its environmental impacts
Ana Paula Bortoleto

Waste Prevention Policy and Behaviour

New approaches to reducing waste
generation and its environmental impacts

Ana Paula Bortoleto

LONDON AND NEW YORK

First published 2015
by Routledge

2 Park Square, Milton Park, Abingdon, Oxon OX14 4RN
711 Third Avenue, New York, NY 10017, USA

Routledge is an imprint of the Taylor & Francis Group, an informa business

First issued in paperback 2016

British Library Cataloguing in Publication Data
A catalogue record for this book is available from the British Library

Library of Congress Cataloging in Publication Data
Bortoleto, Ana Paula.
Waste prevention policy and behaviour : new approaches to reducing
waste generation and its environmental impacts / Ana Paula Bortoleto.
    pages cm
    1. Waste minimization. I. Title.
    TD793.9.B67 2015
    363.7´0561–dc23   2014012112

ISBN 978-0-415-73758-6 (hbk)
ISBN 978-1-138-22599-2 (pbk)

Typeset in Goudy
by HWA Text and Data Management, London

To my family

Contents

Figures

Tables

Preface

As Tom Jobim once wrote 'Tristeza não tem fim, felicidade sim …' (Sadness has no end, happiness yes), avoiding pain and suffering is the wish that follows us everywhere we go. But what is truly happiness? How do we deal with it? Although philosophy has been searching for its meaning since the ancient Greeks, there are still more questions than answers. In the twenty-first century, we live divided between enlightened and materialistic happiness. Nowadays, our culture involves mainly the acquisition of things linked to the culture of status. This makes us believe that buying a certain car will give us freedom or that youth is inside the new beauty product. This materialistic happiness comes from the emptiness created by the things we do not have and we are told they are necessary for living. The list of things needed for us to survive is getting bigger and bigger. And the result of this is waste. A mountain of things that we thought we needed and, after a brief space of time, fail to give us the promised happiness. Do not be confused; this book is indeed about waste prevention policies. But how can I write about this urgent topic without acknowledging the importance of why waste is created in the first place? Waste prevention is not only about waste and how to decrease its generation. It is about changing how we deal with waste, from something that needs to be burnt or buried to something resourceful that can be reused or repaired. It is thinking about what we consume and how we perceive the value of these things. Waste managers need to start addressing these questions, nevertheless, in an effective way. Technology alone is not capable of running at the same speed that waste is generated. It cannot treat this amount of waste or even tackle its environmental impacts. How can we achieve a sustainable society without understanding all facets of the problem? This book aims to open this door showing how important it is to comprehend human behaviour prior to the implementation of any waste prevention programme. More importantly, how it is possible to merge this knowledge for future research not only in waste prevention policies but also in technology innovation for waste management. As a former Marie Curie Fellow, and an admirer of this amazing researcher, I would like to use one of her quotes to explain what is urgent for us to achieve in waste prevention policies:

You cannot hope to build a better world without improving the individuals. To that end, each of us must work for our own improvement and, at the same time, share a general responsibility for all humanity, our particular duty being to aid those to whom we think can be most useful.

(Marie Curie, physicist 1867–1934)

Only when we adopt this approach to waste management will we be able to bring the situation under control.

Acknowledgements

My interest on waste started when I was an undergraduate looking for a research topic for my first scientific project. In 2001, waste issues were beginning to challenge Brazilian local governments and, as an engineering student, it seemed logical to me that this was a problem which could be solved with the right technology and management. Recycling was promised at that time and I decided to study how the university's hospital could improve their recycling rate to decrease the costs of waste management. After securing financial support, I started accounting the materials used in one of the hospital wards and also searching through the non-hazardous waste collected in plastic bags. My first week opening the bags would be the last one. Inside the plastic bags were food leftovers, office paper, plastics, beverage cans, and, to my surprise, medical waste contaminated with patients' blood. Because of the obvious risks, I was not allowed to open the bags anymore but this stimulated my interest in finding out why the waste was being mixed despite strong regulations. For this day on, I was talking to the nurses, the cleaning staff and anyone could give me any information as well as taking pictures and documenting everything. At the end, doctors, nurses, cleaning and office staff were mixing the waste mainly because of the distribution of the waste bins in the ward. In the end, I was able to understand that recycling had its downside but also that waste was the linking factor among all those actors. I am grateful to my dedicated supervisor, Dr Egle Novaes Teixeira for this opportunity which stimulated my passion for researching this topic and also to Professor Paulo Franco Barbosa, who opened the doors of the scientific world as his student on the former PET programme.

My adventure as a researcher led me to the opposite side of the world, Japan, my second home. I lived in Tokyo for almost six years and there I discovered that an engineer could and should be a social scientist not only looking for technological improvements but also for a better life for the ordinary citizen. The Japanese culture gave me a different perspective of our planet and how we live our daily lives. And for that, I am forever grateful to my supervisors Professor Keisuke Hanaki and Dr Kiyo Kurusi. They supported me throughout my masters and PhD research with their wisdom and perseverance and allowed me to work in my own way. Their ideas and constructive observations were most precious and, without their advice, I would not be here, writing this book. One simply could not wish for better or friendlier supervisors. I also want to thank Professor Yukio Hirose for his valuable comments on my thesis and for his kindness in listening to my questions. My sincere gratitude goes to Professor Maria Cecilia Loschiavo dos Santos, who not only opened the doors for me at the University of São Paulo but also opened my eyes to the fragile human side of our waste management system, the scavengers. The fruits of my PhD thesis led me to the United Kingdom, more precisely to Sheffield to work, for the first time, with human geographies. I am immensely grateful to Professor Nicky Gregson and Dr Matt Watson who gave me a leap of faith and accepted me to work with them. I also want to thank Professor Jean Grugel and Ms Gill Johnson for their support while was working at the University of Sheffield.

Over the last few years, many dedicated and knowledgeable researchers in Germany have helped me understand what waste actually is through their perspectives. At the Otto-von-Guericke University Magdeburg, my deepest gratitude goes to Professor Florian Kaiser who welcomed me to their department and graciously answered my numerous questions and discussed my research for such long hours. I would like to extend my gratitude to Dr Siegmar Otto, one of the co-authors of this book and a great listener of my several research doubts. At the Max-Planck Institute for Human Development, my sincere appreciation goes to Dr Konstantinos Katsikopoulos who gave me the opportunity to work with this great team of researchers at ABC. Thanks go as well to Dr Mirta Galesic and Astrid Krausse for the valuable insights and their direct contribution to this book. I feel fortunate for so many people showing interest in my research, and thank them all for what they have given me. Their contributions were substantial, because it has not always been easy for me with a subject weighing heavily on me.

In particular I would like to show my appreciation of the European Commission through the Marie Curie Actions which provided me with an invaluable fellowship (2011–2012) that allowed this book project to grow roots. That research fellowship took me to the UK and to the Department of Geography in the University of Sheffield. But most importantly, an enormous debt of gratitude goes to the thousands of people across the globe who volunteered to join me on this research. They responded to the questionnaires, welcomed my research and shared their opinions and stories with me. And I also thank the helpful people at Routledge who have done their bit to get the book right.

I owe my deepest gratitude to my beloved family who listened to and understood my concerns and fears for the future and whose understanding right from the beginning has been of great value throughout much of the writing. They gave me much more than that and I only hope that, by the time these words are printed, I shall have thought of an adequate way to thank them.

Ana Paula Bortoleto

2014

1 An introduction to the book

This book is for those readers with some interest in trash or rubbish or, more politely, waste and are concerned about contemporary threats to environmental and social well-being posed by the way humans deal with waste. Some brief observations are enough to show that waste management impacts the environment on every level, from local to global. Human population growth and human activities are rapidly increasing waste generation both in developed and developing nations. Recent quantitative assessments of waste production in urban areas give a sobering picture: in a new report on municipal solid waste, the World Bank (Hoornweg & Bhada-Tata 2012) found that the world's cities currently generate around 1.3 billion tonnes of waste a year, or 1.2 kg per city-dweller per day, nearly half of which comes from OECD countries. That is predicted to rise to 2.2 billion tonnes by 2025, or 1.4 kg per person per day. The Bank estimates China's urbanites will throw away 1.4 billion tonnes in 2025, up from 520 million tonnes today. By contrast, America's urban rubbish pile will increase from 620 million tonnes to 700 million tonnes. Many people hope that technology will solve this problem, but the reality is that while looking for technology efficiency and other innovations might feel more comfortable, it is unlikely they can offer a sustainable solution. While technology will certainly be needed to reverse environmental impacts, just as the technological revolution was needed to produce it, the impacts that threaten our society and environment are too enormous and complex to be solved by technological innovation alone. Although human beings have always produced waste (and will continue to do so), the pace and scale of the current waste production knows no precedent. To sum up, betting on the smaller odds of technology efficiency, the worse the problems become, the more difficult it will be to find a real solution. More importantly, confining waste-management research to engineering and natural sciences misses the primary cause of the current rise of waste generation: human behaviour. It is critical to examine the sociological and psychological dimensions of this problem, because waste problems are deeply related to consumption and, therefore, are caused by human behaviour relating to our beliefs, values, social interactions and the context of where we are living. It is human behaviour that determines how efficient a waste prevention programme will be. Waste problems are literally threatening people's lives not only in developing countries but also in developed countries. The incidence of homelessness is everywhere, perhaps more than at any time in human history. This is an acute issue which has created a survivalist informal economy based on the collection and selling of recyclable wastes, i.e. the waste from our throwaway society. Yet, most people proceed as though their normal lives will continue, and the threat coexists peacefully with the vague sense of pessimism about the future. Thus, solutions for waste generation will have to start through waste prevention, and that will require more than technological answers. We will have to change our way of life, the ways we behave, how we see ourselves, how we experience our relationship with nature, and even, how we understand consumption.

I was driven to write this book not only by the challenge of waste issues, which links all of us, but also by the perspective that engineering alone will not be successful in solving them regardless of all the effort. Despite being recognised as a sustainable approach to waste management, waste prevention is still not effective in addressing waste generation issues. Studies suggest that waste is a dynamic system where materials move in and out in many different ways apart from kerbside collections. Waste prevention occurs before a product is recognised as waste. If we focus on how waste is produced, our attention will be drawn away from the waste bin and concentrated on human behaviour. Waste is created through the recognition of value, i.e. everything that comes to the end of its life will require a decision. As our everyday life has rapidly changed throughout the last decades, so has this process of defining what waste is. Essentially, we can choose to reduce our waste by not buying certain products, by reusing what we have bought or by participating in recycling programmes. However, by far, our most favoured option is still to throw our waste into a dustbin (or plastic bags). As the major direct and indirect producers of waste, we, as householders, have the power to decide whether to participate in waste prevention programmes on a regular basis. And that is the main challenge of waste prevention programmes: how to stimulate householders to buy less, reuse as much as they can and only throw away what can be recycled, composted or incinerated to produce energy. Behaviour change is the cornerstone of waste prevention. And to promote this change, waste prevention research needs to be interdisciplinary. There are many other disciplines (e.g. psychology, sociology) that are relevant to waste issues and should be considered when designing waste prevention policies. Interdisciplinary research is still at best midway into effectively putting its resources at the disposal of decision makers working for a more sustainable waste-management policy. It is necessary and imperative to see a sea change in the work of 'waste researchers' towards addressing human behaviour, waste generation and consumption. Although this is a significant challenge, this is the kind of wake-up call I hope this book will provoke and inspire others.

Waste management and sustainable development

Our society is overloaded with challenges to mitigate global and local environmental impacts through sustainable development. In 1987, the

Brundtland Commission (WCED 1987) defined sustainable development as 'development that meets the needs of the present without compromising the ability of future generations to meet their own needs'. This ambitious statement integrates environmental, social and economic goals that need to be reached for its practical implementation. Donella H. Meadows (Meadows *et al.* 2004) wrote: '*sustainability is a new idea to many people, and many find it hard to understand. But all over the world there are people who have entered into the exercise of imagining and bringing into being a sustainable world. They see it as a world to move toward not reluctantly, but joyfully, not with a sense of sacrifice, but a sense of adventure. A sustainable world could be very much better than the one we live in today*'. The major challenge for researchers and policy makers today is the social facet of sustainability. It is increasingly recognised that environmental problems stem from the millions of choices that people make in everyday life. Until the majority of people change their attitudes and behaviour towards nature conservation, the search for a sustainable future for the planet will elude us. The implementation of any environmental policy needs ordinary people's active involvement and, as a result, it poses significant difficulties for policy makers. The prospect of using social understanding of environmental issues is one that has the potential to achieve sustainable development.

At the present time, humanity is involved in an unparalleled situation: we are turning ourselves into an urban species. Large cities, not villages and towns, are becoming our main habitat, and where the future of the biosphere will be determined. It is crucial to understand that our urban areas need to be socially just, participatory and economically viable while being environmentally sustainable. Agenda 21 (UNCED 1992), the main product of the Rio Earth Summit in 1992, states that dialogue about local sustainability policies must be undertaken with all citizens. The majority of the world's local authorities have initiated Agenda 21 programmes, but while many useful things have been said, very little has been done to implement them. Generating interest and action from individuals (i.e. increasing intrinsic motivation) is probably the most important and difficult aspect of sustainable development on the ground. Sustainable development at the local level must be implemented in a way which inspires people and which gives them a sense of ownership and direct involvement.

Urban areas take up 2 per cent of the Earth's surface, with 53 per cent of the world's population using 75 per cent of all natural resources and discharging similar amounts of waste (Girardet 1999). Much effort has gone into addressing the problems of scarcity, crime and the accumulation of social discontent. However, an issue which has received less thought is the large use of resources by urban areas and the resulting urban wastes. Chapter 17 of Agenda 21 sets out waste as a key problem in the search for sustainable development. In most metropolitan cities, there has been a substantial increase in waste produced per capita. There is confirmed evidence of absolute growth in material requirements, products used, and ultimate waste generation throughout the OECD area and beyond (OECD 2011). Further, waste composition has become even more complex and hazardous. Household waste is, traditionally, one of the hardest sources of waste to manage effectively. However, now, its composition has become more diverse in terms of raw materials and contamination and, increasingly more difficult to segregate and to recycle.

Environmental concerns over the management and disposal of waste can be divided into two major areas: conservation of resources and pollution of the environment. The consequences of these environmental impacts can be easily understood by using systems' theory. This theory assumes that everything exists as part of a larger system, in other words, that everything is connected. Accordingly, any urban area is a subsystem of the Nature's ecosystem and for that reason these subsystems need to work inside the limits of their parent system. Nature's own ecosystems have an essentially circular metabolism in which every output discharged by an organism also becomes an input to sustain the continuity of the whole living environment. On the other hand, the metabolism of most urban areas is essentially linear, with resources being injected through the urban system without much concern about their origin or about the destination of wastes, resulting in the discharge of vast amounts of waste products incompatible with natural systems. Inputs and outputs are largely unconnected. This linear model is unsustainable and undermines the overall ecological viability of urban systems, for it has the tendency to disrupt natural cycles. Waste is the most visible output by cities that keeps growing against the limits of cities' capacity to manage it in a sustainable way. A sustainable waste-management system must be environmentally effective, economically affordable and socially acceptable. Taking waste to landfill outside the cities is a misuse of both space and resources that could be used more beneficially. Many cities in developing and developed nations have chosen incineration as the most convenient solution for their waste-management systems. It reduces the volume of waste and energy recovery can be added as bonus. But incineration is far away from being the solution for urban waste problems. Incinerators compare badly with recycling in terms of energy conservation. Recycling is three to six times more energy efficient than incineration (Young *et al.* 1994). Some European cities are now investing in a combination of recycling and composting facilities with minimal incineration for waste products that cannot be further recycled.Nevertheless, not all waste materials can be recycled and, in general, it is unlikely that recycling alone will be able to contend with the ever-mounting waste challenge. As a consequence, concerns over conservation of resources have led to calls for, first, general reductions in the amount of waste generated (i.e. waste prevention), and second, for ways to recover the materials or energy from the waste, so they can be reused.

Waste prevention

Waste prevention has been regarded by policy makers and environmental agencies as the sustainable option to decrease the impact of waste generation. However, waste prevention is not only the result of administrative activities but also from the millions of choices that people make in daily life. Consequently, policy makers are now dealing with more and more complex ways to implement waste prevention. This has led progressively to a greater focus on the contribution that waste prevention can make to mitigate waste generation and, so, the costs and impacts from landfill sites, incineration plants and kerbside collection. During the early 1990s, many environmental agencies fully embraced 'source reduction' and 'pollution prevention' as overarching goals after realising the limits of downstream and end-of-pipe approaches. This meant, among other things, that as little waste as possible was to be finally disposed of, and this objective was to be achieved with priority focus on preventive efforts, generally followed by recycling and incineration. Based on these premises, waste prevention has been accepted as an essential waste-management policy for nearly five years in developed countries and, more recently, in developing countries (e.g. Brazil).

While it is true that the principle of waste prevention is universally accepted, the practice has a considerable distance to travel in achieving its full potential. Despite the groundswell of municipal governments and environmental agencies in tackling waste prevention policies, the amounts of waste being produced continue to rise across the globe. Neither the community nor the national targets set in the past have been satisfactorily met and many initiatives have been faced with considerable difficulties in maintaining individuals' engagement. The quantity of waste generated in the OECD area has risen strongly since 1980, and exceeded an estimated 650 million tonnes in 2009 (540 kg per capita) (OECD 2011). In most countries for which data are available, increased affluence, associated with economic growth, and changes in consumption patterns tend to generate higher rates of waste per capita. That is why waste prevention entails modified consumption patterns and modified production with concomitant reduction of waste generation in the upstream portions of the product lifecycle. The definition of waste prevention by the OECD (2000) emphasises this complexity, by highlighting that: (i) waste prevention is a multi-faceted construct, and is far from being a single homogeneous behaviour; (ii) individual preferences and choices can guide many different manifestations of waste prevention behaviour; (iii) waste prevention should be a collective and universal responsibility; and, (iv) the value of individual waste prevention actions can be judgemental and vary according to perspective.

Given its multi-faceted nature, waste prevention is often poorly understood by policy makers. Still, it is not clear to them how to promote relevant awareness and behavioural change of individuals' waste prevention behaviour. This can be attributed to several causes, but mainly because of the lack of comprehension of the psychological mechanisms which influence intrinsic motivation to engage in waste prevention behaviour. Individuals' decisions on waste prevention actions are often made under substantive uncertainty. They do not have all necessary information to fully comprehend the effects of their actions. Because of that, understanding how waste prevention behaviour occurs and how this affects individuals' engagement have become necessary in recent years.

Although people's behaviour has a huge impact on the environment and on the efficiency of waste-management systems, little research attention has been paid to this crucial issue. This book is about understanding the interface between waste prevention policies and individuals' behaviour. It aims to show the way people conceptualise waste problems by looking at the consequences of these perceptions for making decisions on waste prevention behaviour.

Priorities for waste prevention research

As it is evident that there has been a profound change in urban areas, city dwellers have also changed, with technologies now merged into our daily life and the experience of nature has become ever more distant. And this new urban society has a crucial role in waste prevention policies. In 2000, the OECD (2000) established a consensus understanding of waste prevention: 'waste prevention refers to three types of practical actions: strict avoidance, reduction at source, and product reuse. All societal actors including product manufacturers, businesses and institutions, and individuals and communities may express specific waste prevention behaviours. The practical value of waste prevention will be circumstance-specific and will depend on the characteristics of the material, product, waste stream or target audience in question'. Following this definition, the implementation of waste prevention policies requires ordinary people's active involvement.

Householders can make a number of decisions regarding what to do with the materials they have already purchased and even whether to purchase them. Essentially, they can choose to reduce their waste, reuse what they bought and participate in recycling schemes. However, the most favoured option is still to dispose of the rubbish produced into black plastic bags. For this reason, the challenge for waste prevention policies is how to intrinsically motivate the ordinary people to buy less, reuse as much of their consumed products as they can and only throw away what can be recycled, composted or incinerated to produce energy. They need to engage in these actions on a regular basis or a decrease in waste generation or even waste stabilisation will be difficult to achieve. In essence, a fundamental shift in individuals' behaviour is required if the targets of sustainable development are to be accomplished.

Although householders have a vital role to play in achieving sustainable waste management, the research for a 'social solution' has been the effort of relatively few academics and research institutions. One of the main arguments is that the relationship between awareness campaigns and actual behavioural change is complex and most of time weak and many different factors can interfere preventing a long-term effect in terms of waste reduction. In that case, the role of technology innovation and economic strategies has been seen by both academics and policy makers as the most feasible and acceptable option on which they should focus when confronting waste management issues. There is a compulsion to address the question of why campaigns for waste prevention and even recycling are not capable of intrinsically motivating the population. Further, why do certain people hold a positive attitude toward the environment, but do not act? It seems logical to understand why people partake in waste behaviours, how they act and what influences their decisions before trying to change those behaviours through informational campaigns. As will be outlined in more detail on the following chapters, behaviour change is only likely to result from tangible shifts in attitudes towards waste prevention within the context of a clear programme for a sustainable waste management system.Another research dilemma is how to evaluate waste prevention achievements or failures. Assessment is a difficult and complex task. It is not clear how to measure something that is not being produced in the first place. What can be measured? Unlike recycling, where the amount of recyclable waste can be quantified, waste prevention actions often result in the elimination of waste. The aim of monitoring and evaluating waste prevention is to assist policy makers and to ensure them that these programmes are being effective in promoting the required behavioural change.

It is crucial for researchers to develop reliable methods to monitor, measure, evaluate and compare waste prevention programmes and their benefits by assessing the effectiveness of actions aiming to promote behavioural change.

However, there has only been limited effort devoted to the establishment of evaluation tools, such as indicators and performance evaluation. So far, the developed methods have their own advantages and disadvantages and it is too difficult to decide which is best. Insufficient attention to this issue has likely contributed to a lack of understanding of, and investment in, waste prevention. In following chapters, this topic will be also discussed as an efficient form to engage individuals in waste prevention actions.

The organisation of this book

This book applies psychological theory and research to waste prevention. I think this endeavour is important because there is no solution for the rise of waste generation without considering human behaviour. This problem is mainly caused by the mismatch between how humans meet their needs and wants, and the natural order of our environment. Chapter 2 (the history of waste) outlines how waste management was developed and describes the current nature of our waste. Here, I argue, that, because of the rapid change of waste composition in the last century, waste management needs to be an integrated system. Chapter 3 is a revision of the origins of waste prevention policies, highlighting the problems of defining waste prevention per se and also its measuring and evaluation tools. Examples from different countries are also presented. Chapters 4 and 5 examine a particular perspective in psychology as applied to pro-environmental behaviour. Chapter 6 introduces the framework-model for waste prevention behaviour and the psychological theories and hypotheses assumed to shape the behaviour while Chapter 7 shows the application of the framework-model in three different areas of study (São Paulo, Sheffield and Tokyo) and analyses and compares the results. Chapter 8 introduces another approach to understand waste prevention behaviour which uses a measurement instrument in which pro-environmental motivation becomes tangible in individual actions. This chapter provides empirical examples (São Paulo and Sheffield) of such methodology to help verify people's motivation and the level of difficulty for all behaviours associated with waste prevention. The third part of the book introduces in Chapter 9 and 10 two new topics of research in waste prevention behaviour, respectively, rebound effect and bounded rationality. Finally, Chapter 11 summarises the insights from the whole book, compares the different approaches offering a broad perspective on the key concepts and analytical issues in the study of waste prevention behaviour and waste management. This chapter emphasises the importance of considering individuals' behaviour in waste management decisions. The utility of this approach will be emphasised and discussed in the context of previous research that has applied two different quantitative approaches. Finally, the chapter will end with a perspective on the future of waste prevention behaviour research and its implications on waste prevention policies.

References

Brundtland, G. (1987) *Our common future: Report of the 1987 World Commission on Environment and Development*. Oxford: Oxford University Press.

Girardet, H. (1999). *Creating sustainable cities in Schumacher briefings*. Chelsea Green Publishing, 1999 Devon, UK.

Hoornweg, D., & Bhada-Tata, P. (2012). *What a waste: a global review of solid waste management*. Urban Development Series: Knowledge Papers no. 15. Washington, DC: World Bank.

Meadows, D., Meadows, D., & Randers, J. (2004). *The limits to growth: The 30-year update*. London: Green Publishing.

OECD. (2000). OECD reference manual on strategic waste prevention. Paris: OECD.

OECD. (2011). 'Municipal waste'. In OECD Factbook 2011–2012. Economic, Environmental and Social Statistics. Paris: OECD.

UNCED. (1992). *Agenda 21 – action plan for the next century*. Endorsed at UNCED. Rio de Janeiro: UNCED.

Young, J. E., Sachs, A., & Ayres, E. (1994). *The next efficiency revolution: Creating a sustainable materials economy* (Vol. 121). Washington, DC: Worldwatch Institute.

Part I
Waste prevention policies

An overview

2   The history of waste

Few things are as certain in life as waste. It is something humans have always produced and have always had to figure out what to do with. In this sense, little is new about waste management problems. Our society produces more waste than ever before, but none of the ways we traditionally deal with it – landfilling, incineration, recycling, composting, biogas – are fundamentally different from what has been practised for thousands of years. For much of human history, people mostly just dropped their waste on the ground wherever it suited them. Many ancient cities (e.g. Rome) and even some modern ones literally rose above their waste by building on top of it. In Manhattan, for example, the ground level today is six to fifteen feet higher than it was in colonial times, as the result of enormous amounts of waste being used as filling for construction projects. The practice of using land from the sea in Tokyo and other coastal cities in Japan can be seen as a time-honoured exercise in waste management.

> *Waste:* 1. to use more of something than is necessary or useful; to give, say, use, etc.; 2. materials that are no longer needed for a particular process and therefore thrown away; 3. something good where it is not valued or used in the way that it should be; 4. to not make good or full use of something.
>
> (Hornby & Wehmeier 2000)

So, what is waste? Definitions of waste (as described above) invariably refer to lack of use or value or useless remains. Waste is a by-product of our society. Any human activity generates waste materials that are often discarded because we consider them useless. Physically, waste contains the same raw materials as are found in useful goods and it only differs by how we perceive its value. The lack of value in many situations can be related to the conditions of the product and the unknown composition of the waste. However, many of these wastes could be avoided or reused if they were managed properly and perceived in a different way by individuals and local authorities responsible for dealing with our waste.

Landfilling has never been the only means of handling our waste. Recycling and incineration were always important processes in preindustrial societies, just as they are today. Before the Industrial Revolution, recycling was done informally by scavengers who collected the materials people threw out and either burnt them for heat, reused them, or sold them. This is still what happens in some developing countries (e.g. Brazil, India). Food waste is another example of informal recycling. Historically, people have recycled food leftovers by feeding them to domestic animals. This practice is still quite common in rural areas as a moral justification of not wasting food. In large urban areas, it turned out to be incompatible with contemporary urban lifestyles and health standards. The use of food waste as animal feed can cause frequent outbreaks of disease. And to avoid that in the present day, many local authorities have been adopting home composting as the main option to reduce household food waste.

Then, what is new or different about the waste problem today? In the twenty-first century, individuals have different reasons for throwing things out – reasons that, if not entirely new, operate on an unprecedented scale. The total quantity of municipal waste now generated is certainly larger than it once was. More often, people, from both developed and developing countries, discard goods simply because they do not want them anymore. The continuous increase of technological innovation created a new generation of consumers eager to buy things that will be obsolete before they hit the market. Gilles Lipovetsky, a French philosopher, wrote: 'Today, we feel we have a natural right to new objects. We know nothing but the ethic of consumption' (Lipovetsky 2002). This phenomenon promotes a veneration of newness filling the waste bins with perfectly good things that are simply not new anymore. Household waste is only a part of this problem once we realise that most of the wastes generated in our society have moved upstream from households to industry. This has happened simply because the number of people consuming at high levels has increased since the Industrial Revolution. The world population continues to multiply and so does the proportion adopting hyper-consumption patterns. Needless to say, industrial waste often causes even worse environmental damage than municipal waste, and the quantities involved are considerably greater.

Thus, waste generation has become one of the most significant problems of our time because our way of life produces enormous amount of waste and most of us want to preserve our lifestyle while we also demand environmental protection and public health. In recent years, many countries have passed more laws dealing with waste generation and management than with any other topic on their legislative agendas. There is a growing concern from local authorities, industry and even citizens to search for means to reduce the growing amount of waste discarded every single day. Although this problem appears severe, it must be borne in mind that there is time to change, but this will depend on political will and more importantly, the will of the population.

A brief story of waste management

Historically, waste management has been an engineering function. The evolution of waste management has followed humankind's development and progress as it moved from an agricultural base, through the Industrial Revolution, and now to the information age (see Figure 2.1). The transition of the waste management movement revolved around two initiatives; first, the protection of public health and second a shift to the protection of the environment. Regulations, policies and methods were created as societies addressed the critical waste management needs that were associated with these transitions.

The Neolithic revolution was the first agricultural revolution and was the starting point for the transition from nomadic hunting and gathering communities and bands, to agriculture and settlement. The concept and need for waste management was not a key concern. Back then, waste was made up of food scraps, bones, broken household items and clay shards. It can be assumed that these people established sites for dumping to escape the nuisances of vermin, odour, and wild animals. What is known is that societies operated under a convenience mentality, lacking guidelines or regulations related to waste management. During this time frame, most households and small communities deposited waste within or just outside their villages based on group consensus. In antiquity, in many European and Asian cities, waste was collected in clay containers and hauled away. In many other areas, pits were used to collect waste and faeces which were emptied and cleaned periodically. The first recorded landfill sites were discovered in the Cretan palace complex, Knossos, in 3000 BC. Waste was placed in large pits and covered with earth at various levels.

The first documented solid waste management regulation occurred in the city of Athens, Greece, in 500 BC. At that time, the city of Athens organised the first municipal dump in the Western world where waste haulers were required to dispose of their waste at least 2 kilometres from the city walls. There are also records of regulations from 320 BC for the daily sweeping of Athens' streets by residents, even though at that time the link between hygiene and diseases, such as the plague, cholera and other epidemics was not known. The physician and Greek scholar Hippocrates (around 400 BC) was one of first to suspect the link between hygiene, contaminated water, mouldy food and epidemics. By 300 AD, there were 144 public toilets in Rome, with running water underneath to carry away the waste.

With the decline and fall of the Roman Empire and the turmoil of the Great Migration, much of the technological knowledge and the early hygiene of antiquity were lost for more than a thousand years. Roads, rivers, and ground water were contaminated by human and animal waste until the beginning of the nineteenth century. Not until the fifteenth century did city councils require the paving of streets, so that no one would have to wade through faeces and waste. While breathing city air meant a taste of freedom, it also smelled to no end. Under threat of stiff penalties, strict requirements for cleanliness were imposed upon the citizens. Rubbish bins were introduced at that time; the streets were cleaned regularly, animal carcasses were collected, and the possessions of people who had died from the plague were burnt.

During the late eighteenth and early nineteenth centuries, the world economies underwent a major shift from an agricultural base to an industrial one. The Industrial Revolution was a period when major changes in agriculture,

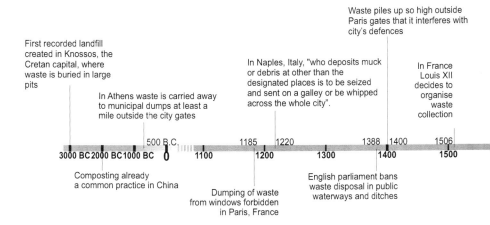

Figure 2.1 A history of waste management in a few selected anecdotes

Source: Bournay (2006)

manufacturing, and transport had a profound effect on socioeconomic and cultural conditions around the world. This shift had major impacts on the types and amounts of waste being generated. In the late nineteenth century, a breakthrough in waste management occurred due to the research of physicians and scientists like Louis Pasteur and Robert Koch. They demonstrated that the spread of diseases could be controlled by the presence or absence of public health measures. The link between public health measures and mortality was recognised and the weight of the scientific evidence silenced the opposition. It was during this century that waste management shifted toward a cleanliness and public health movement to eradicate diseases. Engineers and technicians were now challenged to develop the technologies that would alleviate and solve these problems. Among other measures, this led to the construction of the first waste incinerators in Britain in 1876, the so-called 'destructor', at Nottingham. Another 250 would be built during the next 30 years. Recycling of household waste was first introduced around the turn of the century. In 1898, the first manual material recovery facility was built in New York City, for processing the waste of over 115,000 residents. At the same time, similar facilities were operating in Berlin, Hamburg and Munich.

In the kitchens and parlours of British homes, waste avoidance was a highly developed art. In the Victorian house (Flanders 2004); nothing was thrown

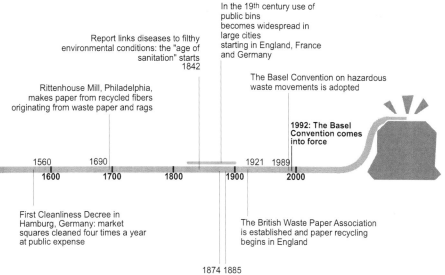

In the 19th century use of public bins becomes widespread in large cities starting in England, France and Germany

Report links diseases to filthy environmental conditions: the "age of sanitation" starts 1842

The Basel Convention on hazardous waste movements is adopted

Rittenhouse Mill, Philadelphia, makes paper from recycled fibers originating from waste paper and rags

1992: The Basel Convention comes into force

1560   1690   1921 1989
   1600   1700   1800   1900   2000

First Cleanliness Decree in Hamburg, Germany: market squares cleaned four times a year at public expense

The British Waste Paper Association is established and paper recycling begins in England

1874 1885
In Nottingham, England, First waste incinerator
"destructors" burn garbage and produce electricity built in the United States

away that was not beyond all hope of further use. In the kitchen, fish heads, plate scrapings and vegetable water went into soups and gravies, and stale bread into puddings. Anything left would be recycled as pigswill. Soiled paper was thrown on to the fire, while clean paper was torn up either to serve as lavatory paper or to twisted into spills for lighting candles or fires. Worn-out sheets became bandages. Rag-and-bone men took other textiles and bones, and the back door received a steady flow of dealers ready to buy paper and anything else for which human ingenuity could devise a future. Only the careless, the drunk or the reckless would leave very much for the sifters to find at the yards. In 1921, the Association of London Waste Paper Merchants was founded with its self-interested but nonetheless worthy ambition to recycle paper.

World Wars I and II marked the beginning of wartime economies around the globe. Wartime economies are very different from peacetime economies since all resources must be mobilised and conserved to support the war effort. The war effort led to some major material exchanges to reuse items. The British government established the earliest documented industrial waste exchange, called the National Industrial Materials Recovery Association, in 1942. This waste exchange was created to conserve materials for the war effort during World War II. Tin cans and other metal objects were collected and processed through scrap merchants to supply the country's steel industry. Bones had also a high commercial value for the production of compost. Even dust – still the principal component of the household waste bin – was sold for brickmaking or fertilizer. During this period, the first landfills were established to dispose of waste and initial recycling efforts began to aid the war effort.

Upon the end of World War II, world economies began to shift back toward normal production. Paper, for example, was starting to become a problem. The production of plastics from petroleum-derived chemicals had started in the 1930s but now began to rise sharply, the perfect symbol of the twentieth century. People had made their contribution through austerity and were eager for a chance to consume. The explosion in consumption unleashed an eruption of waste which was to be swallowed up by holes in the ground. As a consequence of the enormous growth in the post-war era, the waste generated by the 1970s had become a 'waste avalanche', and was largely fuelled by the increases in both industrial production and private consumption. Waste managers were primarily faced with the question of how to deal with the problem of waste volume. Waste policy was driven by the politics of discard. Until the end of the 1960s, waste was simply disposed of in a multitude of small dumps. Also, during this time, more information became available on the dangers of pollution and contamination. The closing of a large number of small dumps was therefore given a high priority, and the construction of sanitary waste disposal facilities was required.

The information revolution served as a catalyst to quickly disseminate environmental issues around the world and pinpoint negative impacts on nature for further analysis. Waste managers were requested to prevent any threat to the health and welfare of the human and animal population. The waste movement shifted from a public health and wartime conservation focus to an environmental protection and natural resource conservation one. Initiatives and focus on the environment exploded, with many governments taking a very active role in establishing policies and regulations. Continuous improvements were made in the technological standards for waste management. The creation of environmental regulations during this period greatly surpassed all previous ones.

While the original goal of proper waste disposal was essentially met, the goal of controlling the waste volume had not been achieved. In the 1980s, the term waste avoidance was introduced to waste regulations, particularly in Europe. This term not only includes the development of low-waste technologies, but also the recovery and reuse of products, the creation of a product design conducive to recycling, and an increase in the overall life of a product. Since the mid-1980s, the trend has therefore been toward source-separation of waste for recycling rather than waste avoidance. To this day, recycling of household waste is still primarily limited to materials such as glass, plastics, and metals. Technology for the recovery of other substances has not yet been technologically optimised.

Although recycling is an economically profitable business, the commercialisation cycle has kept it on the margins of legality, where the work of waste pickers is the initial link in an economic chain. The existence of people who work in and with waste is almost commonplace in the landscape not only of Brazilian cities, but of Tokyo, New York, Los Angeles and Paris (dos Santos 2005). There is no precise date for when waste picking first became a form of work within the Brazilian context, however, reports of its existence dated from the end of the 1930s. At that time, waste pickers as a group were socially invisible, stigmatised for being street dwellers and for collecting waste and individuals' leftovers. Initially, waste picking became a form of work in the large urban areas and was restricted to paper, glass and scrap metal, which were sold first to middlemen and then to recyclers. Waste pickers became visible in Brazil as a workforce in the middle of the 1980s when the recycling industry started to involve the large number of people who were surviving on the collection of recyclable waste. They were used as the base of the system, offering cheap labour for collecting and sorting waste and, consequently, serving as facilitators for the recycling industry's establishment in Brazil. By the 1990s, waste picker associations and cooperatives were a common thing in many cities and organisations with public authorities established to improve selective waste collection programmes. It is worth saying that this process was marked by numerous social conflicts, and in some cities, the relationship between local governments and these associations are still problematic, marked by repression and omission.

The worldwide view of the presence of waste pickers in urban areas varies. In some cases, it inspires humanitarian sentiments, but in others repulsion and indignation. Social prejudice still exists, particularly in developed countries (e.g. Japan, the USA) and usually oversimplifies the vision of many public authorities who often invest massively in technology to overcome this situation. Above all, it does not take account of their worthy efforts and the benefits that they promote for the city. As an economic activity, with a strong environmental bias, recycling has become a concrete alternative for the promotion of pro-environmental behaviour and social inclusion with the slogan of being a social-green effort. However, this view is quite perverse. Currently, it depends on labour with minimal remuneration and old sorting technology. However, to improve the system, it is threatened by the gains of economics of scale which require a profitable system with new technology and not depend on waste pickers' labour. At the end, what is left is a struggle between these two forces for a more efficient recycling programme and social justice.

Mostly there has been a failure in the last two decades to create sufficient disposal capacities and treatment technologies and the waste generation crisis is becoming more and more acute. In the twenty-first century, the volume of waste is rapidly increasing with the development and introduction of new technologies every year. Waste management is now related to the evolution of our technological society, which, along with the escalation of mass production, has also created problems that require a different approach to handling municipal wastes. The reduction of waste generation is a current need that our society has to satisfy immediately. A sustainable waste management system today has to have two fundamental requirements: less waste and an integrated system for managing effectively the waste still produced.

The current nature of waste

Most of us are first aware of the issues related to waste when, as children, we are asked to take out out the family rubbish. By performing this simple action, we learn that rubbish consists of broken, spoilt and old things we do not longer want or need, all wrapped in a plastic bag or and put in a dustbin. It was not necessary to know what happened next. This story that we have grown up with has trained us to not to think about the dust cart, the vehicle that calls at our house once a week and collects all those things we do not want any more. And we have chosen not to think about what is inside the plastic bag. There are occasions when the mountain of leftovers breaks through our fences and we have to think about them. But we still continue to carefully make them invisible and unthinkable by avoiding them at any opportunity. Bauman defines waste as *'the dark, shameful secret of all production'* (Bauman 2004). Throughout the years, the plastic got bigger and bigger and cannot remain as a secret any more.

So, what is inside the black plastic bag today? Currently, municipal waste includes things such as durable goods, containers and packaging, food scraps, garden rubbish, and miscellaneous waste from residential, commercial, and institutional sources. Examples of waste from these categories include appliances, newspapers, clothing, boxes, paper, and food waste. Waste composition varies dramatically across countries with different income levels (see Figure 2.2). Developing countries (e.g. Brazil) have a very high proportion of organic waste while paper waste is the single largest component in developed countries.

Our waste has changed deeply in its composition since the 1920s when coal ash figured prominently in the municipal waste stream. Most of this ash has not disappeared entirely but has merely moved upstream from households to industry after the arrival of electrical energy. Its major replacement is packaging. It accounts, on average, for a little over a third of municipal waste by weight. In the UK, packaging waste reached 175 kilos per capita in 2011 and in Germany 200 kilos per capita (Eurostat 2014a). The US Environmental Protection Agency's report on waste shows that paper waste (34 per cent of total waste) in the US comes mainly from corrugated cardboard used for packaging (US EPA 2013). This category is increasing rapidly and includes metal cans, cardboard boxes, glass bottles and plastic containers of all types. Several forces were responsible for making packaging such an important part of our waste stream.

In the early history of humanity, containers for packaging were not required, as food was immediately consumed and human waste was just left on the ground to biodegrade naturally. Later, pottery was developed and used to hold food and grains or items for barter and trade. Pottery and similar vessels were reused and repaired until they wore out or were broken. Paper was first used as packaging in the first century BC by the Chinese to wrap foods. The technique advanced and it was introduced in England in 1310 (Hook & Heimlich 2007). But paper was a luxury item and most store owners asked their customers to bring their own bags. Little was wasted and almost nothing thrown away. Broken items would be repaired or used to create other items. The first paper bag was made in Bristol, in 1844 by Francis Wolle who invented the paper bag-making machine. But it was Walter H. Deubner who took the paper bag idea further. He realised that his customers only purchased what they could carry home, and in an attempt to increase his sales, he took the traditional paper bag and put a cord through it to serve as a handle. This allowed the bag to carry up to 35 kilos of groceries (Great Idea Finder 2014). No one knows exactly who invented the plastic bag. The first clear plastic bag began to appear in bakeries and grocery shops in 1957 (Gogte 2009). Quickly, consumers began to use a different bag to separate each type of purchase they made, one for potatoes, another for apples, and so on. Eventually, the opaque paper bags were substituted by translucent plastic ones. Although paper and plastic materials are most commonly used for containers; metal, aluminium and glass packaging also comprises a considerable percentage of the municipal waste stream. In 1944, a Swedish designer, Ruben Rausing, developed a new kind of milk container made of plastic-coated paper board that could be filled and sealed at dairies as an unbreakable alternative to glass. This was one of the wellsprings of the packaging industry. This paperboard drinks carton

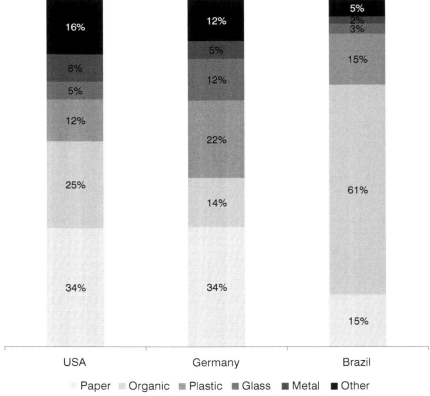

Figure 2.2 Waste composition in Brazil, Germany and the USA

Sources: USA EPA (2012), Abrelpe (2012) and Eurostat (2014b)

transformed Rausing's company Tetra Pak (now part of Tetra Laval) into the most profitable packaging company. , Nowadays, it is the only way to carry fruit juice and milk over distances. In 2012, Tetra Pak worldwide sold 173,234 million items of packaging and 77,307 million litres of products were sold in Tetra Pak packages (Tetra Pak 2014). They are used not only for drinks but also for ice cream, dry foods, cheese and even pet food.

By definition, it is assumed that all containers and packaging are discarded in the same year they are manufactured. The sudden rise of disposable packaging after the 1950s was also possible due to the declining cost of natural resources such as wood, aluminium and oil. Cheaper and more durable packaging improved conditions for distribution and storage of goods. Even more fundamentally, packaging became 'the producer's sole representative at the sales decision point' (US EPA 1988). This new kind of packaging encouraged a throwaway lifestyle. By the 1960s the 'no deposit, no return' era of packaging was the norm in most Western countries. In 1977, another breakthrough took place. Soft drinks started to be sold in PET (polyethylene terephthalate) bottles and by 1980 this was the main means of selling them. These bottles were never meant to be reused or recycled, just to be disposable. The advent of this new consumer/littering behaviour put pressure on the manufacturers to market disposable products as well. Figure 2.3 shows the share of packaging waste in total household waste. Other disposable products, besides packaging, began taking up a larger share of the municipal waste stream. For example, disposable nappies were practically non-existent some decades ago but today they account for 8 per cent of household waste in the UK (Freyberg 2012). Actually, these figures should be considered carefully, since it is not possible to accurately measure how much waste is being thrown away every day. As the World Bank report points out, reliable waste data is not easy to gather and methodologies vary from country to country. The lack of robust, standardised waste data underscores how difficult it can be to hold countries accountable for waste generation. Nevertheless, packaging and disposable waste have undoubtedly become much more important in the past 50 years.

Another major addition, during the last century, to our municipal waste stream was food waste. Food waste was a non-existent problem until the late nineteenth century when several experts pointed out that that a lot of imported food was becoming inedible within short time period due to unhygienic conditions in the households and the grocery shop. Before the late 1800s, nothing was wasted. Leftovers from the upper classes were sold to be reused in popular restaurants for the lower class (Porter & Prince 2005). It is reported that leftovers were also taken home by court servants who could subsist on them for several days with their families and even donate some to beggars and hospitals (Bauer 2009). It was also used to feed animals. In the late nineteenth century, Professor Atwater conducted a series of food diet studies in the USA. Food waste was defined in his studies as 'the so-called edible portion of food which may for any reason be rejected'. The studies showed that food waste in US households was a serious problem at that time, stating that: '*even in some of the most economical families*

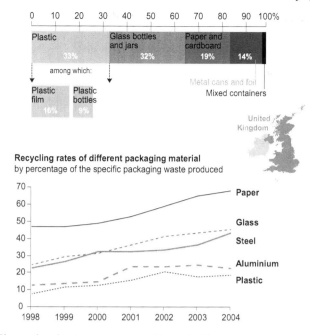

Figure 2.3 Share of packaging waste in total household waste

Source Bournay (2006). Designer Emmanuelle Bournay© with permission from http://www.grida.no/graphicslib/detail/share-of-packaging-waste-in-total-household-waste-oecd_6a84

the amount of food waste, if it could be collected for a month or a year, would prove to be very large, and in many cases the amounts would be little less than enormous' (Atwater 1895). Nevertheless, he also observed that some American families would use the leftovers carefully, mainly due to financial restrictions (Atwater & Bryant 1902).

It was during World War I that the population was first asked to consume food economically by efficient use of materials as well as by separating all waste components and recycling. Food was an important resource for the troops and the morale of both the troops and the population. Worldwide, awareness campaigns for the population were introduced to restrict food imports to a minimum. Children were taught to eat all the food on their plate and thus to leave a clean plate. Target groups were not only housewives but also the husbands at home. The situation changed dramatically during the 1950s and 1960s. Small grocery shops were converted into self-service shops where consumers had to take the packaging sizes offered instead of quantity required by the individual customer. Refrigerators were introduced to the households and, for the first time, it was possible to keep food fresh. Householders were able to eat salads, fresh fruit and vegetables without having access to a garden or allotment. Imported food from far-off countries increased and frozen foods, previously a luxury item, became commonplace. But it was the freezer that allowed people to buy food in bulk and eat it at leisure. Processed and convenient food arrived on supermarket shelves and the population began to eat less healthily. By the late 1990s, things had worsened, and the food manufacturing sector was estimated to be generating over 8 million tonnes of food waste annually (Gunning & Holm 2007).

Recently, many studies and projects have been carried out to estimate the amount of food waste produced by householders, retailers and producers as well as the reasons for that behaviour (WRAP 2008). The Swedish Institute for Food and Biotechnology (SIK), in its 2011 report, estimated the total of global food loss and waste to be around one-third of the edible parts of food produced for human consumption, amounting to about 1.3 billion tons per year (Gustavsson *et al.* 2011). The report also differentiates between industrialised and developing countries. In the latter, the larger losses are due to the post-harvest and processing stages, while, in the former, they occur at retail and consumer levels. Thus, due to inefficient production, poor transportation systems, packaging, hygienic standards and individuals' behaviour, food is wasted or is not used for human nutrition. Our consumption attitudes 'fresh is beautiful' and 'buy bulk and save money' are not a unique result of our contemporary affluent society but have their roots in how food is handled and valued (Pudel & Westenhöfer 1998).

Integrated waste management

As mentioned above, waste management practices were initially implemented to ensure safety and safeguard public health by preventing the spread of diseases that were being caused by the increasing amounts of waste being discarded with appropriate collection or disposal. Essentially, waste management practices must reduce environmental impacts as much as possible. They must also operate at an appropriate cost for society and, in a manner that is acceptable for the majority of people. In other words, they must be sustainable (environmentally effective, economically affordable and socially acceptable). Clearly, it would be difficult to minimise these three factors simultaneously. It is likely that a balance must be achieved among them through a well-designed system.

A system approach to waste management was proposed by W. R. Lynn in 1962. It was described as 'viewing the problem in its entirely, as an interconnected system of component operations and functions' (Lynn *et al.* 1962). Lynn has recognised the full complexity of waste management which led to the application of systems analysis and mathematical modelling to optimise waste management operations and strategy development. This was the foundation of the concept of integrated waste management (IWM). Tchobanoglous and Kreith (2002) have defined an IWM system as 'the selection and application of suitable techniques, technology and management programs to achieve specific waste management objective and goals'. Today the concept of IWM is broader and includes the use of different treatment technologies depending on situations, and an overall approach being taken with respect to the analysis, optimisation, and management of the whole system. According to McDougall *et al.* (2003), an 'Integrated solid waste management system combines solid waste streams, solid waste collection, treatment and disposal methods, with the objective of achieving environmental benefits, economic optimisation and societal acceptability'. Thus, in a sustainable IWM system all strategies are interactive combining different technologies which are designed to process a specific component of the solid waste stream.

The concept of lifecycle assessment (LCA) is an appropriate tool to infer environmental impacts since it is based on a holistic and systematic approach and covers all the phases of the lifecycle from cradle to grave (Tchobanoglous & Kreith 2002). LCA is defined as a methodology to assess the potential environmental impacts and resources used throughout a product's lifecycle, i.e. from raw material acquisition to waste management (ISO 14040 2006). LCA and other lifecycle approaches (e.g. lifecycle cost assessment) have become an important tool for policies and implementation of IWM systems since they can provide qualitative and quantitative information on energy and resources consumption, production, and emissions concerning the system. They can also consider the environmental benefits related to the implementation of different management options, such as recycling and incineration. In this manner, LCA can be used in policy and decision-making to compare various potential management strategies in different situations and regions. This comparison is achieved by a scenario evaluation, i.e. a comparison of a set of scenarios defined according to a scientific approach accounting for current and future possibilities. Many researchers (Ekvall *et al.* 2007) have already developed complex models integrated in a lifecycle perspective. This approach helps to deal with the LCA's steady-state problem which prevents verification of the optimum mix of waste management options. For example, if recycling is considered the best solution, this is not always true. With increasing amounts of waste, the better solution might be different due to the distance from plant, transportation costs, etc.

The waste hierarchy is the basis for selecting priorities in waste management (see Figure 2.4). It usually gives the following order of preference: prevention, reuse, recycling, biological treatment, thermal treatment and landfilling. It does not attempt to assess the environmental impacts of a specific IWM system; it only gives guidelines for the preferred strategy for waste management. This strict priority of options has serious limitations and has no scientific justification to explain why one option is always a better option. As pointed out before, recycling does not always have less environmental impact than energy recovery if we consider its LCA. Thus, it is of little use when a combination of options is required. These limitations were also addressed by the United Nations Environmental Programme (UNEP 1996) as the hierarchy cannot be followed rigidly, since in a particular situation the cost of a prescribed activity may exceed the benefits when all financial, social and environmental considerations are taken into account. Besides, it does not address costs, so consequently, it cannot help assess the economic affordability of solid waste systems. Rather than following a hierarchy of preferred options, IWM systems must be designed using an all-inclusive approach which recognises that all options can have an equal

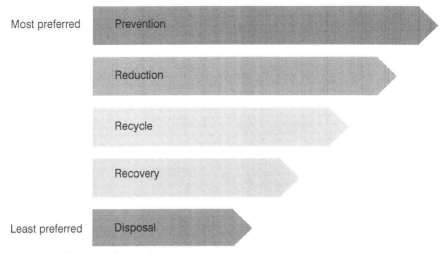

Figure 2.4 The waste hierarchy for waste management

Source: UNEP, UN DESA and FAO (2012)

chance to be considered depending on specific local conditions (Gustavsson *et al.* 2011). There is not a unanimously ideal system. There will always be geographic differences in composition, the quantities of waste generated, the size of the recycling market, and; in the availability of some management options. Figure 2.5 illustrates the interrelationship of the system's parts.

A sustainable IWM should be flexible and always consider waste prevention above and within any management option. Flexibility will allow the system to adapt easily to any changes in the current social, economic and environmental conditions. These are likely to change over time with or without warning, mainly because all waste management systems are a part of a larger system: Nature's ecosystem. This flexibility will also guarantee an effective implementation of waste prevention policies within the whole system (see Figure 2.5). All options are clearly interconnected and the concept of waste prevention (avoidance, reduction and reuse) must be applied to all of them. For instance, the collection and sorting methods employed in the system might affect the quality of the recyclable material which might also affect the ability to recycle it and/or to produce a marketable good. Similar to a domino effect, this might as well increase or decrease the percentage of waste disposed at the landfill. That is why waste prevention is not a part of the IWM system but rather a management rule to be followed in the design/operation of each system's part. This is one of the main requirements to reduce waste generation, and, to develop and implement a sustainable IWM system.

The IWM is a complex system and involves carefully evaluating local needs and conditions to determine the most suitable options for all aspects of the system. Besides that, all its processes (e.g. collection, transportation, and disposal) have to be carried out within existing legal and social guidelines and they also need

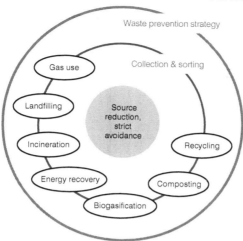

Figure 2.5 The interrelationship among the elements of an integrated solid waste management

to be aesthetically and economically acceptable. Equally important, it needs to provide public education and awareness. This will likely develop trust and gain support from the community which needs to be involved in every step of the process. For the management to be responsive to public attitudes, engineering and administrative disciplines need to communicate and interact with sociological and psychological disciplines in a positive interdisciplinary relationship. As a result, implementing an IWM plan is an ongoing process, which requires being in constant evaluation to make adjustments to improve or expand its management services along the way.

The issues of municipal waste management

Waste management is the most important and expensive service a city provides. Our cities generate enormous amounts of waste and the volumes are likely to increase beyond 2100. Ten years ago, there were 2.9 billion urban residents who generated about 0.64 kg of municipal solid waste (MSW) per person per day (0.68 billion tonnes per year). This World Bank report estimates that today these amounts have increased to about 3 billion residents generating 1.2 kg per person per day (1.3 billion tonnes per year). By 2025, this will likely increase to 4.3 billion urban residents generating about 1.42 kg/capita/day of municipal solid waste (2.2 billion tonnes per year) (Hoornweg & Bhada-Tata 2012). Waste volumes are increasing even faster than the rate of urbanisation. A city that cannot effectively manage its waste is rarely able to manage more complex services such as health, education, or public transport. Improving waste management is one of the most effective ways to strengthen overall municipal management and is usually a prerequisite for other, more complicated, municipal services.

In the era of sustainability, waste managers are charged with one of the most challenging task in urban areas: make the waste disappear from the streets in the most economically, socially and environmentally optimal way possible. And the task also involves: waste composition, transboundary waste movements, awareness campaigns, employment generation, partnerships and contracts, and budget allocation. It is an intensive service that often falls completely within the local government's purview. In most cities, waste management is the single largest budget item and source of employment. According to the World Bank, it represents 1 per cent to 5 per cent of all urban employment. This situation is likely to get worse: in 2013, the world's population surpassed 7 billion and it is projected to reach 9 billion by 2050. More than half of the world's population now lives in urban areas. By 2050, the urban population will reach 6.4 billion with an approximate growth of 1.5 per cent per year. This will add challenges to waste disposal. It is likely that citizens and corporations will need to assume more responsibility for waste generation and disposal, specifically, waste prevention and separation.

Waste is inextricably linked to urbanisation and economic development; consequently, there is a strong correlation between waste generation rates and greenhouse gas (GHG) emissions, local flooding, soil and water contamination. As standards of living and disposable incomes increase, consumption of goods and services increases, resulting in a corresponding increase in the amount of waste generated. Waste is an inevitable outcome of a resource-intensive, consumer-based economic lifestyle. And this wasteful way of life has been already disseminated in developing countries. In 2004, China surpassed the US as the world's largest waste generator (ISO 14040 2006). The rise in waste generation is a by-product of urbanisation and increasing affluence. This link is quite similar to other urban inputs/outputs such as wastewater and total energy consumption.

There is no 'disappearing' in waste management. Throwing away something means that the system will have to allocate a collection process and a treatment technology less harmful to the environment to deal with the wasted material. And an optimal solution for this combination is not easy to find. Most of the time, solving one problem often introduces a new one, and if not well executed, it backfires creating a new problem of greater cost and complexity. Improperly managed waste usually results in down-stream costs higher than what it would have cost to manage the waste properly in the first place. This is the reason why waste prevention seems the desirable solution for waste generation. Avoiding waste is avoiding management.

Without a doubt the most popular form of 'green' waste management policy, currently, is recycling. For several decades, local governments have advocated industrial reprocessing of household waste as a way of returning some value from what has been used. Yet, recycling is way down the waste hierarchy in comparison to waste prevention. Downcycling is one of the collateral damages of recycling. It is the process of converting waste materials or useless products into new materials or products of lesser quality and reduced functionality. McDonough and Braungart, in their book *Cradle to Cradle*, wrote: 'As we have noted, most recycling is actually downcycling; it reduces the quality of a material over time' (McDonough & Braungart 2002). Most recycled industrial nutrients (materials) lose viability or value in the process of recycling. This means they can only be used in a degraded form for components other than their original use. White writing paper, for example, is often downcycled into materials such as cardboard and cannot be used to create more premium writing paper. Some of these downcycled products are so poorly designed and made from such low quality materials that, at the end of their useful life, they cannot be recycled and go directly to the incinerator or landfill. While recycling rates are increasing worldwide, waste generation rates also increase. In the end, recycling has only enabled our society to consume more and even more waste.

Another issue is the lack of clear definitions, regulations and standards for waste prevention. To date, the lack of clear definitions has been a significant impediment to the development of sound waste prevention programmes. At a fundamental level, it has resulted in confusion as to what constitutes waste prevention and how it differs from waste minimisation. Consistent definitions form a basis for an effective evaluation of the programme. They allow a body to track progress and to compare its progress with other bodies. They facilitate quality dialogue with all affected and interested parties. Moreover, what is measured is managed, so if the reduction of waste materials is not measured it is unlikely that policy makers will be able to infer the efficiency of waste prevention actions. Waste managers must give significant attention to definitions and they must collaborate in giving a clear definition to not only waste prevention but to all waste management options. All future legislation, regulations, scientific research and public dialogue will depend on these definitions. This must be an open public process to establish appropriate definitions early in the strategy developing process of the waste management system. A significant effort was made on this subject by the European Commission with its Waste Framework Directive (EU Waste Framework Directive-2008/98/EC) which came into force in 2008.

Despite progress in waste management practices during the last few years, fundamental institutional, financial, social, and environmental problems still exist. Although each country and city has their own site-specific situations, nonetheless, general improvements for waste management are still necessary to meet the challenges of the new urban areas. Waste is still wasted as a result of inefficiencies of urbanisation and the economies urban areas drive. The traditional vision to reduce waste volumes – to reduce economic activity – still persists in managers' beliefs and, of course, it is not a generally attractive option. It is necessary to change this perspective. And technological innovation will not help us reach this goal. Waste managers have to pay close attention to householders (the waste producers) and understand how they perceive and behave towards their waste. Engaging householders to rethink their behaviour is the only way in which waste prevention can be successful.

References

Abrelpe. (2012). Panorama dos resíduos sólidos no Brasil, 2011. Retrieved from http://www.abrelpe.org.br/Panorama/panorama2011.pdf

Atwater, W. O. (1895). *Methods and results of investigation on the chemistry and economy of food*. Bulletin no. 21, US Department of Agriculture, Office of Experiment Stations, Government Printing Office. Washington, DC.

Atwater, W. O., & Bryant, M. S. (1902). *Dietary studies in New York City in 1896 and 1897*. Bulletin no.116, US Department of Agriculture, Office of Experiment Stations, Government Printing Office. Washington, DC.

Bauer, C. (2009). *Hofküche and Hofkeller*. Cultural magazine for Viennese guides. Vienna Guide Service. Available at http://www.touristguides-austria.at/de/publikationen/hofkueche-und-hofkeller.pdf

Bauman, Z. (2004). *Wasted lives, modernity and its outcasts*. Oxford: Polity Press.

Bournay, E. (2006). *Vital waste graphics 2* (Vol. 2). UNEP/Earthprint. Available at http://www.grida.no/publications/vg/waste2/

dos Santos, M. C. L. (2005). Design, waste and homelessness. *Design Philosophy Papers*, 3(3), 155–165.

Ekvall, T., Assefa, G., Björklund, A., Eriksson, O., & Finnveden, G. (2007). What life-cycle assessment does and does not do in assessments of waste management. *Waste Management, 27*, 8, 989996.

EU Waste Framework Directive 2008/98/EC of the European Parliament and of the Council of the European Union. *Official Journal of the European Union*. Strasbourg, France.

Eurostat. (2014a). Packaging waste statistics. Eurostat statistics explained. Retrieved fromhttp://epp.eurostat.ec.europa.eu/statistics_explained/index.php/Packaging_waste_statistics#

Eurostat. (2014b). Waste statistics. Eurostat statistics explained. Retrieved from http://epp.eurostat.ec.europa.eu/statistics_explained/index.php/Waste_statistics

Flanders, J. (2004). *The Victorian house: Domestic life from childbirth to deathbed*. London: HarperCollins.

Freyberg, T. (2012). Nappy recycling is the UK ready to run, walk or crawl? *Waste Management World, 13*, 5.

Gogte, M. (2009). Are plastic grocery bags sacking the environment? *International Journal for Quality Research, 3*, 4.

Great Idea Finder. (2014). Shopping bag. Retrieved from http://www.ideafinder.com/history/inventions/shopbag.htm.

Gunning, J., & Holm, S. (2007). *Ethics, law and society*. Aldershot: Ashgate Publishing.

Gustavsson, J., Cederberg, C., Sonesson, U., Otterdijk, R., and Meybeck, A. (2011). *Global food losses and food waste*. Rome: Food and Agriculture Organisation of the United Nations.

Hook, P., & Heimlich, J. E. (2007). *A historystory of packaging*. CDFS-133. Ohio State University Fact Sheet. Columbus, OH: Ohio State University.

Hoornweg, D., & Bhada-Tata, P. (2012). *What a waste: A global review of solid waste management*. Urban development series: knowledge papers no. 15. Washington, DC: World Bank.

Hornby, A. S., & Wehmeier, S. (2000). *Oxford Advanced Learner's Dictionary*, 6th revised ed. Oxford: Oxford University Press.

ISO (2006). *ISO 14040. Environmental management: Life cycle assessment. Principles and framework*. ISO, Geneva.

Lipovetsky, G. (2002). *The empire of fashion: Dressing modern democracy.* Princeton, NJ University Press.

Lynn, W. R., Logan, J. A., & Charnes, A. (1962). System analysis for planning wastewater treatment plants. *Journal of Water Pollution Control Federation, 34,* 565–581.

McDonough, W., & Braungart, M. (2002). *Cradle to cradle: Remaking the way we make things.* New York: North Point Press, ed.

McDougall, F., White, P., Franke, M., & Hinde, P. (2003). *Integrated solid waste management: A life cycle inventory.* Oxford: Blackwell.

Porter, D., & Prince, D. (2005). *Frommer's Vienna & the Danube Valley.* Hoboken, NJ: Wiley .

Pudel, V., & Westenhöfer, J. (1998). *Food psychology: An introduction.* Göttingen: Verlag für Psychologie.

Tchobanoglous, G., & Kreith, F. (2002). *Handbook of solid waste management.* New York: McGraw-Hill, NY.

Tetra Pak. (2014). Tetra Pak in Figures 2012. Retrieved from http://www.tetrapak.com/ about-tetra-pak/the-company/facts-and-figures

UNEP. (1996). *International source book on environmentally sound technologies for municipal solid waste management.* International Environmental Technology Centre Technical Publication Series, 6. United Nations Environmental Programme.

UNEP, UN DESA and FAO. (2012). *SIDS-focused green economy: an analysis of challenges and opportunities.* Available at http://www.unep.org/greeneconomy and www.unep.org/ regionalseas.

US EPA. (1988) *Report to Congress: Solid Waste Disposal in the United States* (Vol. 2). Washington, DC.

US EPA. (2012). *Municipal solid waste generation, recycling, and disposal in the United States: facts and figures for 2012.* EPA-530-F-14-001. Washington, DC.

US EPA. (2013). *Municipal solid waste in the United States.* EPA530-R-13-001. Washington, DC.

WRAP. (2008). *The food we waste. Food waste report.* Banbury, UK: WRAP

3   The roots of waste prevention policies

In the late 1980s and early 1990s, waste prevention captured the imagination. Many cities in different countries were looking for waste disposal options that were preferable to incineration or to dumping in old, sub-standard landfills. Recycling was beginning to grow as one way to manage waste that was produced. But waste prevention was the ideal promise: the amount of waste prevented would not have to be managed at all! Unnecessary packaging, take-away food containers, disposable cameras, any single-service item, disposable batteries, catalogues, probably anyone could make a list of products that seemed reasonable targets for achieving measurable waste prevention. Worldwide, local governments and environmental agencies put waste prevention at the top of their waste management hierarchy. Hence the order was to reduce, reuse and recycle.

In 1989, this new waste management hierarchy was formalised in the European Commission's Community Strategy for Waste Management. This was further endorsed in the Commission review of the strategy in 1996. In France, the concept of prevention was introduced in the 1992 waste law in order to 'prevent or reduce the generation and harmfulness of waste, in particular by acting on product manufacture and distribution...' (Loi No. 92–646). In the same year, the US Environmental Protection Agency put waste prevention at the top of its hierarchy of methods to handle waste. In 1993, the California Integrated Waste Management Board published its Statewide Waste Prevention Plan (Local Assistance and Planning Committee 1993), prepared under contract from Gainer Associates under Contract No. IWM-C107 8 with subcontract assistance from Tellus Institute, RGB Consulting Services, and Waste Reduction Research, including recommendations for legislative action to promote waste prevention; actions to improve product design; actions to develop and implement product durability standards, and actions to reduce toxicity of products.

Targets for waste prevention were adopted by many public authorities despite the speculative character of these estimates. They were based on a series of tentative assumptions about the possible impacts of different policies or factors: (i) waste disposal fees; (ii) waste generation fees; (iii) local or national packaging regulations, and (iv) material use and reuse. At that time, even waste consultants were sceptical about the projected figures of waste reduction (Springer 1994) and many questions have arisen related to waste prevention efficacy. It was in this atmosphere that many environmental administrations fully embraced source reduction and pollution prevention policies as overarching goals for waste prevention.

With respect to measurement, there is always something of an unknown quality of quantifying something that does not happen. For waste prevention programmes, at that point, it turned out that only some had outcomes that could be measured clearly. Others had impacts too diffuse or non-specific to track with reasonable costs. Still others showed considerable uncertainty about amounts of waste potentially saved that could not be predicted well (e.g. paper saving through electronic information systems). Thus, aggregate measures of waste prevention became a mix of likely and uncertain measures. They provided a basis for comparing programmes but were not operationally reliable enough to apply to the tangible waste management system as a whole.

These challenges and limitations may shed light on why some waste management plans (New York State 1998) suggested that waste prevention initiatives should focus on implementation, rather than on measurement. As to amounts of waste preventable, these plans did not suggest a near-term potential to prevent a sizable portion of the waste stream. For households, the programmes that could be measured with relative certainty had benefits that were relatively small. In the public sector, product and agency reviews have contributed ideas for improvements in purchasing and contracting, and even some ideas for improved recycling, but did not indicate great waste stream reductions. And in the private sector, success stories are mixed with difficulties in getting businesses to participate sufficiently and to spend resources on waste prevention documentation, even when offered free waste prevention technical assistance (Science Applications International Corporation 2000).

To be against waste and to advocate consumption patterns that generate less waste are roles that are intuitively appealing. And on an *a priori* basis, at that moment, it might have seemed as if there would be countless ways to reduce waste and save money at the same time. But in reviewing the many waste prevention efforts that local governments and environmental agencies worldwide have supported in all sectors and documented in these studies, it was possible to learn that they had not been sufficient toward counteracting a significant and growing waste burden.

Despite all odds, waste management policies have continuously evolved over the past 30 years to pursue the goal of waste prevention, shifting their focus from pollution control mandates to voluntary strategies that promote resource efficiency. In 1998, the OECD refined the scope of its work programme on waste minimisation to squarely focus on the prevention component (OECD 2000). A driving force behind this move was the recognition that adequate attention to waste prevention needs to be assured not only in principle, but also in the analyses and practical advice provided to governments. Currently, waste prevention initiatives seek to reduce the quantity of waste at the source by redesigning products, changing patterns of production and individual consumption. The target is not only to avoid increasing costs but also to reduce greenhouse gas emissions. In this matter, a two-fold benefit is expected to occur: First, to decrease GHG emission associated with material and product manufacture and, second, to cut emissions associated with the avoided waste management activities. While it is true that the principle of waste prevention is universally accepted, the practice still has a considerable distance to travel in achieving its full potential.

Defining waste prevention

Waste prevention is usually mistaken as waste minimisation due to its multi-faceted and often poorly understood nature. Research using focus groups in the UK suggests that the public often include recycling activities as reduction actions that minimise the amount of waste put in residual waste bins or sacks, rather than reducing the amount of waste produced overall (RECAP 2008). This terminology not only leads householders to believe that they are already undertaking waste prevention activities (and possibly limiting further interest or action) but also makes it more difficult for policy makers and lawmakers to establish effective waste prevention policies. Cox *et al.* (2010) noted that stakeholders sometimes could not make a clear distinction between recycling and prevention. Terms should not be used loosely or interchangeably. Vancini (1997) highlights that every effort should be made to have a common understanding of terminology when discussing waste policy.

According to terminological work undertaken at OECD (2000), waste minimisation is a broader term than waste prevention in that it includes recycling, large-scale composting and, incineration with energy recovery (see Figure 3.1). As discrete activities, they are distinct from waste prevention. The OECD (2000) defines waste minimisation as 'Preventing and/or reducing the generation of waste at the source; improving the quality of waste generated, such as reducing the hazard, and encouraging re use, recycling, and recovery' while it refers waste prevention to three types of practical action: strict avoidance, reduction at source, and product reuse. As shown, waste minimisation is a broader term; however, waste prevention also involves the waste management measures of 'quality improvements', such as reducing the hazard (EPA 1997).

It is important to stress that the potential contribution of waste prevention to overall waste minimisation has not still been realised. While waste prevention will never make recycling obsolete, the application of both will generally have a greater impact on waste generation than the singular application of one or the other. For instance, there are numerous applications of source-reduced packaging made with recycled materials, which can also be recycled. The interaction of both policies may cause two possible outcomes: (i) high rates of waste prevention could result in fewer materials available for recycling or (ii) the potential increase in the value of recyclable waste may act as a disincentive to waste prevention. Still, the US Environmental Protection Agency's studies clearly show the considerably higher greenhouse gas mitigation potential associated with waste prevention in comparison with waste minimisation, particularly in the case of recycling (EEA 2002).

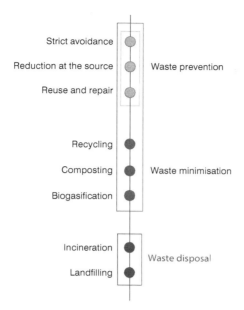

Strict avoidance

Reduction at the source   Waste prevention

Reuse and repair

Recycling

Composting   Waste minimisation

Biogasification

Incineration   Waste disposal

Landfilling

Figure 3.1 Waste prevention in the context of waste management

Along with the OECD (2000) report, the Waste Framework Directive (WFD-2008/98/EC), expressly in Article 3, clause 12–13, states that prevention means taking action before a material or product has been recognised as waste, that reduce: (i) the quantity of waste, including the reuse of products or the extension of the life span of products; (ii) the adverse impacts of the generated waste on the environment and human health; or (iii) the content of harmful substances in materials and products. Reuse is defined as any operation by which products or components that are not waste are used again for the same purpose for which they were conceived. The directive also highlights that waste prevention should be the first priority of waste management, and then in descending order, reuse, recycling, recovery (including energy recovery) and safe disposal.

An additional source of confusion is determining where some activities (e.g. home composting) fit into the waste prevention definition. Despite UK evidence that the greatest tonnage diversions can be achieved on food waste through home composting, Defra UK does not consider home composting to be a strict waste prevention measure as the waste is still produced even though it reduces the amount of waste that needs to be collected (Defra 2013a). However, the National Resource and Waste Forum has included home composting (as well as community composting) in its definition of waste prevention since it reduces the amount of the waste and the compost can be reused as fertiliser for gardens (National Resource and Waste Forum 2003). The former CIWMB also recognised garden composting as waste prevention because garden rubbish is managed on-site and does not enter a collection system (Local Assistance and Planning Committee 1993). Home composting, according to Wilson (2005) will be, eventually, included into waste prevention regulations.

The consensus understanding of waste prevention achieved by the OECD in 2000 can be broken into three types of action: (i) strict avoidance, which involves the complete prevention of waste generation by virtual elimination of hazardous substances or by reducing material or energy intensity in production, consumption, and distribution; (ii) reduction at source, which minimises the use of toxic or harmful substances and/or material or energy consumption, and; (iii) product reuse, which involves the multiple use of a product in its original form, for its original purpose or for an alternative, with or without reconditioning (OECD 2000).

The OECD (2000) report also emphasises that: *'all societal actors including product manufacturers, businesses and institutions, and individuals and communities may express specific waste prevention behaviours. The practical value of waste prevention will be circumstance-specific and will depend on the characteristics of the material, product, waste stream or target audience in question'.* This statement is extremely important in the sense that it draws attention to the multi-faceted construction of waste prevention since it is far from being a single homogenous behaviour like recycling. Its heterogeneous nature can influence individual preferences and choices translating into many different manifestations of waste prevention behaviour. And in influencing individuals, their waste prevention actions can be judgemental and vary according to their perspective.

Due this complexity on waste prevention actions, the Waste Framework Directive (WFD-2008/98/EC) recommends using lifecycle assessment not only for the waste phase but also for products and materials in order to better anticipate how to reduce environmental impacts of waste generation and waste management, thereby strengthening the economic value of waste. By taking into account the whole product lifecycle, WFD highlights that waste prevention is not only about waste, but also about efficient and innovative ways of dealing with resources. The long-term objective is to develop the EU into a society with a closed cycle and waste management policy, which aims to both prevent waste and utilise waste as a resource.

The targets of waste prevention programmes

An important aspect of waste prevention is that its goal is much more complex than only decrease waste generation. It involves decreasing impacts on the environment and human health by improving resource use efficiency and by reducing overall hazardousness of the content substances in materials/products and in the management of waste. According to the Waste Framework Directive (WFD-2008/98/EC), waste prevention programmes must: *'take into account the whole lifecycle of products and materials and not only the waste phase, and to focus on reducing the environmental impacts of waste generation and waste management, thereby strengthening the economic value of waste. (…) The aim of*

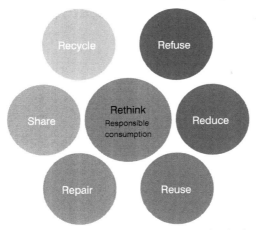

Figure 3.2 Proposed waste prevention policy guidelines to individuals

such objectives and measures shall be to break the link between economic growth and the environmental impacts associated with the generation of waste'. These targets are not ends in themselves, rather they are the foundation for the effective implementation of waste prevention programmes that will give support to achieving the main goal, i.e. to decrease waste generation. The generation of waste needs to be comprehended as a consequence of economic growth directly related to environmental protection by taking into account the overall impacts of the whole lifecycle of waste from the production of goods until their final disposal. Assessing the whole product/waste lifecycle implies that waste prevention is not only about waste, but an innovative approach to handling resources, defining consumption and decreasing environmental impacts. Given the complexity of defining how to achieve waste prevention specific targets (e.g. to decrease food waste), it is important to develop a systemic approach that takes into account not only these interdependencies but also individuals' behaviour towards waste prevention actions. By doing this, it is possible to assess which particular measures support each other, to identify the areas in which measures may be missing and how the most efficient combination of measures can be effective to shift people's behaviour and, consequently, to decrease waste generation.

Measuring, monitoring and evaluating

Waste prevention is notoriously difficult to measure and yet reliable and robust monitoring and evaluation methods are essential to enable policy makers, local authorities and other stakeholders to ensure that waste prevention initiatives are being effective and delivering behaviour change. WRAP's Monitoring and Evaluation Guide (WRAP 2006) explains that monitoring and evaluation are two distinct activities with monitoring being impartial and factual while evaluation tends to be more qualitative/interpretative. Monitoring is the systematic collection and analysis of information as a project progresses. The purpose is usually to track progress against targets set and activities planned during the planning phases of work. It is aimed at improving the efficiency and effectiveness of a project. Evaluation is the comparison of actual project impacts against the agreed strategic plans. In other words, it means drawing conclusions from the monitoring data on how well the schemes, initiatives or campaigns are performing.

To situate the issue of waste prevention evaluation, it will be useful to consider the following question: 'how is it possible to measure something that has not been created?' Indeed, establishing a link between the progress on waste reduction and waste prevention actions is problematic, since waste generation is linked to many parameters whose weight is not easy to assess. For instance, in many European countries, the decrease of waste generation observed in 2009 was mainly due to the 2008 economic crisis. In this context, it is difficult to assess the role of waste prevention policies in the reduction of waste generation. This is the reason why waste prevention evaluation is so challenging. Traditional waste management indicators are not capable of assessing the quantity of material diverted from the waste cycle. It requires assessment and hypothesis leading to uncertainties. Therefore, a completely different evaluation approach has to be established, focusing on assessing these policies or actions efficiency considering sustainability indicators.

Waste prevention has a multi-faceted nature that is often poorly understood. And this contributes to the absence of any widely accepted indicators for its evaluation. Although waste prevention characteristics were addressed before, they are discussed here to help provide a richer context for thought. To demonstrate how these characteristics relate to waste prevention evaluation, we consider the links between them and the more commonly recognised constraints to waste prevention evaluation.

There can be different ways of defining *success* in waste prevention. It may therefore be difficult to agree whether waste prevention is occurring. A good example is the case of food packaging. Recently, the amount of food packaging has declined per capita, mainly due to a shift from glass and paper to plastic. But the lifecycle energy use required and the GHG emissions to create the packaging increased. As a result, there is quantitative, but not qualitative, waste reduction. Since there can be a variety of ways to evaluate waste prevention, stakeholders may not easily agree on a methodology or even the relevant input data to determine whether waste prevention is actually occurring.

Waste prevention effects may also add difficulties to developed suitable indicators. First, there is the matter of *timing*. Unlike recycling, waste prevention decisions are made before products or materials are recognised as waste. This implies that direct macro-level data on waste prevention will be tricky to gather. Second, waste prevention effects are *diverse* and depend on the nature of the policy intervention. This diversity may influence waste generation, energy use and hazardousness. Secondary effects may also occur such as reduced air and/or water pollution. While all potential effects must be kept in mind, it is not usually practical and cost-effective to measure them all since sufficient baseline data on these effects will not be easily collected.

There is a considerable *heterogeneity* in waste prevention actions and they can be implemented at different points during the product's lifecycle. Waste prevention comprises products with less or no packaging, product design, appliance repair, home composting or product's reuse. Even governments themselves may pursue waste prevention initiatives such as green procurement. With such a wide range of actions contributing to waste prevention, it can be challenging to decide which policies should be included in the monitoring and evaluation processes in order to generate the most relevant information for policy makers and other stakeholders.

Finally, efforts at waste prevention evaluation may also be aggravated by the fundamental *complexity* of waste prevention activities. In opposition to recycling, which is more easily predicted, waste prevention aims for behavioural change interventions to raise environmental awareness and to modify consumption patterns. This complexity often means that waste prevention will not always be easily observable and that its implementation is sometimes slow, and that data may not be available for a long period (Vancini 1997).

Many studies have discussed a number of commonly recognised *constraints* that restrict progress in developing waste prevention indicators. Such constraints include lack of data, absence of specific methodology and protocols or guidelines, inconsistent definitions, and, inadequate financial investments on waste prevention programmes. These constraints result mainly from institutional, legal, and political processes. Hence, if institutional support is followed with a focused recognition of the characteristics of waste prevention, strategies may be better linked to reduce more systematically these constraints that inhibit waste prevention evaluation.

With the increasing importance of waste prevention policies and the Waste Framework Directive (WFD-2008/98/EC) stressing the need for consistent monitoring of waste prevention, a number of reports (WRAP 2006) and studies (Sharp *et al.* 2010a) were published on the issue of waste prevention indicators. The development of waste prevention indicators is not a goal in itself. Indicators are best viewed as intimately tied to promoting policy change, to ensure that policy programmes remain dynamic, and to create attention so that emerging issues as well as existing problems can be treated effectively. Previous studies showed that waste prevention indicators must be structured together with policy objectives and targets, focusing on sustainable development goals.

In 2004, OECD (2004) published a report on the topic of waste prevention indicators as part of their work on waste prevention and recycling. The report stresses the importance in designing waste prevention indicators according to specific targets and focusing on sustainable development goals. It introduces the Pressure-State-Response model where: (i) *pressure* covers the concern to address waste generation and its drivers; (ii) the *state* deals with environmental threats, and (iii) *response* tackles the efforts and disbursements going toward waste prevention. Population and private final consumption were chosen as standards drivers for municipal waste. GDP and number of households were dismissed due to lack of data or of logical relevance. Municipal waste generation per inhabitant and on private final consumption were identified as direct pressure indicators. Several response indicators were given as well, such as the number of companies with certified environmental management systems, inventories of several waste prevention actions, existence of national waste prevention plans, extended producer responsibility schemes or variable rating pricing for household waste collection.

The report also introduces other indicators based on Material Flow Accounts (MFA) that consists in integrating waste management as part of material management. Thus, to make this material management sustainable, waste generation has to be reduced and generated waste has to be reintroduced in the material cycle as much as possible. This method considers the material flow for each branch of the economy: inputs, production, consumption and outputs.

Both the PSR model and the MFA approach provide relevant elements toward waste prevention monitoring and evaluation. Yet, it is only possible to apply them on national scales rather than in local situations. The report does not cover local indicators and their link to pressures and drives; such information could be extremely important to determine the impact of waste prevention policies on the environment. And, consequently, it could facilitate the evolution of waste prevention indicators.

Following the revision of the WFD-2008/98/EC, in 2009, the European Commission published a report on waste prevention indicators in order to assist Member States in evaluating their waste prevention programmes. Accordingly, waste prevention indicators have two main goals: to identify priority waste streams to be reduced and, to monitor the results in comparison with targets. The report considered the most usual indicators for waste management and established three core elements as waste prevention indicators in household, construction and biodegradable waste.

For household waste prevention indicators, the report mainly focuses on national indicators and material intensity, with the objective to measure the evolution of several household activities regarding material consumption. Since size of household is one of the most important parameters of waste generation, three core indicators are proposed: (i) weight of total waste generated; (ii) household expenditures on selected consumption categories, and (iii) the total number of households. Other indicators are engagement in waste prevention actions (e.g. home composting) and, the amount of waste directly sent to elimination or not recycled. These indicators mainly consider material intensity but to implement them in one specific waste prevention action can be difficult considering that data on specific consumption is hard to obtain.

Thus, as the OECD (2004) report shows, this one also focuses more on national indicators rather than local indicators (i.e. indicators for a given waste prevention action). The same situation appears in another report published by Fondazione Ei Enrico Matte (Mazzanti & Zoboli 2008). The monitoring is very much dependent on the goal of the prevention policy and, by focusing on different goals, each report comes up with different indicators. The availability of data seemed also to be a key parameter for the choice of these indicators.

In previous reports, waste prevention monitoring is generally perceived as an assessment of waste quantity reduction. And this type of assessment has its downside and limitations: lack of reliable data, no common methodology and issues on qualitative assessment. However, as pointed out by the WFD-2008/98/EC, waste prevention is also defined as all measures that reduce 'the adverse impacts of the generated waste on the environment and human health'. And reducing waste generation does not automatically mean reduction in environmental impacts. For example, plastic (a lighter material) can generate a greater impact during its lifecycle than glass (a denser material).

Thus, it is important to focus on environmental impact as an indicator for waste prevention monitoring and evaluation. Instead of reasoning on quantities, environmental impact allows for a comparison on quantitative waste prevention actions as well as qualitative ones. In general, sustainability indicators (environmental, social and economic aspects) should be considered for waste prevention evaluation. A sustainable waste prevention programme needs to be implemented considering these three aspects. For example, the cost of a waste prevention action can be easily understood by comparing it with the avoided waste quantities and environmental impacts.

Many studies have assessed the impact of waste prevention actions beyond quantity reduction, focusing on environmental impacts using a lifecycle assessment (LCA) based approach. LCA allows assessing the impact of waste prevention at the different stages of the material or product lifecycle. Most of LCAs focus on environmental impact, so for these studies, a LCA based approach is generally used, allowing assessment of the impact of prevention at the different stages of the lifecycle of the product in question. To achieve that, the inventory assessment must lead to the amount of prevented waste, potential by products as well as the action's impact on other stages of the lifecycle in question, relying on various calculations and precision data. Local specificities might have an impact, so the LCA needs to be as flexible as possible to allow taking into account these specificities. Thus, a good balance between the precision of the calculation and the reliability of the data has to be established through studying the sensitivity of the different parameters.

As far as economic impacts are concerned, data from financial resources allocated to the action are necessary to monitor these impacts since financial outcomes might be more complicated to gather. Social impacts represent an important issue for waste prevention, yet it appears to be one of the most difficult parts to evaluate, since very few previous experiences can be found. Direct impacts on employment, poverty or population engagement seem to be standard indicators to monitor. For other social indicators, a case-by-case approach will probably be necessary.

Pre-Waste project (Prewaste ORDIF 2012) has developed a framework of waste prevention indicators based on environmental, economic and social impacts. Its main goal is the monitoring of one prevention action. Indicators are organised in three groups: (i) resources indicators, to monitor the resources allocated to the action (e.g. financial resources, staff, communication, equipment); (ii) results indicators, to monitor the targets of the waste prevention action (e.g. change individuals' behaviour, evolution of waste generation, waste composition); (iii) impact indicators, focusing on further impacts of the waste prevention actions on the three cornerstones of sustainable development (e.g. GHG emissions, avoidable costs, participative actions, employment rates).

While the definition of a common set of indicators is relatively simple, it is more difficult to define a common method to calculate these indicators. Previous studies tend to show that there is no universal method to assess the efficiency of waste prevention. Sharp *et al.* (2010b) argue that there appears to be an emerging consensus that no single approach is sufficient on its own, but rather a 'hybrid' method using a suite of monitoring approaches is recommended.

The main purpose of waste prevention programmes is to change the behaviour of the targeted population in order to decrease waste generation. Therefore, it is also interesting to monitor and evaluate these changes in order to assess the efficiency of the action. Several types of behaviour-changing indicators can be employed, such as awareness, engagement, and the evolution of waste prevention activities. WRAP, in its Good Practice Guidance (WRAP 2006), established three important sources of data gathering: (i) inputs (e.g. number of hits on the website); (ii) outcomes (e.g. number of householders aware of the policy) and; (iii) impacts (e.g. the number of householders engaged in the policy).

The aim is to assess householders new to performing waste prevention behaviour. This engagement indicator is essential to measure behaviour change and to assess diverted waste quantities. Indicators such as 'population reached by the action' only allow assessing the efficiency of communication activities. It is important to note that part of the targeted population might not be able to perform certain actions for different reasons (e.g. no access to a garden for home composting). This happens when the targeted population is greater than potential participants. Another important point is the difference between the 'reached population' and the 'level of awareness of the population'; this can vary depending on the type of instruments used and the initial state of awareness within the targeted population.

Thus, depending on the objectives of the monitoring process, it can be interesting to perform an assessment of the initial participation in the territory targeted by the waste prevention action. For example, how many households with access to a garden are already composting their garden waste prior to a promotion action? If previous data are not available, then this initial state will have to be assessed using behaviour surveys. Depending on the scale of the action and the number of potential participants, it can be done either by the entire panel or only by a representative sample.

Behaviour surveys can provide interesting qualitative and quantitative data on a large scale and are an interesting tool to monitor changes of behaviour. However, they do require important resources especially for polls and face-to-face interviews. Moreover, they give declarative data which can be subjective and biased. Self-completed questionnaires can be a less expensive solution but they increase the risk of uncertainties since the panel will not necessarily be representative of the total targeted population. Then again, according to WRAP (2007), these issues can be taken into account by (i) having a good sample design, including large sample sizes; (ii) estimating the risk for small samples in some engagement models; (iii) avoiding self-selecting and unrepresentative samples and; (iv) checking for self-reporting bias, including a tendency to over-estimate waste reduction impacts.

Finally, the main idea behind the use of waste prevention indicators is not new or even unfeasible. Yet, its practical application requires time, money and a strong methodology. It is unlikely that every indicator presented here will apply to every waste prevention action. Some actions will be more difficult to monitor than others because of the availability of data or the possibility of linking these data to waste generation. Thus, establishing a research panel is an important step to find the appropriate questions and to develop a reliable measurement instrument. Waste prevention indicators must be set up in relation to the goals of monitoring and evaluation. It is important to have an idea of what the purpose of the monitoring is before starting it, in order to ensure sufficient and consistent data collection. On the other hand, it might not be relevant to have an exhaustive and time-consuming monitoring system if nothing is done with the indicators. Combining quantitative and qualitative measures is highly recommended in order to get a full picture of the impact of the implemented waste prevention programme.

Examples of waste prevention policies

A waste prevention programme consists of a set of organised activities with a specific time schedule and budget to put waste prevention policies into action. A waste prevention programme would create conditions to reduce waste generation and ultimately contribute to the sustainability goals. A programme for waste prevention may take different forms. It may draw from a wide range of instruments, target many different types of stakeholders, and may or may not include quantitative reduction goals. Moreover, different national, regional and/ or local waste prevention programmes can be created to explicitly complement each other, though in practice such co-ordination remains largely indefinable.

Constructive measures to reduce waste can be taken by all societal players, by consumers just as much as suppliers. There are no shortages of advice and suggestions as to what might be done. Key reports such as NRWF's Household Waste Prevention Toolkit (NRWF 2004) and published papers (Coggins 2001) provide much useful analysis. There are also many other published guidelines on what waste prevention activities could be undertaken, and on the ways to encourage people to engage in those activities. Most local authorities, waste campaigners and NGOs, for example, provide lists and tips for household waste reduction on their websites. This chapter does not propose to refer or review all

Table 3.1 Household reduction and reuse activities

Reduction and reuse tctivities	How
Avoid over packaging	Buy loose products and the right amount, saving packaging. Buy in larger containers rather than in small packages.
Shopping for food	Plan beforehand what you want to buy. Favour foodstuffs produced locally.
Sustainable cleaning	Use the right amount, just a little is enough. Use cleaning product refill packages.
Cooking and eating	Reuse every bit of food. Do not put more than you can eat on your plate.
Machines and appliances	Consider repairing old appliances before buying new ones. Try also to rent or lease the appliance.
Clothes	Repair old clothes for reuse. Wool and silk are self-cleaning when properly aired.

Source YTV Helsinki Metropolitan Area Council website

that material in the literature, but simply notes, by way of example, some of the materials typical to those commentaries. Table 3.1 summarises the information posted on the YTV Helsinki Metropolitan Area Council website (YTV 2007). Clearly the presented material, aimed at the householder, focuses on the small practical everyday activities that might be accommodated easily within householders' lifestyles.

In 2006, anticipating the requirement to prepare a waste prevention programme, the Austrian Lebensministerium (Ministry of Life) has decided to make waste prevention a focus of its Federal Waste Management Plan (Lebensministerium 2006). The Waste Prevention and Recycling Strategy (Umweltbundesamt) was developed and implemented in 2007 (Reisinger & Krammer 2007). This strategy was based on five core functions: motivation, enablement, encouragement, engagement and, example. The waste prevention programme accounts for five main areas of waste management: construction and demolition waste, industrial waste, household waste, food waste and, waste repair and reuse. In the case of household waste prevention policy, the package of measures consists of: internet based fact sheets on prevention actions and technologies; an information campaign on waste prevention options for householders; printed fact sheets to promote eco-products and eco-events initiatives, and waste consultants' support for municipalities. Employee training, online best-practice examples, incentive systems and donation schemes were also established for food waste prevention. To encourage repair and reuse, the programme helped to create new markets for reuse activities within the public administration by initiating reuse of equipment/furniture campaigns and introducing public purchasing reuse criteria. A national campaign on reuse was also introduced with new collection points, a new networking of waste municipalities and social institutions, new quality standards and new concepts for shops selling secondhand goods and market development.

The strategy is implemented at regional level by the Austrian Provincial Waste Management Plan, which calls for regional authorities to analyse the waste generated locally and design waste prevention campaigns based on local circumstances. The plan also advises on public engagement through awareness campaigns and on the promotion of home composting. Based on the national strategy, the city of Vienna is using three distinct initiatives to help reduce household waste. The first is the web flea market, an internet based exchange platform for consumer goods, construction tools and materials and gardening equipment. Twenty-three local repair and service centres (RUSZ) were established to provide affordable repair services for electrical household appliances, and to break down appliances for material recycling. The city also has a campaign to promote lifestyle change, encouraging individuals to spend money on services and culture instead of material goods. Currently, the RUSZ centres repair nearly 400 tons of appliances per year and the internet flea market sells 450 tons of used appliances. The Vienna authorities estimate that around 11,000 tonnes of waste was prevented by the RUSZ centres while the flea market saves about 1,000 tonnes per year. In 2099, an estimated €34 million was saved with over 100,000 tonnes of waste prevented (EU 2009).

In 2013, the UK Department for Environment, Food and Rural Affairs (Defra) published a *Waste Prevention Programme for England* (Defra 2013c) which sets out the government's view of the key roles and actions which should be taken to tackle waste generation. The waste prevention programme is a requirement of the revised Waste Framework Directive (WFD-2008/98/EC). The main objectives of the British programme are to (i) encourage the contribution from the businesses sector by including waste prevention into design, offering alternative business models and delivering new and improved products and services; (ii) encourage a culture of valuing resources by making it easier for householders to find out how to reduce their waste, to use products for longer, repair broken items, and enable reuse of items by others; (iii) support action by central and local governments, businesses and civil society to capitalise on these opportunities. Thus, the purpose is to contribute to breaking the link between waste arising and the environmental impacts associated with the generation of waste by increasing the level of resource efficiency and preventing waste.

Many of the actions proposed in this programme are relevant across different sectors and materials, but some areas were identified as priorities to help provide direction to local governments, businesses, and other stakeholders when determining where to focus action on waste prevention. Food will be continue to be a key source of waste prevention, and the national government will continue to support voluntary action focused on food waste aiming to reduce household food and drink waste by 5 per cent by 2015 from a 2012 baseline. As far as paper is concerned, the programme recommends actions to improve packaging design through the supply chain to maximise recycled content as appropriate, while ensuring there is no increase in the carbon impact of packaging by 2015, from a 2012 baseline. Another proposed action is to reduce packaging waste in the grocery supply chain by 3 per cent by 2015, from a 2012 baseline. Plastic bag distribution will be reduced by imposing a manadatory 5p purchase charge, by developing a more sustainable biodegradable plastic bag and by giving incentives for businesses to minimise packaging. Waste prevention and reuse will be included in Government Buying Standards and a web-based postcode locator will be developed to provide a practical tool to enable householders to find their local reuse and repair services.

Some examples of ongoing waste prevention policies in the UK include (Defra 2013c): (a) Wandsworth Council's household bulky waste reuse service, which diverts around 6 tonnes each month, saving approximately £870 per month in avoided disposal fees and providing affordable white goods and furniture, and so on to low-income households; (b) the paint reuse scheme at Nottinghamshire, which has collected and diverted 17,000 litres of paint from householders from (specialist) disposal, saving the council £17,000 to date and saving local community groups £69,700 on the cost of new paint; (c) the Greater Manchester Waste Disposal Authority WEEE reuse schemes, which repaired 582 items from 813 collected and diverted 30.7 tonnes of WEEE making it available for reuse by the community, and (d) the Real Nappies scheme in London (City of London 2014) provides an incentive of £50 per family when they purchase reusable nappies, preventing 1 tonne of waste per child.

In 2004, Japan developed its waste management initiative, called 'A Sound Material Cycle Society' (MoE 2003), focused on reducing the environmental load and minimising consumption of natural resources. The plan was developed in response to the increasing volumes of waste generated in Japan, ongoing rapid industrial development, and the limitations imposed by Japan's relatively small land mass. The country has extensive waste-related legislation and other sustainable production and consumption policies under the 3Rs (reducing, reusing and recycling) umbrella. And Japan's 3Rs are heavily weighted towards waste prevention. These include laws setting targets for general waste prevention, waste recycling and avoidance of final disposal. The emphasis of waste prevention policies is not only on reduction and reuse activities; but also on eco-design, lifecycle assessment, and on extended producer responsibility (EPR). This means that waste prevention is addressed from the design stage, sharing the responsibility among all stakeholders (including consumers), and taking the Integrated Product Policy (IPP) into account.

The particular Japanese definition of waste is 'discarded materials which cannot be sold to other people'. Thus, according to the Basic Act for Establishing a Sound Material-Cycle Society, citizens are responsible for making efforts to prevent waste (reduce and reuse) as well as for using products as long as possible, using recycled articles, and cooperating in the separation and collection of recyclable materials. In addition, the law determines that local governments are responsible for controlling the disposal of and the adequate cyclical use of municipal waste, and to take the initiative in promoting waste prevention.

Recently, Tokyo's municipal governments are advancing efforts to control waste generation with the cooperation of householders, businesses and shopping districts. A new secondhand market was developed by holding eco-events and flea-markets where disused articles and bulk waste are sold. Another example is the Shinjuku Eco Jiman Point, an eco-point card (Environment of Tokyo 2010). The card serves as proof of their waste prevention behaviour in which the consumer accumulates points every time s/he declines a shopping bag or undertakes a waste prevention action while shopping. They can exchange these points at eco-events organised by the local government or for privileges/prizes offered by stores. Through this policy, Tokyo aims to encourage consumers to refuse plastic shopping bags and also to raise householders' awareness regarding waste and general environmental issues. In Tokyo, householders have to put their waste out in translucent bags segregated into three types: bulky wastes, packaging and paper, combustible and non-combustible, at a place shared by 10 to 20 households. Thus, this policy not only encourages the habit of separating waste at source but also makes waste generation visible among residents.

In France, the law of 12 July 2010 (Ministère de l'Écologie, du Développement durable et de l'Énergie 2010) (known as the Grenelle 2 legislation) made it mandatory for local governments, responsible for waste collection and treatment, to set up a local prevention programme as from 1 January 2012. These schemes have a broader scope than under the previous legislation, covering all household and similar waste, including bulky waste. According to the National Prevention Plan, local authorities have to set up operational local waste prevention programmes aimed at reducing household waste generation by 7 per cent within five years. Various strategies were proposed to achieve these objectives: tariff incentives, such as per-service waste management fees; mandatory sorting by producers of large amounts of organic waste; development of extended producer responsibility and application to a broad range of products. To support this plan, the French government has increased taxes on landfill waste and has adopted an incineration tax.

To promote these policies at the local level, Île-de-France has elaborated its Regional Prevention Plan transposing the National Prevention Plan while taking into account regional specificities. This plan primarily aims at rallying all societal actors involved in waste prevention schemes by promoting cooperation among them. The Île-de-France prevention programme sets actions around five main topics: awareness raising; promotion of waste prevention within the local government's departments and offices; actions that directly avoid waste generation such as responsible consumption and reuse; qualitative prevention or industrial waste prevention, and home composting. The target is to reduce household waste from 490 kilos per inhabitant in 2005 to 440 kilos per inhabitant in 2019 (Bel 2011).

In 2013, the Ministry of Ecology, Durable Development and Energy has published the first draft of the National Waste Prevention Plan for 2014–2020 (Ministère de l'Écologie, du Développement durable et de l'Énergie 2013). The plan reviews past waste prevention efforts from 2004 through 2013, and then discusses 55 actions that France will undertake during the next six years. The plan organises specific waste streams into three levels of priority based on factors such as tonnage generated and environmental impact. Industrial packaging is in the first priority level and household packaging second. The 13 main strategies include: extended producer responsibility, reuse and repair, food waste prevention, responsible consumption and waste prevention awareness campaigns.

In Germany, the realisation that waste can be a useful source of raw materials and energy is not new. Since 2012, through the Closed Cycle Management Act (Kreislaufwirtschaftsgesetz, KrWG), local waste management plans have adopted the closed cycle management policy by assigning disposal responsibilities to manufacturers, introducing new disposal technologies and increasing recycling capacities. These actions have also made householders even more aware of the necessity to separate waste. Economic instruments were also adopted to promote resource efficiency, such as the Material Input Tax project that encourages lower raw material demand through the taxation of resource extraction.

In 2013, the German Cabinet approved the German Government's Waste Prevention Programme (Dehoust *et al.* 2013). The programme sets out a systematic and comprehensive approach for waste prevention in the public sector by recommending specific instruments and measures. The Waste Prevention Programme examines various approaches to waste prevention throughout the various stages of a product's lifecycle, including measures that address production, product design, retail, trade, and the use of products. Alongside the key criteria of waste prevention potential and ecological impacts, the analysis also considers economic, social and legal criteria. Only measures that are expected to have a beneficial effect in view of all these criteria are recommended for inclusion in the Waste Prevention Programme. Some of the recommended measures of preventing waste include: reusing products, designing minimal-waste products, and extending the lifespan of products. The German waste prevention programme also emphasises the importance of information and awareness campaigns, coupled with research and development, as well as providing organisational and/or financial support for reuse and communal schemes (to encourage the more intensive use of commodities by a larger group of users).

Düsseldorf has implemented a number of policies in different areas of waste prevention. Over the past two decades, the city has worked in close cooperation with different charitable institutions in the area of reconditioning used furniture, kitchen equipment and consumer electronics. On its website, the city promotes a variety of opportunities to sell or exchange used objects on a private basis. This policy also benefits lower-income families who have the opportunity to buy low-cost furniture at the outlets. The amount of bulky waste from private households has decreased from 319 kilos per capita in 2000 to 262 kilos per capita in 2010 (Lindert 2012). The local waste management programme specifies a number of guidelines for administrative and operational work. The internal purchasing standards are determined by a series of central operational guidelines to ensure the procurement of long-life, low-pollutant products and materials.

In addition, Düsseldorf's council actively pursues a policy of selling vehicles and furniture that have been scheduled for replacement. The programme also provides householders with detailed information on waste prevention. The local government promotes the involvement of householders and other stakeholders in policy decisions, which leads to forward-looking legislation, more investments, and changes in behaviour.

Many other developed and developing countries are also pursuing the objective of decreasing waste generation. These are just some of the countries that are investing massively in their waste prevention programmes with the objective of reducing or preventing the increase of the total amount of waste. However, despite all efforts presented above, waste prevention programmes are still struggling to effectively decrease waste generation and to maintain householders' engagement. Many studies reveal that even when conventional environmental and solid waste policy approaches have succeeded in attaining their own specific objectives, they have not been sufficient toward counteracting a significant and growing solid waste burden. While it is true that the principle of waste prevention is universally accepted, the practice has a considerable distance to travel in achieving its full potential.

The challenge of waste prevention programmes

The multiplicity of waste prevention measures that have already been demonstrated in the examples above shows a very broad range and could provide good bases for any waste prevention programme. Therefore the focus should particularly be on behavioural change policies. It is clearly identified in the examples above that there are significant challenges in relation to the implementation of these waste prevention programmes and many of them are concerned about how individuals' behaviour will affect the effectiveness of these policies. Despite achievements on the recognition of the importance and the further approved regulations on waste prevention, there has been little change in the total waste generated. Volumes of waste are likely to increase since consumption patterns are unaffected. More attention needs to be paid to why waste prevention programmes have been not successful in achieving goals established in the dominant discourse of the integrated waste management system that permeates these programmes. That means looking more carefully at the causes and consequences of this ineffectiveness of governance. There are other reasons for the lack of success of waste prevention programmes that relate to the very conception and definition of waste and they are evident in the alternative discourses of zero waste and resource efficiency in the policies presented above. Unsurprisingly, given the unpopularity of any requirements to modify behaviour, there is reluctance among elected officials to engage directly with the issue of consumption that leads to the production of waste. Yet the whole waste lifecycle centres on consumption practices and here lies the contradiction. Given the reticence of governments to address conspicuous consumption, new waste management technologies (e.g. biogasification) are being proposed as solutions for increasing volumes of waste. While the potential advantages are indicated by these technologies in terms of reduction the volume of residual waste, they permit the continued consumption of resources. The issue of waste generation cannot be solved as an isolated problem. Thus if waste prevention programmes are to decrease waste generation the preoccupation with behavioural changes policies need to be regarded as a priority and the dimension of consumption in relation to waste tackled.

References

Bel, J.-B. (2011). Waste prevention strategy – Île-de-France Region, France. International Pre-waste workshop. Brussels.

City of London. (2014). Waste Strategy 2013–2020 – Planning a sustainable future for the City of London. London. Retrieved from http://www.london.gov.uk/sites/default/files/Municipal%20Waste_FINAL.pdf

Coggins, C. (2001). Waste prevention – an issue of shared responsibility for UK producers and consumers: Policy options and measurement. *Resources, Conservation and Recycling, 32*, 181–190.

Cox, J., Giorgi, S., Sharp, V., Strange, K., Wilson, D. C., & Blakey, N. (2010). *Household waste prevention – a review of evidence. Waste Management & Research: The Journal of the International Solid Wastes and Public Cleansing Association, ISWA, 28*(3), 193–219.

Defra. (2013a). *Prevention is better than cure – the role of waste prevention in moving to a more resource efficient economy*. London: Defra.

Defra. (2013b). *Waste prevention programme for England – call for evidence*. London: Defra.

Defra. (2013c). *Waste prevention programme for England, household waste prevention in action – examples from across England*. London: Defra.

Dehoust, G., Jepsen, D., Knappe, F., & Wilts, H. (2013). *Substantive implementation of Article 29 of Directive 2008/98/EC – scientific-technical foundation for a national waste prevention programme*. Report No. (UBA-FB) 001760 E. Heidelberg, Germany.

EEA (European Environment Agency). (2002). Case studies on waste minimization practices in Europe, Topic report 2/2002, Copenhagen.

Environment of Tokyo. (2010). 3Rs in Tokyo – present state of wastes and recyclables. Retrieved from http://www.kankyo.metro.tokyo.jp/en/attachement/3Rs%20in%20Tokyo%202009.pdf

EPA – Environmental Protection Agency. (1997). *Source reduction program potential manual – a planning tool*. EPA530-R-97-002. Washington, DC.

EU. (2009). Waste prevention programme – Vienna, Austria. Waste Prevention Best Practice Factsheets. Retrieved from http://ec.europa.eu/environment/waste/prevention/pdf/Vienna_Factsheet.pdf

Lebensministerium. (2006). Federal waste management plan 2006. Vienna.

Lindert, M. (2012). *Waste prevention – municipal practice in Düsseldorf*. Paper presented at ISWA International Conference, Florence, Italy.

Local Assistance and Planning Committee. (1993). *Statewide waste prevention plan*. California Integrated Waste Management Board, Sacramento, CA.

Loi No. 92-646 du 13 juillet 1992 relative à l'élimination des déchets ainsi qu'aux installations classées pour la protection de l'environnement (in French). Law No 92-646 of 13th July 1992, concerning the disposal of waste and registered organisations for the protection of the environment.

Mazzanti, M., & Zoboli, R. (2008). Waste generation, incineration and landfill diversion. Decoupling trends, socio-economic drivers and policy effectiveness in the EU. *Environmental & Resource Economics*, 44, 2, 203–30.

Ministère de l'Écologie, du Développement durable et de l'Énergie. (2010). Grenelle Environment, Grenelle 2 Law. Paris, France. Retrieved from http://www.developpement-durable.gouv.fr/IMG/pdf/Grenelle_Loi-2_GB_.pdf

Ministère de l'Écologie, du Développement durable et de l'Énergie. (2013). Projet de plan national de prevention des dechets: 2014–2020. Paris, France. Retrieved from http://www.consultations-publiques.developpement-durable.gouv.fr/IMG/pdf/PNPD_2013-11-15.pdf

MoE, Ministry of Environment, Japan. (2003). *Fundamental plan for establishing a sound material-cycle society* (English version).

National Resource and Waste Forum. (2003). *Towards a UK framework for household waste prevention*, Phase 1 report. National Resource and Waste Forum, London.

New York State, Department of Environmental Conservation, Division of Solid & Hazardous Materials. (1998). New York State solid waste management plan: 1997/98 update. New York (State). Albany, NY. x, 52, ENV 214-4 SOLWM 87-30439 1997/98 update FINAL.

NRWF – National Resource and Waste Forum. (2004). Household Waste Prevention Toolkit (Unpublished Version). UK

OECD. (2000). *Strategic waste prevention*. ENV/EPOC/PPC(2000)5/FINAL. Paris: OECD.

OECD. (2004). *Towards waste prevention performance indicators*. ENV/EPOC/WGWPR/SE(2004)1/FINAL. Paris: OECD.

Prewaste, ORDIF (2012). PREWASTE: waste prevention indicators – a general framework. CP4: Final note on PREWASTE indicators. Retrieved from http://www.prewaste.eu/images/stories/prewaste/Virtual_library/pre_waste_indicators_general_framework_report.pdf

RECAP. (2008). Waste prevention plan for Cambridge and Peterborough 2008–2022. Retrieved from www.recap.co.uk

Reisinger, H., & Krammer, H.-J. (2007). *Weißbuch Abfallvermeidung und verwertung in Österreich [Whitebook on waste prevention and recycling in Austria]* (Report, REP- 0083). Klagenfurt, Vienna: Umweltbundesamt.

Science Applications International Corporation. (2000). *NYC WasteLe$$ summary report*. Newport, RI: Science Applications International Corporations.

Sharp, V., Giorgi, S. G., & Wilson, D.C. (2010a). Delivery and impact of household waste prevention intervention campaigns (at the local level). *Waste Management & Research*, 28, 256–268.

Sharp, V., Giorgi, S. G., & Wilson, D. C. (2010b). Methods to monitor and evaluate household waste prevention. *Waste Management & Research*, 28, 269–280.

Springer, T. (1994). *Source reduction measurement methods for cities and counties*. Sacramento, CA: California Integrated Waste Management Board.

Reisinger, H., & Krammer, H.-J. (2007). Weißbuch Abfallvermeidung und verwertung in Österreich [Whitebook on waste prevention and recycling in Austria] (Report, REP-0083). Klagenfurt, Vienna: Umweltbundesamt.

Vancini, F. (1997). Effective approaches to waste minimisation. In *Changing consumption patterns: Waste prevention and minimisation*. Proceedings of an International Conference, Korea Environment Institute, Seoul.

Waste Framework Directive 2008/98/EC of the European Parliament and of the Council of the European Union. (2008) *Official Journal of the European Union*. Strasbourg, France.

Wilson, C. D. (2005). *The evidence base for household waste prevention: How best to promote voluntary actions by households*, Imperial College London and Research Managing Agent, Defra Waste and Resources Evidence Programme, United Kingdom.

WRAP. (2006). *Improving the performance of waste diversion schemes, a good practice guide to monitoring and evaluation*. Banbury: WRAP.

WRAP (2007). *Possible method for estimating the landfill diversion attributable to home composting for use in LATS calculations: A discussion paper by WRAP.*

YTV – Helsinki Metropolitan Area Council. (2007). It's smart with less waste campaign. Retrieved from from http://www.hsy.fi/en/wastemanagement/Pages/default.aspx.

Part II
Waste prevention behaviour
Conceptual issues

4 Waste prevention behaviour and social psychology

Consider the following situation, you are in the supermarket and you see one of your friends carrying her reusable carrier bag. You stop to say hello and she starts to talk about the local campaign to raise awareness about the environmental impacts of using plastic bags. Your friend explains that she has decided to actively participate on this campaign and that her group is distributing free cloth bags to involve people on waste prevention actions. You do not know much about the issue, but you trust your friend, so you decide to accept the fabric bag and attempt to practise this new way of shopping. After all, it does seem reasonable to try to avoid using plastic bags do so much harm to the natural environment. Her argument that we should not generate so much waste makes sense. You meet her again next week and she invites you to a meeting the following week to support the new legislation and the efforts to forbid the free distribution of plastic bags at the supermarkets. As she is talking, you start to remember the TV news you watched earlier that morning. The reporter was interviewing a prominent lawyer who was defending the right of consumers to use the free plastic bags. He believes that the new legislation would impose on the consumer the burden of having to cope with environmental protection by paying for the purchase of reusable bags. You thought that the lawyer had had delivered a strong argument about the unfairness of the plastic bags ban, especially because consumers would have to pay for something that was free only few days ago. Now you feel uncomfortable. What do you tell your friend? Will you go to the meeting to support the plastic bags ban? Are you more likely to support it because you are using the cloth bag you accepted last week? To what extent does your relationship with your friend and the lawyer's argument influence your decision? How important is protecting the environment for you? Would you spend more money and effort carrying out this action?

This example shows some of the influences we commonly face today about protecting the natural environment we live in. Even when we are on our own, these influences keep working because we internalise what we learn from others, including beliefs about who we are, and how to think about everything (e.g. environmental degradation) that surrounds us. Although we like to think that our decisions are based on rational and logical assessment of the available facts, environmental psychologists have shown in their studies that there is a great influence of different factors which generally goes unrecognised in our daily lives. And they will affect how we view a given environmental action both in the way it is regarded generally and the consequences of particular actions. From an environmental psychological perspective, understanding the environment and its interplay with humans is largely necessary to help change pro-environmental behaviour. The definition of environment includes ecological, social and cultural aspects. Environmental psychology defines the term environment broadly, encompassing natural environments, social settings, built environments, learning environments, and informational environments. There are different definitions of pro-environmental behaviour. In this book, it is defined as the behaviour which people adopt with an explicit goal of doing something beneficial for the environment (Greve 2001). Waste prevention behaviour is one of the categories of pro-environmental behaviour.

As defined in the previous chapter, waste prevention is a multi-faceted construct in which individual preferences and choices can guide many different manifestations of waste prevention behaviour. There are many different opportunities for householders to prevent potential waste from entering the system, but there are also ways that waste can be avoided in the first place. One example is changing shopping habits by reducing the amount of packaging waste and buying refillable products. Another is repairing old appliances or renting them instead of buying new ones. Taking a reusable bag to the supermarket instead of accepting a plastic bag is another useful way to prevent waste. There is also the opportunity of reusing packaging, such as glass jars or plastic containers, or looking for packaging that can be recycled easily. Other materials (e.g. paper, clothes) may also be reused for different purposes rather than their original objective. Thus, waste prevention can be judgemental and vary according to one's perspective.

This chapter will examine the influences on waste prevention behaviour in the context of major topics that have received much research attention by environmental psychologists. It includes: values, attitudes, norms, affect, identity, status, response efficacy and environmental uncertainty. It provides a definition and discusses these features and how they can affect how an individual acts with regard to environmental protection.

Values, attitudes, norms

Values

Is environmental protection important to you? Most people would probably answer 'yes'. Some might be more specific and say, 'it is important also for future generations'. What actions are you carrying out to protect the environment? Many people engage in different behaviours that threaten the environment as well as protect it. You can separate your waste for recycling but at the same time you prefer to use plastic bags instead of taking your own reusable bag to the supermarket. So, how do you know that you are really concerned about the environment? How do you show your environmental values? The first set of variables that researchers have linked to pro-environmental behaviour constitute the most fundamental bases of human subjectivity towards the environment in which we live in. Values can be defined as the underlying guiding principles in the life of a person (Schwartz 1992). Values includes beliefs about the desirability of consequences; they are rather abstract constructs and transcend specific situations; and, they serve as guiding principles for the evaluation of people, events and behaviours. Values are ordered in a system of priorities which implies that the most important value for a specific situation is chosen. Values are a relevant starting point for changing behaviours. Through influencing or activating certain values, it is possible to influence a range of environmental behaviour-specific beliefs, norms, intentions, and behaviours (Thøgersen & Ölander 2006). The fact that values are extremely abstract complicates its measurement. For example, based on the same value, a person may decide to buy water in returnable glass bottles or may decide not to buy bottled water anymore. A considerable number of studies have attempted to link values and pro-environmental behaviour. However, a review of the literature presents few results to demonstrate the direct influence of values and their role in promoting pro-environmental behaviour. Thus, behaviour-specific attitudes and norms are generally better predictors of behaviours than values (De Groot & Steg 2007).

The Value-Belief-Norm (VBN) theory (Dietz *et al.* 2005) underscores the pivotal role of values by outlining them as basic in two ways: (i) values influence other elements in the model, exerting their effects on beliefs, which in turn affect norms and then predict behaviours; (ii) values are also basic because they are the most stable determinants of pro-environmental behaviour and thus the hardest to change. This means that values have the most far-reaching effects. They influence how we interpret information, what we think we are responsible for and what we actually do about it. Schwartz (1992) proposes in his value theory, a general and comprehensive taxonomy of 56 values which can be plotted in a two-dimensional space where the different motivational value types can be identified as separate clusters of values. In Schwartz's theory, scores on the importance of values have little meaning on their own, but reflect the relative priorities of values compared to other values, and their motivational content is revealed more clearly when forming value clusters or value orientations (Schwartz 1992). The first dimension in Schwartz's value structure is 'openness to change' versus 'conservatism', which distinguishes values that stress openness to new things and ideas from values that emphasise tradition and conformity. The second dimension is 'self-transcendence' versus 'self-enhancement' which is comparable to the distinction between altruistic and egoistic values. *Altruistic values* reflect the concern for society and other people and *egoistic values* reflect the concern for oneself. This means that egoistic values may lead to concern about the environment because of direct impacts on the individual rather than its relevance for the society in general (altruistic values). Schwartz has validated this value clusters structure in a survey across 44 countries (Schwartz 1994). Stern *et al.* have separated *biospheric values* from altruistic values, which reflect the concern with the quality of natural environmental for its own benefit. Those with biospheric values regard ecological systems as important in themselves, beyond what they mean for human welfare or personal interests. Both altruistic and biospheric values are likely to promote pro-environmental behaviour; both reflect self-transcendence being in line with Schwartz's value theory. According to Stern, these three values are particularly relevant to understand and promote pro-environmental beliefs, norms and behaviours (VBN theory). Values also differ across different cultures. European and US samples show a priority of egoistic over biospheric values whereas Latin American countries tend to show higher biospheric than egoistic values (Schultz 2002). In contrast, altruistic values are common in most cultures. In addition, analyses of the relationship between values and environmental behaviour show evidence for norm activation only for self-transcendence; results for self-enhancement show a consistently negative relationship (Schultz et al. 2005).

Attitudes

Attitudes are mental dispositions to evaluate an object (a person, place, thing or event) with some degree of favour or disfavour. In other words, it is an evaluative reaction to an object or behaviour based on ideas about this object or behaviour. Attitudes arise out of values and beliefs and are more immediate predictors of behaviour. Within social psychology, attitudes have been studied as an important antecedent to pro-environmental behaviour. Pro-environmental attitudes serve as a catalyst to integrate our values and beliefs as they apply to environmental issues. In this way, the main assumption is that positive attitudes toward the environment would result in pro-environmental behaviour.

At the most general level, attitudes toward the environment have been conceptualised by many researchers as *environmental concern*. It is often described as a general attitude towards the environment and it reflects a personal evaluation of environmental issues. Previous studies (e.g. Hines et al. 1987) have shown that, in general, environmental concern is positively associated with conservation behaviours. Yet, few researchers (who have statistically tested the relationship between environmental concerns and environmental behaviours) have found general environmental concern to be a significant factor in the participation in any pro-environmental behaviour. Thus, while most people admit to having positive beliefs toward environmental protection, only a portion of them appear to behave accordingly. This discrepancy between attitudes people possess and their overt behaviour has stimulated a lot of discussion among researchers. Hines et al. have shown that although a positive relationship does exist between attitudes and behaviour, this relationship is moderate. Vining and Ebreo found direct relationships between attitudes and behaviour to be very weak or not significant at all (Vining & Ebreo 1990), including no fundamental differences in pro-environmental attitudes held by recyclers and non-recyclers (Vining & Ebreo 1992). Wicker (1969) in his study on the relationship of attitudes to behaviour concluded that barely 10 per cent of the variance in behavioural measures can be accounted for by attitudinal data. One explanation for this discrepancy is the fact that pro-environmental behaviour is influenced by a multiplicity of factors (e.g. norms, demographics) in addition to attitudes toward the environment. For example, the context-situation in which behaviour takes place has a direct effect on it since individuals are constrained by physical, social, institutional, and financial factors. Guagnano *et al.* (1995), for example, suggest that the attitude-behaviour link may only operate in certain social contexts. Additionally, Oskamp (1995) argues that many mediating factors can affect the relationship and thus attitudes and beliefs must become more specific towards individual behaviours before any strong correlations will emerge. Tucker and Douglas (2006) affirm that general environmental concern has become more widespread across the whole population and that most people nowadays claim to have at least some concern. Aspirations very rarely reflect reality and, while environmental values/concerns logically underlie pro-environmental behaviour, they are merely the starting point when analysing pro-environmental engagement. Dunlap *et al.* (1983) claim that environmental values held by practitioners and non-practitioners of pro-environmental behaviours now appear to have converged, while Schultz *et al.* (1995) suggest that any historical correspondences linking general environmental attitudes to pro-environmental behaviours have disappeared.Previous research has also found that more-specific pro-environmental attitudes can exert some influence on pro-environmental behaviours. For example, recycling behaviours have been found to be supported by attitudes in favour of resource conservation, litter reduction, energy conservation, reduction of landfill space (Vining & Ebreo 1989); satisfaction from saving natural resources, reducing litter, decreasing landfills, saving energy (Hopper & Nielsen 1991); or saving landfill space, reducing pollution, saving natural resources, reducing litter and saving energy (Kilner 1992). Motivation to act toward a specific environmental action (e.g. recycling) can be increased if the environmental issue in question (e.g. recognition of waste generation impacts) is a sensitive matter to the individual. However, in the absence of such external stimuli, pro-environmental attitudes still appear to be relatively correlated to pro-environmental behaviours.The search for a general predisposition toward the environment has generated many different ways of measuring environmental attitudes. One of the best-known measurement scales for environmental attitudes is the New Environmental Paradigm scale (NEP) developed by Dunlap and Van Liere (1978). The NEP scale measures general beliefs about the relationship of human beings to the environment, considering an emerging ecocentric system of beliefs (i.e. humans are seen as being part of natural systems and constrained by that fact). The scale is theoretically based on the contrast of this new ecocentric system represented by NEP and the traditional Dominant Social Paradigm (DSP), an anthropocentric system of beliefs where humans are seen as being independent from, and superior to, other organisms in nature. Despite its wide application, Hawcroft and Milfont (2010) argue that there is a lack of empirical and theoretical integration in studies employing this scale, particularly related to the lack of necessary information, sample type and variation in scale length and item content. The NEP scale is theoretically related to Schwartz's Theory of Cultural Values (Schwartz 1999) which represents the relation of humans to the natural and social environment.

On the contrary, Kaiser *et al.* (2010) argue that the inconsistency between attitudes and behaviour has led researchers to cease to believe 'in either a tight and simple or an axiomatic connection between a general attitude and a specific behaviour'. Campbell (1963), when addressing the attitude-behaviour gap, argued that verbal claim and other behavioural responses toward attitude object arise from a single 'acquired behavioural disposition'. So, the apparent discrepancy between what individuals say and their behaviour is due to the difficulties or costs of the behaviour in question. Kaiser *et al.* (2010) developed the Campbell Paradigm for attitude research that is grounded in Campbell's idea. The paradigm explains the probability of a person engaging in a pro-environmental behaviour as a function of (i) that person's pro-environmental attitude and (ii) the difficulty of that behaviour. Kaiser and Wilson (2004) developed a unidimensional measure of goal-directed pro-environmental behaviour within the Campbell Paradigm. The underlying idea of this measurement is that individuals generally favour the easiest behaviours rather than the more difficult ones. The more obstacles an individual overcomes and the more effort that person puts into implementing his/her goal, the stronger is his/her commitment to environmental protection goal. On the other hand, when an obstacle prevent someone from taking a more difficult pro-environmental action, his/her commitment to protecting the environment is likely to be weak.Conceptually defining an attitude within Campbell's paradigm thus involves carving out a uniform set of behaviours linked by one underlying goal (i.e. environmental conservation). This set of behaviours in turn is thought to represent the means people can use when implementing their personal levels of an attitude. However, the definition of an attitude is dependent not only on the set of behaviours but also on the order or structure of the behaviours which are distinct only in terms of their difficulties. Kaiser and Wilson (2004) mapped in one dimension six categories of pro-environmental behaviours, such as waste avoidance, recycling and consumer behaviour. The Rasch Model is the mathematical tool used to describe the Campbell Paradigm. The model orders pro-environmental behaviours in a data set from the easiest to the most difficult, assuming that individuals adopt behaviour cost-effectively. Thus, this measurement represents as much a measure of an individual's pro-environmental attitude as well as their overall behavioural performance. However, this measurement assumes that behaviours are linked by a single goal which conflicts with the notion that pro-environmental behaviours may be motivated by different antecedents (Vlek 2000). Part III of this book will discuss this later with more details.

Norms

Norms are rules for expected behaviour, i.e. 'an expected standard of behaviour and belief that is established and enforced by a group' (Park & Allaby 2013). Norms guide individuals' actions by suggesting what is normal, expected or correct. It is what you accept as commonly done or disapproved. Whether we are conscious or not, we are constantly reading social settings to determine appropriate speech, gestures, manners, topics of discussion, etc. Sociologists describe norms as informal understandings that govern society's behaviours (Scott & Marshall 2009). Psychologists have adopted a more general definition, recognising that smaller group units (e.g. a team) may also endorse separate norms in addition to cultural or societal expectations (Jackson 1965). There are several types of norms, which exert their influence through different mechanisms.

Social norms, the customary rules that govern behaviour in groups and societies, have been extensively studied in the social sciences. Anthropologists have described how social norms function in different cultures (Geertz 1973), sociologists have focused on their social functions and how they motivate people to act (Hechter & Opp 2001), and economists have explored how adherence to norms influences market behaviour (Akerlof 1976). Also legal scholars have touted social norms as efficient alternatives to legal rules, as they may internalise negative externalities and provide signalling mechanisms at little or no cost (Posner 2002). Psychologists define social norms as standards of behaviour 'that are understood by members of a group which guide and/or constrain the behaviour without the force of laws' (Cialdini & Trost 1998). This definition emphasises social norms' behavioural component by stating that norms have two dimensions: (i) how much behaviour is shown by most group members and, (ii) how much the group approves or disapproves of that behaviour. The latter are called *injunctive norms* while the former are *descriptive norms*. For example, littering is a socially disapproved behaviour and there is an injunctive norm against doing so. An interview on the TV news with a local government officer stating that flooding problems have increased in São Paulo partially because people are still throwing waste in the streets or into streams, gives descriptive norm information. The interview shows the situation (flooding) and the extent to which certain behaviour is still common (littering).

Descriptive social norms can either increase or decrease pro-environmental behaviour (Cialdini 2003). Usually, recycling campaigns advertisements show how the kerbside collection works and how easily the population are contributing to it. These campaigns are intended to encourage people to contribute to recycling policies by presenting descriptive norms (e.g. recycling rates, kerbside collections). Cialdini (2003) argues that highlighting descriptive norms is effective when the prevalent behaviour is environmentally beneficial (e.g. recycling); however this approach is detrimental when the prevalent behaviour is harmful to the environment (e.g. water pollution). For example, if a campaign promoting waste reduction reveals the average amount of waste generation by each resident in a specific street, chances are that those above the average limit will eventually decrease their waste generation while those below the descriptive norm would produce more. Schultz *et al.* (2007) have demonstrated this effect in their study of energy consumption. Injunctive norms are beliefs about the approval or disapproval of others. And many types of pro-environmental behaviours, particularly those related to waste management, are affected by the approval or disapproval of others. Consequently, if the majority of citizens approve a pro-environmental behaviour, the campaign developers should incorporate this injunctive normative information in parallel with descriptive norms (Cialdini 2003). That is why, many recycling campaigns portray citizens speaking positively about recycling and the kerbside collection and negatively of someone who failed to recycle and contribute to environmental protection. Both injunctive and descriptive norms have to operate in parallel, otherwise injunctive norms can be subverted by destructive norms. If you see your neighbours mixing their recyclable and disposable waste (descriptive norm), and later on a sign saying 'Separate your recyclable waste! It is your responsibility!' you will easily ignore the injunctive norm. The cross-norm inhibition effect (Keizer *et al.* 2008) states that the influence of an injunctive norm is inhibited when violations of another injunctive norm is observed. Although norms can exert a powerful influence on pro-environmental behaviour, people tend to underestimate their effects. We believe we act because of common sense, or through logical decisions, rather than because of social pressure to conform to others' behaviour. *Subjective norms* refer to what Fishbein and Ajzen (1975) regarded as a primary influence on behaviour. The awareness of others' behaviour, along with an acceptance of that behaviour, was, according to them, a crucial factor affecting personal decision to take action. Oskamp *et al.* (1991) asked respondents whether their friends and neighbours recycled waste in their evaluation of the kerbside collection. They found that social awareness of others' recycling was a significant predictor of recycling behaviour. There is also evidence from the experimental literature that social pressure can have positive effects on pro-environmental behaviour. Schultz (1999) introduced normative feedback intervention and results showed significant increases in the frequency of participation and the total amount of collected recyclable material. Even so, people are not very conscious of social influences and pressures on their decisions to act (Schultz *et al.* 2008). Conforming to norms is often associated with social acceptance or rewards, whereas violating norms often entails disapproval and social sanctions. We seek the approval of and fear their disapproval. As a consequence, environmentally appropriate behaviour can be induced through social diffusion, i.e. when people change their behaviour to be in line with what others do. For example, a person will be more likely to accept a reusable bag if another person surrounding her/him at the supermarket also accepts. Rogers (2010) shows that people often change behaviours when they see neighbours, family or friends change theirs. In this case, respondents were using them as their reference group, i.e. people who are liked or respected, and can have a significant influence on environmentally relevant behaviour through the power of normative influence. They serve as models and their behaviours communicate social norms (Bandura & Walters 1963). This is the reason why so many campaigns about climate change are endorsed by well-known people involved in the cause. Most of time, the audience is not paying attention to the facts portrayed in the advertisement; they attend to other variables such as the credibility of the source. According to Flynn and Goldsmith (1999), responsible consumption behaviour is influenced by high status people who know about and choose environmentally friendly behaviours. Al Gore's documentary (*An Inconvenient Truth*) has certainly raised public awareness about climate change (Gore 2006).

Not all pro-environmental behaviours can be influenced by social norms since they are typically not done in public. Waste prevention behaviour is one of them. The decision to not buy, reuse and repair something is done privately by the householder. A good example is home composting which is usually unobservable by neighbours. However, there are alternatives to raise the profile these behaviours. In their study, McKenzie and Mohr found that after asking participants to post feedback that demonstrated their participation in a composting programme, home composting in the neighbourhood increased. In addition, norms are generally specific to a context and they refer to beliefs about the appropriate behaviour in a specific setting. Thus, while it is appropriate to separate recyclable material for the kerbside collection at home, when staying in a hotel people might believe it is appropriate not do so. And in most contexts, there are different norms that are important and the extent to which a specific social norm is relevant determines the degree to which it is activated. Finally, there is a general social norm to obey the law. Legal norms differ from social norms in that they are enforced by specialised agents who typically impose direct punishment. Laws and regulations contribute greatly to social norms by interacting in numerous ways, such as forbidding citizens to drop litter in the streets. According to Elster (2007), when the law prohibits behaviour that imposes negative externalities on others, the social norm of obeying the law may spill over into a norm against that behaviour.

Personal norms are an individual's beliefs about their moral obligation to engage in certain behaviour. According to Schwartz (1970), social norms are far too general and detached to govern behaviour. Instead, the social norms are adopted by each of us on a personal level and hence become personal norms. Though derived from social norms, what distinguishes personal norms is that the consequences of violating or upholding them are tied to one's self-concept. To violate a personal norm would engender guilt and to uphold a personal norm engenders pride. In short, social norms exist on the social structural level, whereas personal norms are strongly internalised moral attitudes (Schwartz & Howard 1980). Thus, personal norms refer to an individual's belief about their moral obligation to engage in the behaviour. They are potent influences on pro-environmental behaviour because people try to avoid the guilt and remorse experienced when they are wrong. Using again the example of the reusable bag, you would feel guilt for not going to the meeting after learning that most of your friends did. We act on personal norms to avoid guilt, whether or not others approve or disapprove of our behaviour. Because of this internalisation process of social norms, personal norms are considered to be deeper and more potent. When people are intrinsically motivated by their own values to act in environmentally friendly ways, they are more consistent and committed, relative to people who act out of extrinsic motivations, such as peer pressure, rewards or convenience (Deci & Ryan 2010). Because it is built through an internalisation process of social and moral norms, personal norms depend both on social norms and on the frequency of the behaviour. When this internalisation process is deeper and so well enclosed into one's behaviour, Thøgersen (2006) refers to personal norms as integrated personal norms. This means that initially you take your cloth bag to the supermarket because you would feel guilty if you did not. After a while, you do it because seems the right thing to do and you do not think consciously about it any more. The norm is integrated and has become a habit.

Personal norms are an integral part of our personal beliefs about what is right or wrong to do. When individuals act in accordance with their personal norms, they experience a strong sense of pride. If, on the contrary, personal norms are violated, individuals undergo a feeling of guilt. Because of this guilt and, consequently, the fact that rewards for pro-environmental actions are more personal than social, waste prevention behaviour and other environmentally responsible actions have been considered as moral or ethical behaviour by some researchers (Thøgersen 2006). The principle of moral reasoning is directly related to environmental concern and environmental justice. The term environmental justice emerged as a concept in the United States in the early 1980s and it is defined by the US EPA as: '*the fair treatment and meaningful involvement of all people regardless of race, colour, national origin, or income with respect to the development, implementation, and enforcement of environmental laws, regulations, and policies. It will be achieved when everyone enjoys the same degree of protection from environmental and health hazards and equal access to the decision-making process to have a healthy environment in which to live, learn, and work*' (US EPA 2014). Environmental justice, by its definition, seems a general moral guideline. However, Koger and Winter (2010) argue that environmental justice can be fragile because it is so difficult to notice threats to the well-being of those who lie outside one's scope of justice. Speciesism (Singer 2009), a form of prejudice against animals, is one good example among others showing a clear division between humans' scope of justice and the rights of animals and wildlife preservation. In the case of waste prevention behaviour, this impasse over environmental justice creates differences among householders on how they are responsible or not for the impacts caused by excessive waste generation. Consequently, individuals may be unwilling to hear moral claims from others who disagree with them and may refuse to accept that their moral judgement relies on denial and moral exclusion.

Identity, status, affect, response efficacy

Pro-environmental behaviour research is almost exclusively done using rational behaviour models which confirms that instrumental reasons underlie behavioural decisions. The Theory of Planned Behaviour (TPB) (one of the most widely applied theories on pro-environmental behaviour) assumes that the decision to behave in a given way is based primarily on a rational assessment of salient information and makes no distinction between the feelings one has concerning a behaviour and one's evaluation of the costs and benefits of performing the behaviour (Parker *et al.* 1995). Thus, the study of identity, status and affect is relatively less in this context.

There is substantial literature within psychology on *identity*, what it is, where it comes from, and what difference it makes. In summary, when norms become very deeply internalised they give rise to identity, the sense of oneself, of who one thinks one is. In other words, identities are frameworks for organising information about a person which can be personal attributes; can involve social roles and relationships; or can place people into social categories. Identities are experienced both internally (a self-concept of ourselves) and externally (defined by others). Social identity is derived from a group and groups can shape important dimensions of one's sense of self, and can thereby powerfully affect environmentally relevant behaviour (e.g. individuals' participation in a social movement in Dunlap & McCright 2008). Different studies have found a strong correlation between being environmentalists and acting in more environmentally friendly manners (Kempton & Holland 2003). Conversely, group membership also inspires stereotypes and distinctions between in-group and out-group members (Tajfel & Turner 1986) which can increase the risk of failure of pro-environmental policies. However, collaborative learning between groups can facilitate the implementation of these policies by shifting group identities and promoting superordinate goals (Samuelson *et al.* 2003). Self-identity refers to the labels individuals use to describe themselves and are formed through a process of self-categorisation and identification (Stets & Burke 2000). We express our self-identity and make inferences about others' identities based on different sources of information including visible possessions and behaviours (Belk 1988). For example, we easily make different judgements about someone dropping litter the street and those who separate their recyclable waste. Identities thus affect the way we respond to the world, both cognitively and emotionally. They can form barriers to pro-environmental behaviours but they can also motivate such behaviour. As suggested by recent studies, adding identity to the TPB model increases its ability to explain behaviour. For example, Mannetti *et al.* (2004) found that self-identity accounted for a significant proportion of variance in recycling behaviour and Clayton (2003) found that environmental identity mediated the relationship between values and behaviour. Manetti *et al.* (2002) developed the identity similarity concept, which measures the correlation between self-attributes that one may infer to oneself and to the typical person who adopts, for example, a pro-environmental behaviour. They found that identity similarity explained behaviours over and above other variables such as attitudes, perceived behavioural control and subjective norms.

People develop their self-concepts by varied means, including social comparison. By comparison to relevant others, people gain information about themselves, and they make inferences that are relevant to their *status*. These social comparisons can be to people who are either higher in status or ability, or lower in status or ability. Status can also be inferred by owning and using the right kind of product which can be an important motivator for behaviour. Christopher and Schlenker (2000), for instance, show that individuals tend to have a higher opinion of the personal abilities (e.g. intelligent, organised) and sophistication (e.g. successful, cultured) of a hypothetical affluent person than a less affluent person. However, the 'affluent person is not nice' stereotype seemed to be evoked, as the affluent person was regarded as less kind and honest than a not-so affluent person. This is mainly related to when people explicitly endorse the accumulation of wealth and possessions as a basic goal in life. Materialism is defined as 'the importance ascribed to the ownership and acquisition of material goods in achieving major life goals or desired states' (Richins 2004). Materialistic values are problematic when considering pro-environmental behaviours. Gatersleben (2011) has found that materialistic people are less likely to indicate they would be willing to reduce their car use. Usually, these individuals consume more due to their lifestyle choices (Brown & Kasser 2005) and they cooperate less in games involving confrontations between personal and group interests (Sheldon & McGregor 2000). An important factor which contributes to increasing materialism is emotion. A growing body of research suggests that individuals are more likely to become materialistic in less emotional situations. Williams *et al.* (2000) found that materialistic children have parents who are less supportive of their needs for autonomy. People raised in more financially straitened times are more materialistic than those raised in more prosperous times. Concomitantly, consumption does not make people happy since it reduces experiences of personal well-being (Myers 2010).

Affect refers to the experience of feeling or emotion (Hogg *et al.* 2010). Taken together, the experience of negative or positive emotions may significantly impact not only people's experiences with the environment, but also their tendency to engage in pro-environmental behaviour. Indeed, Schultz & Tabanico (2007) argue that emotional affinity with nature can be a better predictor of pro-environmental behaviour than beliefs about environmental issues. Grob (1995) argues that one's emotional reaction to the environment, particularly environmental degradation, is a strong predictor of engagement in pro-environmental behaviour. De Young (2000) suggests that some of these behaviours 'are worth engaging in because of personal, internal contentment that engaging in these behaviours provides'. Affect can predict pro-environmental behaviour or because individuals believe that they will elicit positive or negative affective experiences (anticipated affect) or because engagement in this behaviour results in positive or negative affective experiences (experienced affect). Pelletier *et al.* (1998) suggests that people are more likely to engage in pro-environmental behaviour when they believe they will derive pleasure and satisfaction from doing so (anticipated affect), particularly when behaviour is relatively difficult. As a result, anticipated negative affect works as a barrier for individuals to engage in pro-environmental behaviour. If one experiences negative emotions, he or she may be less likely to engage in pro-environmental behaviour, feeling helpless to engage in meaningful behaviour change or to deny the need to change behaviour in the first place. In 1982, B. F. Skinner (1987) publicly criticised the efforts of environmental groups arguing that instead of trying to make people feel guilty or shame people into being more environmentally conscious, groups should focus instead on the benefits of adopting a more eco-friendly lifestyle. According to him, by reinforcing positive outcomes, people's attitudes and perceptions about the environment would change, thereby improving the likelihood of changed behaviours. Arguably, not everyone feels the same emotional reaction to pro-environmental behaviour. Individuals' anticipation about how they may feel if they engage in these behaviours are likely to be influenced by their past experiences (experienced affect) which can be strong motivators or barriers for engagement. This is consistent with research by Manzo and Weinstein (1987), who found that people who have been harmed by some environmental problem are more likely to be active members of an environmental organisation. More recent research (Chawla 1999) confirms that our emotional reaction to environmental problems is stronger when we directly experience the degradation. These effects are probably due to the notion that environmental harms produce distress, which lead us to psychological and behavioural responses aimed at relieving us from negative feelings or emotions (Kollmuss & Agyeman 2002) (e.g. anger or sadness). Yet, one's psychological response to experiencing environmental problems may actually prevent someone from engaging in pro-environmental behaviour. Kollmuss and Agyeman assume that emotional reactions may lead to defence mechanisms such as denial, i.e. refusing to accept the reality of a situation (e.g. global warming exists) and apathy, i.e. feeling that there is little one can do to change the situation (Hines *et al.* 1987). This may also reduce one's intrinsic motivation to engage in pro-environmental behaviour. Although there may be a number of internal factors that inhibit pro-environmental behaviour, it is important to consider how affective motives can encourage this type of behaviour.

Response efficacy refers to the perception of how a given behaviour will impact to reduce a given problem (e.g. I believe that reusing plastic containers will decrease waste generation). Thus believing that recycling is, or, is not an effective means to solve the waste problem constitutes response efficacy. For example, individuals may be sceptical about whether or not the local government recycles what is collected from households; so questioning whether recycling is carried out or not might affect how these individuals view recycling as a means to reduce waste (i.e. an effective response to the problem). In their study, Axelrod and Lehman (1993) found that response efficacy correlated with an overall measure of pro-environmental behaviour and that individuals with high levels of response efficacy were more inclined to behave in an environmentally responsible manner. Additionally, Kim *et al.* (2013) show that response efficacy regarding climate change mitigation was a significant predictor of individuals' intentions to engage in a set of pro-environmental behaviours. Although, Oskamp *et al.* (1991) found an insignificant relationship between response efficacy and recycling behaviour, they did find that response efficacy had a high predictive power for variables that had a predictive power for pro-environmental behaviour, such as intrinsic motivation to recycle. Response efficacy is also linked to group size, i.e. members of large groups tend to believe that their efforts will be insignificant (Kerr 1989). For example, individuals who are active in waste prevention but not part of a defined group express less consistent views about the effectiveness of their actions. Therefore convincing them to join a defined environmental group might strengthen their response efficacy because they would be part of a smaller setting in which to assess the effectiveness of their own actions. People are less likely to act for the common good if they feel that a cooperative act will be wasted. Manzo and Weinstein (1987) show that members of the defined environmental group (activists' group) viewed their actions as effective in reducing waste (response efficacy). In the other study, active members indicated that the efficacy of their actions was most important in their decision to participate, whereas non-active members cited the importance of competing commitments in their decision not to participate (Martinez & McMullin 2004). Thus, belonging to a defined group might strengthen response efficacy by reducing scepticism. At the end, the more a person feels able to make a difference environmentally, the more they are likely to take action.

Implications for waste prevention policies

From a social psychological perspective, waste prevention behaviour is a function of social influence. Hoornweg and Bhada-Tata (2012) define, in plain language, waste as '*the most visible and pernicious by-product of a resource-intensive, consumer-based economic lifestyle*'. Based on that, waste prevention behaviour seems to be moralised, motivated with a strong positive influence of personal norms and negative influence of materialism. Values, attitudes, and norms determine our choices by influencing what we think of as appropriate behaviour to tackle the growing problem of waste generation. Even though we are usually unaware of theses influences, we are influenced by others in our reference group as well as by messages from the media. The fundamental attitudes that support a pro-environmental behaviour (e.g. waste prevention) are believed to conform to a hierarchical structure, starting with fundamental values, through general environmental concerns to specific attitudes towards the activity (Tucker & Douglas 2006). Waste managers and local governments have traditionally relied on end-of-pipe solutions, technology efficiency and convenience to implement their waste management systems without experiencing any effective success in decreasing waste generation. Insights from social psychology can enable waste managers to redesign and optimise norms, reference groups, and social influence mechanisms that may induce environmentally responsible behaviour and reduce overconsumption. One of the messages of social psychology is that changes are much easier to make and keep if social situations are developed to support the behaviour, as stated by Lewin (1948) '*For unless the inclusive group structure is altered, individuals cannot basically be changed*'.

References

Akerlof, G. (1976). The economics of caste and of the rat race and other woeful tales. *The Quarterly Journal of Economics*, 90(4), 599–617.

Axelrod, L. J., & Lehman, D. R. (1993). Responding to environmental concerns: What factors guide individual action? *Journal of Environmental Psychology*, 13(2), 149–159.

Bandura, A., & Walters, R. H. (1963). *Social learning and personality development*. New York. Holt, Rinehart & Winston.

Belk, R. W. (1988). Possessions and the extended self. *Journal of Consumer Research*, 15(2), 139–168.

Brown, K. W., & Kasser, T. (2005). Are psychological and ecological well-being compatible? The role of values, mindfulness, and lifestyle. *Social Indicators Research*, 74(2), 349–368.

Campbell, D. T. (1963). Social attitudes and other acquired behavioural dispositions. In S. Koch (Ed.), *Psychology: A study of a science* (Vol. 6, pp. 94–172). New York, NY: McGraw-Hill.

Chawla, L. 1999. Life paths into effective environmental action. *Journal of Environmental Education 31*(1), 15–26.

Christopher, A. N., & Schlenker, B. R. (2000). The impact of perceived material wealth and perceiver personality on first impressions. *Journal of Economic Psychology, 21*(1), 1–19.

Cialdini, R. B. (2003). Crafting normative messages to protect the environment. *Current directions in psychological science, 12*(4), 105–109.

Cialdini, R. B., & Trost, M. R. (1998). Social influence: Social norms, conformity and compliance. In D. Gilbert, S. Fiske, & G. Lindzey (Eds.) '*The handbook of social psychology*, (4th edition) vol. 2, pp. 151–192. New York: McGraw-Hill.

Clayton, S. (2003). Environmental identity: A conceptual and an operational definition. In S. Clayton & S. Opotow (Eds.), *Identity and the natural environment*. Cambridge, MA: MIT Press.

Deci, E. L., & Ryan, R. M. (2010). *Self-determination*. Hoboken, NJ: John Wiley & Sons, Inc.

De Groot, J., & Steg, L. (2007). General beliefs and the theory of planned behavior: The role of environmental concerns in the TPB. *Journal of Applied Social Psychology, 37*(8), 1817–1836.

De Young, R. (2000). New ways to promote proenvironmental behavior: Expanding and evaluating motives for environmentally responsible behavior. *Journal of Social Issues, 56*(3), 509–526.

Dietz, T., Fitzgerald, A., & Shwom, R. (2005). Environmental values. *Annual Review of Environmental Resources, 30*, 335–372.

Dunlap, R. E., & McCright, A. M. (2008). A widening gap: Republican and Democratic views on climate change. *Environment: Science and Policy for Sustainable Development, 50*(5), 26–35.

Dunlap, R. E., & Van Liere, K. D. (1978). The new ecological paradigm. *Journal of Environmental Education, 9*, 10–19.

Dunlap, R. E., Grieneeks, J. K., & Rokeach, M. (1983). Human values and pro-environmental behavior. *Energy and Material Resources: Attitudes, Values, and Public Policy*, 145–168.

Elster, J. (2007). *Explaining social behavior: More nuts and bolts for the social sciences*. Cambridge: Cambridge University Press.

Fishbein, M., & Ajzen, I. (1975). *Belief, attitude, intention and behavior: An introduction to theory and research*. Reading, MA: Addison-Wesley.

Flynn, L. R., & Goldsmith, R. E. (1999). A short, reliable measure of subjective knowledge. *Journal of Business Research, 46*(1), 57–66.

Gatersleben, B. (2011). The car as a material possession: Exploring the link between materialism and car ownership and use. *Auto motives: Understanding car use behaviors*, 137–148.

Geertz, C. (1973). *The interpretation of cultures: Selected essays* (Vol. 5019). New York: Basic Books.

Gore, A. (2006). *An inconvenient truth: The planetary emergency of global warming and what we can do about it*. New York: Rodale.

Greve, W. (2001). Traps and gaps in action explanation: Theoretical problems of a psychology of human action. *Psychological Review, 108*(2), 435.

Grob, A. (1995). A structural model of environmental attitudes and behaviour. *Journal of Environmental Psychology, 15*(3), 209–220.

Guagnano, G. A., Stern, P. C., & Dietz, T. (1995). Influences on attitude-behavior relationships: A natural experiment with curbside recycling. *Environment and Behavior, 27*(5), 699–718.

Hawcroft, L. J., & Milfont, T. L. (2010). The use (and abuse) of the new environmental paradigm scale over the last 30 years: A meta-analysis. *Journal of Environmental Psychology, 30*(2), 143–158.

Hechter, M., & Opp, K. D. (Eds.). (2001). *Social norms.* Troy: Russell Sage Foundation.

Hines, J. M., Hungerford, H. R., & Tomera, A. N. (1987). Analysis and synthesis of research on responsible environmental behavior: A meta-analysis. *The Journal of Environmental Education, 18*(2), 1–8.

Hogg, M. A., Abrams, D., & Martin, G. N. (2010). Social cognition and attitudes. In G. N. Martin, , N. R. Carlson, & W. Buskist (Eds.), *Psychology* (pp. 646–677). Harlow: Pearson Education Limited.

Hoornweg, D., & Bhada-Tata, P. (2012). *What a waste: A global review of solid waste management.* Urban Development Series. Knowledge Papers no. 15. Washington, DC: World Bank.

Hopper, J. R., & Nielsen, J. M. (1991). Recycling as altruistic behavior: Normative and behavioral strategies to expand participation in a community recycling program. *Environment and Behavior, 23*(2), 195–220.

Jackson, J. (1965). Structural characteristics of norms. *Current Studies in Social Psychology, 301*, 309.

Kaiser, F. G., Byrka, K., & Hartig, T. (2010). Reviving Campbell's paradigm for attitude research. *Personality and Social Psychology Review, 14*(4), 351–367.

Kaiser, F. G., & Wilson, M. (2004). Goal-directed conservation behavior: The specific composition of a general performance. *Personality and Individual Differences, 36*(7), 1531–1544.

Keizer, K., Lindenberg, S., & Steg, L. (2008). The spreading of disorder. *Science, 322*(5908), 1681–1685.

Kempton, W., & Holland, D. C. (2003). Identity and sustained environmental practice. *Identity and the Natural Environment: The Psychological Significance of Nature,* 317–341.

Kerr, N. L. (1989). Illusion of efficiency: The effects of group size on perceived efficacy in social dilemmas. *Journal of Experimental Social Psychology, 25,* 287–313.

Kilner, S. M. (1992). Participating in a recycling program: Does it change attitudes towards solid waste? *Proceedings of the 15th Annual Madison Waste Conference,* 97–108.

Kim, S., Jeong, S. H., & Hwang, Y. (2013). Predictors of pro-environmental behaviors of American and Korean students: The application of the theory of reasoned action and protection motivation theory. *Science Communication, 35*(2), 168–188.

Koger, S. M., & Du Nann Winter, D. (2010). *The psychology of environmental problems: Psychology for sustainability.* Hove, UK: Psychology Press.

Kollmuss, A., & Agyeman, J. (2002). Mind the gap: Why do people act environmentally and what are the barriers to pro-environmental behavior? *Environmental Education Research, 8*(3), 239–260.

Lewin, K. (1948). *Resolving social conflicts; selected papers on group dynamics.* Gertrude W. Lewin (ed.). New York: Harper & Row, 1948.

Manetti, L., Pierro, A., & Livi, S. (2002). Explaining consumer conduct: From planned to self-expressive behaviour. *Journal of Applied Social Psychology, 32*(7), 1431–1451.

Mannetti, L., Pierro, A., & Livi, S. (2004). Recycling: Planned and self-expressive behaviour. *Journal of Environmental Psychology, 24*(2), 227–236.

Manzo, L. C., & Weinstein, N. D. (1987). Behavioral commitment to environmental protection: A study of active and nonactive members of the Sierra Club. *Environment and Behavior, 19*(6), 673–694.

Martinez, T. A., & McMullin, S. L. (2004). Factors affecting decisions to volunteer in nongovernmental organizations. *Environment and Behavior, 36*(1), 112–126.

Myers, D. (2010). *Social psychology* (10th ed). New York: McGraw-Hill.

Oskamp, S. (1995). Resource conservation and recycling: Behavior and policy. *Journal of Social Issues, 51*(4), 157–177.

Oskamp, S., Harrington, M. J., Edwards, T. C., Sherwood, D. L., Okuda, S. M., & Swanson, D. C. (1991). Factors influencing household recycling behavior. *Environment and Behavior, 23*(4), 494–519.

Park, C., & Allaby, M. (Eds.). (2013). *A dictionary of environment and conservation.* Oxford University Press.

Parker, D., Manstead, A. S., & Stradling, S. G. (1995). Extending the theory of planned behaviour: The role of personal norm. *British Journal of Social Psychology, 34*(2), 127–138.

Pelletier, L. G., Tuson, K. M., Green-Demers, I., Noels, K., & Beaton, A. M. (1998). Why are you doing things for the environment? The motivation toward the environment scale (MTES) 1. *Journal of Applied Social Psychology, 28*(5), 437–468.

Posner, E. A. (2002). *Law and social norms.* Cambridge, MA: Harvard University Press.

Richins, M. L. (2004). The material values scale: Measurement properties and development of a short form. *Journal of Consumer Research, 31*(1), 209–219.

Rogers, E. M. (2010). *Diffusion of innovations.* New York: Simon and Schuster.

Samuelson, C. D., Peterson, T. R., & Putnam, L. L. (2003). Group identity and stakeholder conflict in water resource management. *Identity and the Natural Environment,* 273–295.

Schultz, P. W. (1999). Changing behavior with normative feedback interventions: A field experiment on curbside recycling. *Basic and Applied Social Psychology, 21*(1), 25–36. Cambridge, MA: MIT Press.

Schultz, P. W. (2002). Environmental attitudes and behaviors across cultures. *Online Readings in Psychology and Culture, 8*(1), 4.

Schultz, P. W., Gouveia, V. V., Cameron, L. D., Tankha, G., Schmuck, P., & Franěk, M. (2005). Values and their relationship to environmental concern and conservation behavior. *Journal of Cross-cultural Psychology, 36*(4), 457–475.

Schultz, P. W., Nolan, J. M., Cialdini, R. B., Goldstein, N. J., & Griskevicius, V. (2007). The constructive, destructive, and reconstructive power of social norms. *Psychological Science, 18*(5), 429–434.

Schultz, P., Oskamp, S., & Mainieri, T. (1995). Who recycles and when? A review of personal and situational factors. *Journal of Environmental Psychology, 15*(2), 105–121.

Schultz, P., & Tabanico, J. (2007). Self, identity, and the natural environment: Exploring implicit connections with nature. *Journal of Applied Social Psychology, 37*(6), 1219–1247.

Schultz, P. W., Tabanico, J., & Rendón, T. (2008). Normative beliefs as agents of influence: Basic processes and real-world applications. *Attitudes and Attitude Change,* 385–409.

Schwartz, S. H. (1970). Elicitation of moral obligation and self-sacrificing behavior: An experimental study of volunteering to be a bone marrow donor. *Journal of Personality and Social Psychology, 15*(4), 283.

Schwartz, S. H. (1992). Universals in the content and structure of values: Theoretical advances and empirical tests in 20 countries. *Advances in Experimental Social Psychology, 25*(1), 1–65.

Schwartz, S. H. (1994). Are there universal aspects in the structure and contents of human values? *Journal of Social Issues, 50*(4), 19–45.

Schwartz, S. H. (1999). A theory of cultural values and some implications for work. *Applied Psychology*, 48(1), 23–47.

Schwartz, S. H., & Howard, J. A. (1980). Explanations of the moderating effect of responsibility denial on the personal norm behavior relationship. *Social Psychology Quarterly*, 43, 441–446.

Scott, J., & Marshall, G. (Eds.). (2009). *A dictionary of sociology*. Oxford: Oxford University Press.

Sheldon, K. M., & McGregor, H. A. (2000). Extrinsic value orientation and 'The tragedy of the commons'. *Journal of Personality*, 68(2), 383–411.

Singer, P. (2009). *Animal liberation*. New York: Avon Books.

Skinner, B. F. (1987). *Upon further reflection*. Englewood Cliffs, NJ: Prentice-Hall.

Stets, J. E., & Burke, P. J. (2000). Identity theory and social identity theory. *Social Psychology Quarterly*, 63(3), 224–237.

Tajfel, H., & Turner, J. C. (1986). The social identity theory of intergroup behaviour. In S. Worchel & W. G. Austin (Eds.), *Psychology of intergroup relations*. Chicago, IL: Nelson-Hall.

Thøgersen, J. (2006). Norms for environmentally responsible behaviour: An extended taxonomy. *Journal of Environmental Psychology*, 26(4), 247–261.

Thøgersen, J., & Ölander, F. (2006). To what degree are environmentally beneficial choices reflective of a general conservation stance? *Environment and Behavior*, 38(4), 550–569.

Tucker, P., & Douglas, P. (2006). *Technical report no. 1: A critical review of the literature. Understanding household waste prevention behaviour* – project reference number WRT109 (Vol. 44, p. 106). Paisley, Scotland.

US EPA. (2014). Environmental Justice. Retrieved from from http://www.epa.gov/environmentaljustice/

Vining, J., & Ebreo, A. (1989). An evaluation of the public response to a community recycling education program. *Society & Natural Resources*, 2(1), 23–36.

Vining, J., & Ebreo, A. (1990). What makes a recycler? A comparison of recyclers and nonrecyclers. *Environment and Behavior*, 22(1), 55–73.

Vining, J., & Ebreo, A. (1992). Predicting recycling behavior from global and specific environmental attitudes and changes in recycling opportunities 1. *Journal of Applied Social Psychology*, 22(20), 1580–1607.

Vlek, C. (2000). Essential psychology for environmental policy making. *International Journal of Psychology*, 35(2), 153–167.

Wicker, A. W. (1969). Attitudes versus actions: The relationship of verbal and overt behavioral responses to attitude objects. *Journal of Social Issues*, 25(4), 41–78.

Williams, G.C., Cox, E. M., Hedberg, V. A., & Deci, E. L. (2000). Extrinsic life goals and health risk behaviors in adolescents. *Journal of Applied Social Psychology*, 30, 1576–1771.

5   Driving forces and barriers for waste prevention behaviour

To what extent we as individuals and householders live a sustainable life depends on the choices we make in our daily lives. This means that the way we consume, the products we use and the way we handle our waste are the decisions that we make daily and which have serious implications for our natural environment. And, in part, these decisions are tailored by our personal (e.g. demographics, knowledge, experience) and contextual (e.g. culture, legislation, climate) individualities. These factors provide us with the context in which we make our decisions every day. Thus being motivated towards waste prevention behaviour is not enough to undertake the behaviour. For instance, the behaviour may be out of reach for many reasons. It may not be facilitated locally, or might be costly, or it could be faced with barriers too difficult to overcome. One good example is to avoid buying a car. Consider a single woman living in Berlin. Clearly, she does not need a car since the public transport offered by the local government is comfortable enough to move around the city. Besides that, the city also encourages cycling. Now imagine the same woman living in São Paulo, where public transport is overcrowded and does not cover the whole city (including her workplace). The city does not have a strong cycling policy either. Can she comfortably avoid buying a car? And what if she had four children, or lived too far from her workplace or did not know how to ride a bicycle? The balance between these factors and the motivation towards environmental protection gives rise to what some researchers term the difficulty of engaging in certain behaviour. These constraints can either be perceived or not by the individual and may act against carrying out the behaviour by not allowing the opportunities to put it into effect. On the other hand, when these personal and contextual factors are recognised, they can facilitate how a person acts (Tanner *et al.* 2004). There is also the possibility that these factors may affect a person's motivation by confronting her/him with appealing opportunities and breaking down barriers (Stern 2000). They can even bring a non-motivated person to become engaged in certain behaviour. Knowledge of different important barriers and facilitators for daily behaviour is important for understanding why householders may or may not carry out different pro-environmental behaviours. And this is extremely critical for waste managers having to deal with issues of effectiveness and legitimacy, in the design of acceptable waste prevention programmes for the public.

The contextual factors and individuals' perceptions

The human-environment relationship is a complex one, in which behaviour is both a function of the person and their *environment.*[1] Additionally, pro-environmental behaviour (e.g. waste prevention behaviour) is an altruistic focus on environmental conservation and the common good. According to Stern's review (2000), the first type of causal variables influencing environmentally friendly behaviour are contextual factors. They are labelled as external factors and include the physical, economic and social context in which individuals act. Each component of this factor varies between the different types of waste prevention behaviour (avoidance, reuse and repair). As mentioned before, the context in which we perform pro-environmental behaviours specifies the extent to which it is feasible to carry out different behaviours. Hence, the context may be more or less facilitating or hindering for us to engage in, in this case, waste prevention behaviour. In addition, how individuals perceive the context may also provide information on how contextual factors influence behaviours (Stokols & Altman 1987).

Contextual structures can be also be deliberately created by institutions to influence behaviour (Todd & Gigerenzer 2012). Sometimes this is effective, as when governments figure out how to persuade citizens to buy drinks in returnable bottles by default, or design recycling collection in a manner compatible with people's reasons for discarding recyclable waste. In other examples, institutions create environments that are not compatible with people's cognitive processes and instead cause confusion, accidentally or deliberately (Todd & Gigerenzer 2012). For instance, store displays and shopping websites are full of long lists of features of numerous products that can confuse consumers with information overload (Fasolo *et al.* 2007). Additionally, contextual structure can emerge without design through the social interactions of multiple decision makers. Good examples are metropolitan cities such as Tokyo and São Paulo which have grown because of a large number of people seeking job opportunities and a cosmopolitan life. In this case individuals are, through the effects of their own choices, shaping the context in which they and others have to co-habit considering the facilities and restrictions in their daily lives.

By understanding the context structure of certain populations, it is possible to highlight both its effect on behaviour and inherent psychological meaning. And, if reasonable, the context can be restructured by means of different policy measures (e.g. charging for plastic bags at the supermarket). However, it is necessary to understand beforehand the psychological implications of these changes on the targeted behaviour. As stated by Stokols and Altman (1987), an essential aspect of examining contextual factors is to identify the effective context, i.e. the most significant contextual factors for a specific behaviour. Even though it would be impossible to identify all potentially relevant factors there is a need to identify the most important factors and their relative significance, in this case, waste prevention behaviour.

For different consumption behaviours, the shops providing the products are the context in which waste prevention behaviour choices are made. One waste prevention behaviour decision concerns whether or not to purchase vegetables wrapped in cellophane and polystyrene. Studies have shown that several situational factors, such as the price, availability, marketing strategies and quality of the products are important contextual factors. According to Johnson *et al.* (1985) consumers who buy packaged food are concerned about sanitation, often lack sufficient information and have erroneous beliefs about the types of products sold. Landon and Smith (1997) have found that both reputation and collective reputation have a large impact on consumers' willingness, and their slow reactions to, changes in product quality. In a study by Underwood and Klein (2002) to examine the impact of product packaging on consumer's beliefs, results show that consumers use packaging, an extrinsic cue, to infer intrinsic product attributes. Moreover, the correlation between the price and quality of frequently purchased non-durable products is relatively low and that this relationship prevails in four European countries and the USA (Faulds & Lonial 2001). In general, household waste management is carried out inside the home (e.g. reusing, repairing) as well as leaving the waste and recyclable materials for kerbside collection or disposal in public bins and/or shops. Contextual factors of importance for waste prevention are, for example, the availability of space for composting in the home, retail self-dispensing systems, and product repair service systems. Cost can be a motivator for buying low waste products where there is some price advantage. In contrast, if consumers perceive there will be little or no discount, or they think an alternative will be more expensive, this acts as a barrier (Cox *et al.* 2010). As far as food offers are concerned, WRAP's report (2007) shows that these offers can actually contribute to food waste by encouraging people to buy more than they need. Cox *et al.* (2010) also highlighted the lack of visibility of reuse options (donation or purchase) and reluctance to purchase secondhand goods (particularly associated with charity).

While convenience factors are important considerations in the engagement in pro-environmental behaviour as a whole, it is quite common for people to misperceive the actual level of discomfort that those behaviours would entail. Misperceptions of inconvenience often arise prior to the launch of a new waste management programme (Pieters 1991). Such perceptions include reservations about space requirements for home composting, quality and price of unpackaged or loosely packaged products, and the personal costs in terms of time and effort. A study (Lofthouse *et al.* 2007) conducted in the UK explored 15 options for smaller cosmetic refills for a primary cosmetics pack. Results show that consumers expect refills to be cheaper than original products, and regard them as lower quality and think they are getting less value if the package was smaller but with the same quantity as the original. Perceived high personal costs can significantly affect individuals' intentions to participate. Tucker and Spiers (2003) show that prejudice inhibited people from engaging in home composting. However, when individuals are persuaded to carry out the behaviour and, later, confirm positive results, these prior misperceptions usually disappear. Lofthouse *et al.* (2007) found that less weight and space, brand loyalty and the same quality were important factors in encouraging individuals in the UK to use products which can be refilled.

The context is often highlighted when they act as barrier for waste prevention behaviour. In order to understand the role of contextual factors in relation to this behaviour, both physical and socio-cultural factors need to be addressed. Among the physical factors (discussed earlier) availability (e.g. to find refillable products in the supermarket), spatial issues (e.g. space to place a home composting bin), quality (e.g. quality of unpackaged products/food) and the economic cost of acting (e.g. the cost of purchasing a durable product instead of a disposable one) are important to consider. Fewer studies have examined socio-cultural factors within waste management behaviours, even though studies in different behavioural domains have showed that, for example, social norms are not effective in waste prevention behaviour as compared to recycling behaviour (Bortoleto *et al.* 2012). As far as ecological transport is concerned, Kaiser and Biel (2000) found that having a superior public transport system made it effectively easier for the Swiss sample compared to the Swedish sample to abstain from using a car in their respective urban environments. Another example is that climate seems to influence waste consumption differently in northern and southern California (Kaiser & Wilson 2000). Scheuthle *et al.* (2005) found four contextual origins between the Spanish and Swiss samples, such as climate, affluence, quality and availability of certain consumer goods, and culture-specific beliefs. Since Spain has predominantly sunny and warm weather, there is less need for heating and people make less use of solar energy panels than in Switzerland. In Switzerland, however, beverage cans and fabric softeners have extremely negative reputations, and Scheuthle *et al.* (2005) found these behaviours to be typically constrained. These factors may be considered an initial attempted to summarise the effective context of waste prevention behaviour. More structured analyses are, however, needed in order to compare the importance of different factors in relation to different behaviours (avoidance, reuse and repair). Moreover, there is a lack of studies clarifying the process by which different contextual factors influence waste prevention behaviour, for example, the relationship between objective context and subjective evaluations of the context.

Socio-demographics factors and behaviour

The conventional hypothesis that those with similar pro-environmental behaviours would share similar socio-demographics characteristics has been presented in many studies. Marketing research has widely used (and still uses) socio-demographic criteria to distinguish consumers' habits and preferences. And mainly, because of that, the use of socio-demographic data as variables for predicting waste generation is an attractive assumption. Quantifying values, attitudes, norms and behaviours is more complex and requires self-reported and/or observation instruments for an adequate assessment. Selection of suitable socio-demographics relevant for waste prevention behaviour, or for any type of pro-environmental behaviour, is problematical. A number of studies have attempted to establish this link and the results, with exceptions, generally indicate that pro-environmental attitudes and behaviours are more prevalent among people who are better educated (Shen & Saijo 2008), younger (Corbett 2005), politically liberal (Dunlap *et al.* 2000), and female (Stern *et al.* 1993). These results are often ambiguous. For example, some of them show that older (Bowman *et al.* 1998) people are more likely to engage in recycling behaviour while others argue that younger (Vining & Ebreo 1990) people are more involved. Then again, some authors found no significant correlation (Boldero 1995). Educational level has been also widely investigated and researchers found positive correlations with years of schooling and higher education (Lansana 1992). Not surprisingly, Barr (2004) and Oskamp *et al.* (1991) reported no significant correlation. Socio-economic status and occupational status also show mixed correlations with recycling behaviour (Vining & Ebreo 1990), while owning one's home has been positively correlated (Oskamp *et al.* 1991). It has also been noted that recycling behaviour may increase the longer one lives in the property (Tucker 2003). Those living in a single family residence are also more likely to recycle (Derksen & Gartrell 1993). Tucker (2001) found that the presence, number or age of children in the household appears to have a negative correlation with recycling. This was explained by the fact that householders are usually too busy when the children are young but later family pressures to recycle tend to decrease when children become more educated. Many studies show that women tend to show greater pro-environmental attitudes and behaviours than men (Casey & Scott 2006) and these differences hold up across ages (Hunter *et al.* 2004) and countries (Zelezny *et al.* 2000). One answer is that women are more likely to see the connection between environmental conditions and risky situations because they are more accepting than men of messages which link environmental degradation to potential harm to themselves, others and the biosphere (Stern *et al.* 1993).

Overall, the strength of the relationships between socio-demographic factors and recycling behaviour are relatively weak. Tonglet *et al.*'s (2004) study has not found any substantial improvement in the predictability of recycling behaviour by socio-demographic factors. Derksen and Gartrell (1993) argue that a large part of the world's population is relatively aware of environmental degradation and, thus, socio-demographic influences would be expected to be low. Vining and Ebreo (1990) claim that the demographic results tend to support the argument that pro-environmental actions are more likely to take place if caring for the environment is seen as a necessity rather than a luxury. The realisation of this necessity is now becoming much more widespread across all demographic groups.

In the case of waste prevention behaviour, the situation is not different. Tucker and Douglas (2006) argue that they are very poor predictors of behaviour and can only account for around 5 per cent of the observed variation in waste prevention behaviours. Cox *et al.* (2010) reviewed the effects of socio-demographic factors on previous waste prevention studies in the UK stating that 'waste prevention behaviours are more prevalent among individuals who are older, middle to high income; female; living in detached properties; not living with children at home; and more concerned about the environment'. Bortoleto *et al.* (2012) found small effects among some waste prevention measurements in São Paulo. Overall older, highly educated and wealthy individuals are more likely to contribute to waste prevention. In Japan, Kurisu and Bortoleto (2011) observed a positive effect on older people, females, and individuals living in detached houses. As previously pointed out in recycling behaviour, socio-demographics cannot predict waste prevention behaviours either. The assumption of demographic differences in waste prevention behaviour seems acceptable; however, they differ on weights and significances in different population samples with no universal relationship emerging between demographics and behaviour. Although significant demographic correlations can still be found in many empirical studies on pro-environmental behaviour, these identified correlations are not necessarily consistent across these studies and tend to reflect specific situations rather than relate to any particular factor (e.g. educational level, age).

Information, knowledge and competence

Most behaviour models in social psychology assume that individuals make reasoned choices (Chapter 11 discusses the role of bounded rationality). Thus, without a doubt, a requirement for engaging in pro-environmental behaviour is to have the relevant information about the behaviour in question. Information provision is probably the most widely used intervention to promote behaviour change. Generally, two types of information are promoted: (i) information about environmental degradation, and (ii) information about how individuals can take action to alleviate these problems. The knowledge-deficit model holds the assumption that people do not know about a specific environmental problem, or they do not know in detail what to do about it (Schultz 2002). Information intervention policies aim to overcome this knowledge deficit. However, previous studies indicate that information by itself is not very effective. Staats *et al.* (1996) evaluated a mass media campaign in the Netherlands and the results suggest that information and problem awareness may be less instrumental in promoting behavioural change than was assumed before the campaign. Barr argues that when correlations of knowledge to behaviour are not strong, they could be due to issues of questionnaire design or specificity that cause a somewhat unclear relationship. Kaiser and Fuhrer corroborate stating that statistical procedures neither correct for measurement error attenuation nor uncover mediated influences accurately and may keep knowledge's effect undetected.

The dimension of knowledge has also been investigated with respect to individuals knowing what, when and where to perform a pro-environmental behaviour. Knowledge is needed to know how to perform the intended behaviour, to determine responsibility for the intended act and to evaluate the perceived effectiveness of the behavioural act. While the first form of knowledge is composed of *declarative environmental knowledge* (i.e. how environmental systems work), the second consists of *procedural knowledge* (i.e. how to achieve a particular environmental goal) and the third, *effectiveness knowledge* (i.e. about the differential ecological consequences), is particularly relevant when behaviour is instrumental in optimising a person's cost–benefit ratio (Kaiser & Fuhrer 2003). Besides declarative knowledge, Kaiser and Fuhrer (2003) state that *social knowledge* also influences pro-environmental behaviour. Effectiveness knowledge parallels Schwartz's concept of awareness of consequences (Schwartz 1977) while social knowledge considers normative influences and social norms. Appropriate behaviour will not occur without appropriate declarative knowledge though that behaviour will ultimately be determined by more proximal predictors (i.e. values, attitudes, norms). Pro-environmental attitudes will be dependent on an individual's awareness of an issue and so knowledge of the problem should form a fundamental antecedent (Hines *et al.* 1987). However, procedural knowledge is also required in order to comprehend and implement the necessary action strategies that convert the intention to behave into behaviour. This separation into declarative and procedural knowledge is extremely important. Nevertheless, all four different forms of knowledge, according to Kaiser and Fuhrer (2003), have to converge towards environmental conservations and it is the strength of the convergence that will determine pro-environmental behaviour.

Empirical studies, such as Vining and Ebreo (1990) and Gamba and Oskamp (1994), have found that committed recyclers had greater knowledge about the behaviour than non-recyclers, although, the direct influence of knowledge on recycling behaviour was usually weak. According to Kaiser and Fuhrer (2003), this weak influence is partially due to the limited influence that knowledge has on pro-environmental behaviour when strong contextual constraints are effective. Thus, lack of knowledge can be a barrier to pro-environmental behaviours (De Young 2000). Nevertheless, having the wrong knowledge has also important implications (Grob 1995), such as prejudice (e.g. compost smells) and misperception. A motivated individual, who has an incorrect knowledge of the policy, will not participate properly (Pieters 1991). If perceived task knowledge exceeds actual task knowledge, low-quality performance will follow, irrespective of personal motivation (Pieters 1991). But, when perceived knowledge is less than actual knowledge, people may not feel confident in making the right decisions and may under-perform as a result. Ellen (1994) has also found that people with lower levels of knowledge find it more difficult to make recycling behavioural choices because of conflicting messages.

Information and knowledge provision does not necessarily imply that individuals will acknowledge, accept or absorb them. Previous research (Petty *et al.* 1981) has shown that when an individual processes a persuasive message, a number of issue-related beliefs are generated that may support or oppose the advocated position. However, Cook and Berrenberg (1981) show that the impact of information campaigns may be reduced if changes deviate too far from existing beliefs leading to opposing beliefs. Overall, Petty and Priester (1994) suggest that durable behaviour is more likely to occur after concerted information processing (i.e. high cognitive involvement). Arguments in favour are strong, sources credible, topics relevant, the message clear, distractions few, and comparisons favourable.

Linked with knowledge is competence which is defined as abilities and skills that allow individuals to cope effectively and successfully with daily life tasks and challenges, i.e. prerequisites for successful action (Weinert 2001). For example, waste prevention competence consists of those abilities that let a person understand how to reduce waste generation, and be able to execute it in real life. Consequently, pro-environmental competence is formed by those abilities and propensities that result in an improved performance of pro-environmental behaviour. Competence has been found to be a significant predictor of pro-environmental action (Hines *et al.* 1987). Knowledge and competence are both necessary for a pro-environmental behaviour. For instance, the theoretical knowledge of how to compost does not automatically imply practical experience of composting.

De Young (1996) went further, introducing the notion of a motivation competence. This is more than the ability 'to do'. It describes the motive people have for developing and maintaining their skills, for example seeking advice if composting problems arise. Corral-Verdugo (2002) developed the structural model of pro-environmental awareness and defines pro-environmental competence as an influential factor in both skills (i.e. knowing how to do) and conservation requirements (i.e. motives, beliefs, perceptions). In this model, pro-environmental competence is assumed as the predictor of a specific pro-environmental behaviour. The model also includes contextual factors which are anticipated to directly have an influence on pro-environmental competence.

Roczen *et al.* (2013) developed a competence model for environmental awareness which is grounded on people's connectedness with nature and the three forms of environmental knowledge: (i) environmental system knowledge; (ii) effectiveness knowledge, and (iii) action-related knowledge. Only knowledge about the effectiveness of different actions did not have an influence on pro-environmental behaviour. Accordingly, Frick *et al.* (2004) have not found this path significant either. Regarding the relevance of knowledge on influencing the behaviour, Roczen *et al.* (2013) suggest that knowledge forms a foundation, in a way that the necessity of acting on the sense of conservation is recognised. However, it does not seem to be enough to actually motivate pro-environmental action. The authors argue that 'competence formation in environmental education, next to advancements in knowledge and in people's enjoyable experiences in nature, should preferably also involve knowledge integration and, thus, structural development' (Roczen *et al.* 2013). This means that for a pro-environmental behaviour policy to be successful, it is important to also focus on intrinsic motivation rather than focusing campaigning on knowledge and competence. According to Pieters (1991), knowledge is seen as a necessary pre-condition related to the ability to perform a pro-environmental behaviour. Yet, it is not the only sufficient condition for pro-environmental behaviour.

Behavioural interventions

Waste prevention behaviour can be practised by various societal actors, such as manufacturers, commercial businesses, governments, institutions and residences, at various stages in the flow of materials and products, ranging from product design to on-site disposal. However, it is individual behaviour that can stimulate waste prevention at each stage. To prevent waste, conventionally, an individual should evaluate the options to determine the most resource-efficient way to use an item or perform an activity. Waste prevention, in this regard, is unique because it deals with the cause of waste and not the effect. It sets itself apart from other waste management behaviour (e.g. recycling). Manufacturers, on the other hand, can have a significant impact on waste prevention through their design and production processes. This is because once a product is developed, many of its characteristics are permanent. An example is unpackaged products and those with less packaging; when consumers buy these products they can engage in waste prevention with less effort. The reverse is also true, and currently predominant: if a product is designed so it cannot be repaired, when the product breaks it will probably be discarded. While manufacturers are able to design products, packaging and materials more efficiently, they are unlikely to do so without consumer demand for source-reduced items. That is the reason why individuals' behaviours are now the main target in most waste prevention programmes.

And how can waste prevention policies increase the occurrence of such desirable behaviour and decrease waste generation? According to applied behaviour analysis, to change behaviour, one has to analyse the consequences of behaviour. As proposed by Skinner (1987), people are motivated to do things for the promise of what follows. This means that individuals perform certain behaviour to obtain positive consequences or to avoid negative ones. Moreover, individuals repeat behaviours that lead to positive consequences and avoid behaviours that result in negative outcomes. This is the idea underlying the intervention theory which aims to change behaviour by offering rewards and punishments. Skinner and Hayes's *Walden Two* (1976) is a provocative look at how behavioural principles can be used to design a healthier and more sustainable society. He claims that environments should be redesigned to shape more appropriate behaviour to maintain the health of the environment in which behaviour occurs. The behavioural approach is not as popular as it was decades ago, but it still has significant insights to enhance public policies aimed at behavioural change. This section provides a simple overview of previous researches and experiments.

Behaviour interventions are theoretically based on the Antecedent-Behaviour-Consequence (ABC) model which suggests two approaches to encourage pro-environmental behaviour. The first strategy is to introduce or enhance antecedents announcing the availability of pleasant consequences for engaging on pro-environmental behaviour. A second strategy is to introduce new positive or negative consequences (i.e. rewards and penalties) for environmentally destructive behaviour. Note that not all consequences are equal. A consequence is more powerful when it is certain and quick to achieve (Geller 2002). There are many examples of these two approaches. One is the beverage refund in Germany, when individuals perform the desirable behaviour (i.e. return glass/plastic bottles), they receive the new positive consequence of a small financial reward. Another example is the charge for waste collection by weight which penalises those throwing away recyclable materials in the waste bin. However, there are significant risks in relying on rewards and penalties to change behaviour.

Many of the environmentally harmful behaviours have a quick and certain consequence. A good example is disposable paper plates which do not need to be washed after a party. However, not all behaviours have apparent natural consequences (e.g. healthy food > healthy body), and this is the case of waste prevention behaviour as well as other pro-environmental behaviours. In fact, these behaviours can be inconvenient, time-consuming, and uncomfortable. In order to motivate individuals to engage in pro-environmental behaviour, it is necessary to add extra consequences. But how should policy makers apply them? There are many examples where people are aware that their behaviour is harming the natural environment, but they still continue doing it. Thus, providing information in these situations will not help to motivate these individuals to engage in pro-environmental behaviour. They are already conscious of the consequences of their actions. Motivational intervention aims (i) to encourage pro-environmental behaviour through incentives, or (ii) to discourage environmentally harmful behaviours via disincentives. However, rewards effects are hardly durable. To be effective, the potential reward needs to be substantial (Schultz *et al.* 1995). Cialdini (2001) argues that a too high extrinsic reward can lead to over-justification of the action, with a consequent reaction against performing the behaviour in question. Rewarding incentives in waste management activities tend to increase the rates of, for example, recyclers but the amount of recyclable materials collected remains the same (WERG 2006). Gneezy and Rustichini (2000) found that an extra financial penalty actually reinforced undesirable behaviour and they suggest that by paying the fine individuals no longer have the moral obligation to perform the desired behaviour.

Currently, most behavioural interventions are not yet powerful enough to change environmentally destructive behaviours. The reason is partly due to the fact that making the behaviour more attractive by rewards does not increase intrinsic motivation in acting towards environmental protection. People, conventionally, know that their behaviours are irresponsible, but they still choose short-term, personal beliefs with delayed, long-term costs to themselves and others. And, consequently, behavioural interventions on their own have rarely resulted in long-term behavioural change. Werner *et al.* (1995) argue that if the effects of these interventions could be maintained over a long enough period of time then an attitude change could eventually follow. Of course, cues and feedback are needed to facilitate pro-environmental behaviour as well as enhanced social connections that foster a sense of collective responsibility. Human behaviour interacts with the environment promoting changes to it, and as a consequence, the environment changes because of human actions (e.g. climate change). Most environmentally relevant behaviours are also a product of prevailing environmental policies (e.g. infrastructure and product availability); by making them possible through legislation and/or investments, more people would take advantage of them. In that matter, people would simply follow cues for environmentally appropriate behaviour. Not all pro-environmental behaviours can be promoted based on this approach but this new *environment* can be the foundation to stimulate moral responsibility and pro-environmental attitudes.

Note

1 In this context, the word *environment* refers to the total physical, social, political, and economic situation in which a person behaves. This is a wider meaning than the one employed previously in this book; where environment referred to the physical dimensions of ecosystems regarding natural resources and wilderness.

References

Barr, S. (2004). What we buy, what we throw away and how we use our voice. Sustainable household waste management in the UK. *Sustainable Development, 12*(1), 32–44.

Boldero, J. (1995). The prediction of household recycling of newspapers: The role of attitudes, intentions, and situational factors. *Journal of Applied Social Psychology, 25*(5), 440–462.

Bortoleto, A. P., Kurisu, K. H., & Hanaki, K. (2012). Model development for household waste prevention behaviour. *Waste Management, 32*(12), 2195–2207.

Bowman, N., Goodwin, J., Jones, P., & Weaver, N. (1998). Sustaining recycling: Identification and application of limiting factors in kerbside recycling areas. *The International Journal of Sustainable Development & World Ecology, 5*(4), 263–276.

Casey, P. J., & Scott, K. (2006). Environmental concern and behaviour in an Australian sample within an ecocentric–anthropocentric framework. *Australian Journal of Psychology, 58*(2), 57–67.

Cialdini, R. B. (2001). *Influence: Science and practice* (Vol. 4). Boston, MA: Allyn and Bacon.

Cook, S. W., & Berrenberg, J. L. (1981). Approaches to encouraging conservation behavior: A review and conceptual framework. *Journal of Social Issues, 37*(2), 73–107.

Corbett, J. B. (2005). Altruism, self-interest, and the reasonable person model of environmentally responsible behavior. *Science Communication, 26*(4), 368–389.

Corral-Verdugo, V. (2002). A structural model of proenvironmental competency. *Environment and Behavior, 34*(4), 531–549.

Cox, J., Giorgi, S., Sharp, V., Strange, K., Wilson, D. C., & Blakey, N. (2010). Household waste prevention – a review of evidence. *Waste Management & Research: The Journal of the International Solid Wastes and Public Cleansing Association, ISWA, 28*(3), 193–219.

Derksen, L., & Gartrell, J. (1993). The social context of recycling. *American Sociological Review,* 434–442.

De Young, R. (1996). Some psychological aspects of reduced consumption behavior: The role of intrinsic satisfaction and competence motivation. *Environment and Behavior, 28*(3), 358–409.

De Young, R. (2000). New ways to promote proenvironmental behavior: Expanding and evaluating motives for environmentally responsible behavior. *Journal of Social Issues, 56*(3), 509–526.

Dunlap, R. E., Van Liere, K. D., Mertig, A. G., & Jones, R. E. (2000). New trends in measuring environmental attitudes: measuring endorsement of the new ecological paradigm: A revised NEP scale. *Journal of Social Issues, 56*(3), 425–442.

Ellen, P. S. (1994). Do we know what we need to know? Objective and subjective knowledge effects on pro-ecological behaviors. *Journal of Business Research, 30*(1), 43–52.

Fasolo, B., McClelland, G. H., & Todd, P. M. (2007). Escaping the tyranny of choice: When fewer attributes make choice easier. *Marketing Theory, 7*(1), 13–26.

Faulds, D. J., & Lonial, S. C. (2001). Price-quality relationships of nondurable consumer products: A European and United States perspective. *Journal of Economic & Social Research, 3*(1), 59–76.

Frick, J., Kaiser, F. G., & Wilson, M. (2004). Environmental knowledge and conservation behavior: Exploring prevalence and structure in a representative sample. *Personality and Individual Differences, 37*(8), 1597–1613.

Gamba, R. J., & Oskamp, S. (1994). Factors influencing community residents' participation in commingled curbside recycling programmes. *Environment and Behavior, 26*(5), 587–612.

Geller, E. S. (2002). The challenge of increasing proenvironment behavior. *Handbook of Environmental Psychology*, 525–540. New York: Wiley.

Gneezy, U., & Rustichini, A. (2000). Pay enough or don't pay at all. *The Quarterly Journal of Economics, 115*(3), 791–810.

Grob, A. (1995). A structural model of environmental attitudes and behaviour. *Journal of Environmental Psychology, 15*(3), 209–220.

Hines, J. M., Hungerford, H. R., & Tomera, A. N. (1987). Analysis and synthesis of research on responsible environmental behavior: A meta-analysis. *The Journal of Environmental Education, 18*(2), 1–8.

Hunter, L. M., Hatch, A., & Johnson, A. (2004). Cross-national gender variation in environmental behaviors. *Social Science Quarterly, 85*(3), 677–694.

Johnson, S. L., Sommer, R., & Martino, V. (1985). Consumer behavior at bulk food bins. *Journal of Consumer Research*, 12(1): 114–117.

Kaiser, F. G., & Biel, A. (2000). Assessing general ecological behavior: A cross-cultural comparison between Switzerland and Sweden. *European Journal of Psychological Assessment, 16*(1), 44.

Kaiser, F. G., & Fuhrer, U. (2003). Ecological behavior's dependency on different forms of knowledge. *Applied Psychology, 52*(4), 598–613.

Kaiser, F. G., & Wilson, M. (2000). Assessing people's general ecological behavior: A cross-cultural measure. *Journal of Applied Social Psychology, 30*(5), 952–978.

Kurisu, K. H., & Bortoleto, A. P. (2011). Comparison of waste prevention behaviors among three Japanese megacity regions in the context of local measures and socio-demographics. *Waste Management, 31*(7), 1441–1449.

Landon, S., & Smith, C. E. (1997). The use of quality and reputation indicators by consumers: The case of Bordeaux wine. *Journal of Consumer Policy, 20*(3), 289–323.

Lansana, F. M. (1992). Distinguishing potential recyclers from nonrecyclers: A basis for developing recycling strategies. *The Journal of Environmental Education, 23*(2), 16–23.

Lofthouse, V., Bhamra, T. & Trimingham, R. (2007) WR0113: Refillable packaging systems: Key Methods and Processes, WRT151: Objective 6.2, pp.1–31, DEFRA.

Oskamp, S., Harrington, M. J., Edwards, T. C., Sherwood, D. L., Okuda, S. M., & Swanson, D. C. (1991). Factors influencing household recycling behavior. *Environment and Behavior, 23*(4), 494–519.

Petty, R. E., Ostrom, T. M., & Brock, T. C. (1981). Historical foundations of the cognitive response approach to attitudes and persuasion. *Cognitive Responses in Persuasion*, Hillsdale, NJ: Erlbaum, 5–29.

Petty, R. E., & Priester, J. R. (1994). Mass media attitude change: Implications of the elaboration likelihood model of persuasion. *Media Effects: Advances in Theory and Research*, Hillsdale, NJ: LEA, 91–122.

Pieters, R. G. (1991). Changing garbage disposal patterns of consumers: Motivation, ability, and performance. *Journal of Public Policy & Marketing, 10*(2), 59–76.

Roczen, N., Kaiser, F. G., Bogner, F. X., & Wilson, M. (2013). A competence model for environmental education. *Environment and Behavior*. doi: 0013916513492416.

Scheuthle, H., Carabias-Hütter, V., & Kaiser, F. G. (2005). The motivational and instantaneous behavior effects of contexts: Steps toward a theory of goal-directed behavior. *Journal of Applied Social Psychology, 35*(10), 2076–2093.

Schultz, P. W. (2002). Knowledge, information, and household recycling: Examining the knowledge-deficit model of behavior change. *New Tools for Environmental Protection: Education, Information, and Voluntary Measures*, National Academies Press, Washington DC , 67–82.

Schultz, P., Oskamp, S., & Mainieri, T. (1995). Who recycles and when? A review of personal and situational factors. *Journal of Environmental Psychology, 15*(2), 105–121.

Schwartz, S. H. (1977). Normative influences on altruism. *Advances in Experimental Social Psychology, 10*, 221–279.

Shen, J., & Saijo, T. (2008). Reexamining the relations between socio-demographic characteristics and individual environmental concern: Evidence from Shanghai data. *Journal of Environmental Psychology, 28*(1), 42–50.

Skinner, B. F. (1987). *Upon further reflection*. Englewood Cliffs, NJ: Prentice-Hall.

Skinner, B. F., & Hayes, J. (1976). *Walden two* (pp. 18–20). New York: Macmillan.

Staats, H. J., Wit, A. P., & Midden, C. Y. H. (1996). Communicating the greenhouse effect to the public: Evaluation of a mass media campaign from a social dilemma perspective. *Journal of Environmental Management, 46*(2), 189–203.

Stern, P. C. (2000). New environmental theories: Toward a coherent theory of environmentally significant behavior. *Journal of Social Issues, 56*(3), 407–424.

Stern, P. C., Dietz, T., & Kalof, L. (1993). Value orientations, gender, and environmental concern. *Environment and Behavior, 25*(5), 322–348.

Stokols, D., & Altman, I. (Eds.). (1987). *Handbook of environmental psychology* (Vol. 2). New York: Wiley.

Tanner, C., Kaiser, F. G., & Wöfing Kast, S. (2004). Contextual conditions of ecological consumerism: A food-purchasing survey. *Environment & Behavior, 36*(1), 94–111.

Todd, P. M., & Gigerenzer, G. (2012). *Ecological rationality: Intelligence in the world*. Oxford: Oxford University Press.

Tonglet, M., Phillips, P. S., & Read, A. D. (2004). Using the theory of planned behaviour to investigate the determinants of recycling behaviour: A case study from Brixworth, UK. *Resources, Conservation and Recycling, 41*(3), 191–214.

Tucker, P. (2001). *Understanding recycling behaviour* (Vol. 1). Paisley: University of Paisley:

Tucker, P. (2003). *Understanding recycling behaviour* (Vol. 2). Paisley: University of Paisley.

Tucker, P., & Douglas, P. (2006). *Technical report No. 2 – results of a household attitude/ behaviour survey. Understanding household waste prevention behaviour* – project reference number WRT109 (Vol. 44, p. 94). Paisley, Scotland.

Tucker, P., & Spiers, D. (2003). Attitudes and behavioural change in household waste management behaviours. *Journal of Environmental Planning and Management, 46*(2), 289–307.

Underwood, R. L., & Klein, N. M. (2002). Packaging as brand communication: Effects of product pictures on consumer responses to the package and brand. *Journal of Marketing Theory and Practice, 10*(4), 58–68.

Vining, J., & Ebreo, A. (1990). What makes a recycler? A comparison of recyclers and nonrecyclers. *Environment and Behavior, 22*(1), 55–73.

Weinert, F. E. (2001). Concept of competence: A conceptual clarification. In D. S. Rychen, & L. H. Salganik (Eds.), *Defining and selecting key competencies* (pp. 45–65). Seattle, WA: Hogrefe & Huber.

WERG. (2006) Sussex household recycling incentives trials (RRF report). Skipton, North Yorkshire: RRF.

Werner, C. M., Turner, J., Shipman, K., Shawn Twitchell, F., Dickson, B. R., Bruschke, G. V., & von Bismarck, W. B. (1995). Commitment, behavior, and attitude change: An analysis of voluntary recycling. *Journal of Environmental Psychology, 15*(3), 197–208.

WRAP. (2007). Understanding Food Waste – Research Summary. Retrieved from http://www.wrap.org.uk/retail/case_studies_research/report_the_food_we. html

Zelezny, L. C., Chua, P. P., & Aldrich, C. (2000). New ways of thinking about environmentalism: Elaborating on gender differences in environmentalism. *Journal of Social Issues, 56*(3), 443–457.

Part III
Waste prevention behaviour
Case studies

6 A framework-model for waste prevention behaviour

Throughout the years, waste managers have massively relied on technological means to tackle waste generation. Although technological innovation has been useful in the efforts to treat waste and to decrease hazardous waste and volume, waste generation is still increasing mainly because of the weak engagement of individuals to waste prevention policies. And what motivates householders to prevent waste? Environmental psychology, distinctly formed from other psychological disciplines, mainly uses a wide diversity of approaches to answer this question. As is well known, each approach has its strengths and weaknesses. Choosing one rather than the other often involves different conceptions about pro-environmental behaviour. Without doubt, psychology provides the most appropriate background for examining the determinants of human behaviour. Yet, other disciplines have identified factors that can contribute to provide an account of waste prevention action. According to Barr (2008), a number of approaches can be identified and in particular can be grouped into two genres: the *modelling approach* and the *framework approach*. What differentiates them, fundamentally, is that the latter is used by social scientists and the former by psychologists. The difference between these approaches is subtle but important to understand the underlying assumptions that are made about how human behaviour operates.

The *modelling approach* is the more rigid of the two. It is the principal way of explaining behaviours according to a set of rigorously defined criteria that have been theoretically justified and posit a well-defined outcome given a combination of variables within the model (Barr 2008). In other words, this approach seeks to define the relationships between independent and dependent variables based on a set of hypotheses which establishes the association between the factors. Examples of this approach will be described later in this chapter and include the theory of reasoned action, the theory of planned behaviour and Schwartz's model of altruistic behaviour. These models are closed and there is minimum flexibility. Variables cannot be included or excluded and nor can the relationship between them be altered.

In contrast, there is the *framework approach* characterised by far less theoretical rigour than the modelling approach. This loose term can be used as an umbrella label to incorporate most other research into environmental behaviour (Barr 2007). Thus, the difference here is the flexibility of applying a framework over a model. Frameworks are conceptualisations based less on theories and mostly on empirical understanding of the behaviour concerned. There is a significant difference between what has been named a model and what has been recognised as a framework. In the framework approach, the researcher has the liberty of manipulating the variables, i.e. no variables have to be included and their inclusion may depend on the empirical evidence. The relationship between the independent and dependent variable can be changed, and most importantly, the framework can be amended after testing. A research example of this approach was published by Barr *et al.* (2001) regarding waste management behaviour. Their study is based on a model (the theory of reasoned action), which has been mixed into a framework to consider certain empirical circumstances. Other examples include the work of Davies *et al.* (2002), Do Valle *et al.* (2005), Oskamp *et al.* (1991), and Gamba and Oskamp (1994) who examined the impact of various sets of factors on recycling behaviour.

As mentioned before, both approaches have their advantages and disadvantages. The psychological model benefits from a clear logic that can provide a unique understanding of human behaviour useful in informing policy makers about how to potentially change behaviour. These models compensate for the use of few variables by ensuring that the data produced can be generalised since the intention is to track patterns and trends within a large sample. They provide a discussion about the factors influencing the behaviour and propositions regarding pro-environmental behaviour. However, psychological models are not prediction models and usually users (e.g. policy makers) of such models misinterpret the apparent simplicity of the model in question. Although a hypothetical hierarchy can be used, in the framework approach, the researcher can dismiss or add hypotheses and factors if they are found to be appropriate. It offers flexibility and loose assumptions but on the basis of rigorously collected and analysed data. A psychological modeller may criticise this approach as offering nothing to theory development but, despite losses in predictive power and individualist understanding, it gains in flexibility and generalisation (Barr *et al.* 2001).

This chapter will present a hybrid framework-model for waste prevention behaviour. In other words, an integrated model merging insights and elements form well known psychological models (e.g. theory of planned behaviour) to propose a comprehensive structural equation model to explain waste prevention behaviour. It is recognised as a framework-model because it uses a diversity of theories and factors to explain the behaviour. There is a need for a most effective and holistic approach to address not only waste generation problems but also the impact of human actions on the environment. And this framework-model can offer both theoretical insights as well as provide a clear holistic framework of waste prevention behaviour.

Psychological models of behaviour

Environmental psychology mostly focuses on studying pro-environmental behaviour, also often named as environmentally friendly behaviour, ecological behaviour or conservation behaviour. However, this type of behaviour has different meanings. Steg and Vlek define pro-environmental behaviour as 'behaviour that harms the environment as little as possible, or even benefits the environment'(Steg & Vlek 2009), i.e. individuals may act pro-environmentally without any intention to do so, or because the behaviour is habitual or is motivated by other goals. On the contrary, Kollmuss and Agyeman (2002) define it as 'behaviour that consciously seeks to minimise the negative impact of one's actions on the natural and built word'. Thus, people adopt this behaviour with an explicit goal of doing something beneficial to the environment. It is a goal-directed pro-environmental behaviour as described by Kaiser and Wilson (2004). This book assumes the latter and classifies waste prevention behaviour as a subgroup of pro-environmental behaviour since it focuses on the motivation and influential factors to act towards waste prevention rather than the actual impact of these actions on the environment.

The complex structure and relationships underpinning waste prevention behaviour can be visualised but using psychological models. As mentioned previously, these models are essentially a simplified representation of the behaviour in question. Social-psychological models mostly assume that individuals make reasoned choice (Chapter 11 discusses the role of bounded rationality). They test the efficacy of those theorised models through comparing the model outcomes with the observed behaviour of the target. An empirical evidence is, therefore established that will support or deny the specific hypotheses of the model. There is a vast range of cause-effect models throughout the literature which have been applied to explain pro-environmental behaviour. In this chapter, we will concentrate on those models that have particular relevance to pro-environmental behaviour and, more specifically, to waste prevention behaviour.

Theory of planned behaviour

The theory of planned behaviour (TPB) assumes that individuals make reasoned choices, and that the immediate antecedent of any behaviour is the intention to perform it. The stronger your intention to behave, the more effort you will make to conduct a particular behaviour, and the more likely it is that you will engage in the behaviour. The TPB specifies three conceptually independent determinants of intention: attitude towards the behaviour, subjective norms and perceived behaviour control. Figure 6.1 shows a schematic representation of the relationship between constructs in the TPB.

Attitudes, a personal factor, refer to the degree to which a person has a favourable or unfavourable evaluation of the behaviour. They are based on beliefs about the likely costs and benefits, weighted with the extent to which they are considered important. Subjective norms, a social factor, refer to the perceived social pressure to perform or not perform the behaviour. They reflect the extent to which a person believes that important others would approve or disapprove of the behaviour, thus, reflecting the social costs and benefits. Perceived behaviour control (PBC) is defined as 'the person's beliefs as to how easy or difficult performance of the

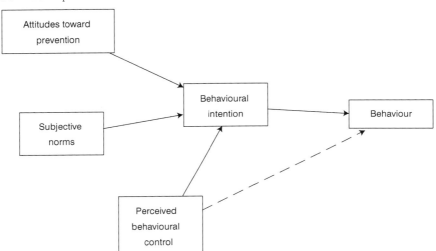

Figure 6.1 The theory of planned behaviour

Adapted from Ajzen (1991)

behaviour is likely to be' (Ajzen & Madden 1986). It essentially refers to the perceived possibility to perform the behaviour, which depends on beliefs about the presence of factors that may facilitate or obstruct the relevant behaviour. PBC can influence the behaviour indirectly (via intention) and directly. The importance of the PBC's influence on the behaviour is obvious. The resources or obstacles facilitating or limiting behaviour will affect the likelihood of achievement. And many factors can interfere, such as skills, abilities, knowledge, time, opportunity and dependence on the cooperation of others.

The TPB is one of the most widely used influential models of the attitude-behaviour relationship during the last 20 years (Eagly & Chaiken 1993). And it has been widely applied to explain many categories of pro-environmental behaviour, such as recycling (Tonglet *et al.* 2004) and green consumerism (Sparks & Shepherd 1992). Although there is considerable support for its use, there are concerns that it does not adequately explain pro-environmental behaviour, and that additional variables should be included with the model (Davies *et al.* 2002). The predictive power of the TPB increases when other motivational predictors are included in the model, for example, personal norms (Harland *et al.* 1999). Bamberg *et al.* (2003) found that personal norms predicted students' car use and bus use, respectively, over and above the TPB variables. Kaiser *et al.* (1999) analysed environmental knowledge and values and found these to be excellent predictors of their general ecological behaviour measure.

The sufficiency of the TPB is one of its potential problems since it suffers from the fact that other variables are involved in the explanatory process and that the attitude-behaviour link in not certain. Ajzen (1991) describes the model as open to further elaboration if important determinants are identified: 'the theory of planned behaviour is, in principle, open to the inclusion of additional predictors if it can be shown that they capture a significant proportion of the variance in intention or behaviour after the theories' current variables have been taken into account'. Bagozzi (1992) argues that the list of new variables is unlimited (they can be constantly added and modified) and that while TPB is able to accommodate a wider spectrum of factors, they may leave the structure of the model random. Another important point raised by Davies *et al.* (2002) is that TPB assumes a straight line between intention and behaviour. This implies the difficulty of measuring intention and behaviour in ways that dissociate the two completely in the respondent's mind, in order to minimise response bias. Most studies rely on self-reported behaviour that can result in a false intention-behaviour relationship. Besides that, the degree to which intentions are well formed affects the way in which attitudes influence behaviour (Bagozzi & Yi 1989). When intentions are poorly formed, the mediating role of intentions is reduced and attitudes have a direct effect on behaviour.

The model of altruistic behaviour

The model of altruistic behaviour proposes that pro-environmental behaviour follows from the activation of personal norms, reflecting feelings of moral obligation to perform or refrain from specific actions. Schwartz (1977) outlined his model as a broad social-psychological framework and not as a purely environmentally based model. What he describes as a process model of activation of moral obligation to altruistic behaviour begins with *social norms* regarding moral behaviour, which people generally agree upon in a sort of abstract way. Social norms includes all pressures from significant others, thus in Schwartz's model they are almost equivalent to subjective norms in TPB. An individual expects others to act in the morally proper way and in return they expect him/her to behave in the same way. When social norms are adopted by the individual at a personal level, they become *personal norms* (internalisation process). The difference between social and personal norms relies on the consequences of violating or endorsing them. To violate a personal norm would cause guilt and to support a personal norm causes pride. Personal norms are a highly internalised moral attitude that is considered to govern an individual's behaviour. Unless the personal norms are defined as relevant and applicable to a given situation, they will not be activated.

Schwartz thus identifies two other variables that influence whether or not personal norms will be translated into behaviour: *awareness of consequences* and *ascription of responsibility*. To act upon a given situation, the individual must be aware of the consequences of their action or inaction and ascribe a personal responsibility for those consequences. When these variables are high, personal norms guide the behaviour. The model implies that basic knowledge and the rationale for the behaviour (or of the consequences of not behaving) must be in place, and that the individual must not only perceive that his/her contribution is effective but must also believe that his/her non-participation will have negative

Figure 6.2 Schwartz's model of altruistic behaviour

consequences for others. In this way, those who feel morally obligated to behave will engage in the act only if they believe in the positive consequences and feel personally responsible for them. Schwartz's model of altruistic behaviour is shown in Figure 6.2.

Schwartz's framework has been extensively used by a number of authors to determine whether a large number of behaviours are altruistic and influenced by moral norms, such as energy use (Stern *et al.* 1985), support for environmental protection (Stern *et al.* 1986), car use (Abrahamse *et al.* 2009), recycling (Vining & Ebreo 1992) and general pro-environmental behaviour (Nordlund & Garvill 2002). In Hooper and Nielsen's study (1991), the belief that personal norms mediate the link between social norms and recycling behaviour was assessed and proved significant; consequently, recycling behaviour was governed by an awareness of consequences and the personal responsibility involved.

Although the TPB contains no theory for the relative importance of attitudes and social norms, Schwartz's model (1977) does provide a different social-psychological framework. This means that when a new behaviour is introduced within an established behavioural domain the individual may first use social norms (alone or in combination with internalised personal norms from related activities) to direct decisions about the proper act. For instance, participation in a waste prevention action (e.g. bring your own bag) may depend on social norms in the introductory phase and on personal norms after the action has been in effect for a period. However, as Blamey (1998) has demonstrated, there are other variables that can be added to the model that enhances its predictive power. This suggests that the altruistic model, like the TPB, could lose its efficacy as a predictive model if additional structural variables are included into the framework.

The model of environmental behaviour

The model of environmental behaviour proposed by Grob (1995) suggests a set of four interrelated determinants of general pro-environmental behaviour: environmental awareness, emotions, personal-philosophical values and perceived control (see Figure 6.3). Environmental awareness relates to the recognition of environmental problems. The model proposes that the more conscious individuals are of the state of their environment, the more appropriately they will act. This involves perception of the environment, i.e. the more a person is aware of environmental problems, they are more likely to behave accordingly. Environmental awareness has also a direct effect on perceived control, i.e. that people necessarily access environmental awareness before making control attributions. Environmental awareness was also hypothesised to be related to knowledge, but Grob has not

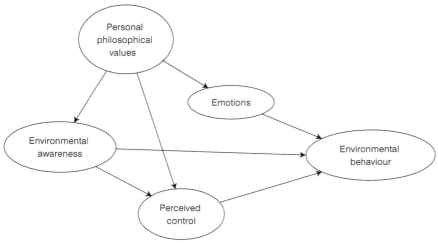

Figure 6.3 The model of environmental behaviour

Adapted from Grob (1995)

found a direct relationship between factual knowledge of the environment and pro-environmental behaviour. However, Kaiser and Fuhrer (2003) have discovered the significance of knowledge for pro-environmental behaviour, in spite of findings seemingly supporting the contrary (Schahn & Holzer 1990).

The model also assumes that emotions are connected to the sentimental value which the individual places on aspects of the environment and the disturbance resulting from his/her perception of the discrepancy between ideal and actual environmental conditions. Thus, the more intensely individuals react to the consequences of environmental degradation, there is a greater chance that they will behave pro-environmentally. Or the more disturbed a person is by the discrepancies between ideal and actual actions, he or she is more likely to do something to protect the environment. Empirical evidence does show that emotional affinity can be a powerful predictor of pro-environmental behaviour (Vining & Ebreo 2002), as in indignation about insufficient protection (Kals *et al.* 1999). Emotional affinity results from positive experiences in wilderness settings, especially in the company of friends and close relations. People's willingness to engage with the natural world is related to their emotional connection with nature and their environmental identity (Hinds & Sparks 2008).

The personal-philosophical variable includes post-materialistic beliefs and readiness to adopt new attitudes. Following Kohlberg's arguments, the model hypothesises that personal-philosophical attitudes affect behaviour in the environmental domain as they do in other areas. This variable accounts for materialistic values and creative thinking. In this way, the more materialistic a person's values, the less appropriately s/he will behave. And if a person is more open to new experiences and able to solve problems creatively, there is a greater possibility that they will act. Theoretical arguments for this hypothesis originate in Gestalt psychology, which states that environmental problems result from the inability to accurately perceive relationships within larger ecosystems. Humans tend to behave in destructive ways because we see ourselves as separate from other species and the natural world as a whole (Winter & Koger 2011). Many researchers have used Gestalt principles to approach ecological problems, such as Abram (1987) and Swanson (2001), but no empirical evidence has been found in the environmental domain. The perceived control, as PBC from the TPB, involves beliefs about self-efficacy and the efficacy of science and technology and the latter stands for the individual's belief that technological innovation will solve environmental problems. Thus, the less people believe in technological solutions, the more appropriately they will behave. Grob has also included social context in the model which proved to be effective to explain pro-environmental behaviour. It was included to gain a more comprehensive pattern of the extent to which pro-environmental behaviours are due to physical, individual, social, societal, historical and cultural influences.

The model of environmental concern

The New Ecological Paradigm (NEP) (Dunlap & Van Liere 1978) scale is the most frequently used measure of environmental concern and Stern *et al.* (1995) has applied it in a theoretical model of environmental concern. They aimed to integrate the relationships among values, NEP, Schwartz-derived belief items, and behavioural intentions. According to this model, five major constructs precede pro-environmental behaviour: behaviour commitments and intentions, specific attitudes and beliefs, general beliefs (worldview and folk ecological theory), values, and position in the social structure (i.e., the institutional constraints and incentives). According to the authors, individuals are embedded in a social structure that has substantial influence on all psychological variables. It shapes early experience and thus an individual's values and general beliefs. It also provides opportunities and constraints that shape behaviour and the perceived response to behaviour (Stern *et al.* 1995). General beliefs about the human environment relationship are measured by the NEP scale and they are antecedents of more specific attitudes or attitudes toward pro-environmental behaviour. Values and general beliefs are causally prior to more specific beliefs and intentions (e.g. beliefs about wilderness preservation). Usually, when responding to a survey, people ignore details and problem-specific information and they classify a topic making reference to general attitudes and values in responding and filtering information (Stern *et al.* 1995). Thus, general beliefs are then predictors of more adjacent causes of specific action, such as intentions, that ultimately determine pro-environmental behaviour.

A framework-model for waste prevention behaviour

The framework-model provides a unique conceptualisation of waste prevention behaviour based on an integrated model, a review of theoretical literature and on the results of the empirical study conducted by Bortoleto *et al.* (2012). Although the framework-model in Figure 6.4 is a conceptualisation, it is possible to apply it to different context-situations in terms of planning, implementation, analysis and interpretation. This is described in Chapter 7 where the framework-model is used as the basis for three studies to analyse waste prevention behaviour in São Paulo, Tokyo and Sheffield. This section introduces the theoretical and empirical hypotheses assumed to determine what factors shape waste prevention behaviour.

The measurement of intention is excluded from the integrated model for two reasons. First, Davies *et al.* (2002) demonstrate that even when all the conditions set out by Fishbein and Ajzen (1975) are met (i.e. precise situational correspondence and continuity between intention and behaviour); the required correlational correspondence between behaviour and intention was not validated. Trumbo and O'Keefe (2005) have also found that intention does not predict behaviour. Expression of intention provides little or no commitment on the part of individuals to engage in pro-environmental behaviour. Besides, their qualitative research, Davies *et al.* found that expression of intention was no more than an expression of support that is subject to change. The presence of behaviour choice (e.g. whether or not to bring your own bag to the supermarket) diminishes the importance of intention as a predictor of the behaviour. Unless the behaviour is mandatory, there is always a choice to be made. In an empirical review of the TPB literature, it was revealed that strong intention is not sufficient for performing a given behaviour (Sheeran 2002). Second, the study (Bortoleto *et al.* 2012) used for the data collection, which formed the basis of the integrated model, only allowed assessment of the respondents' future intention to prevent and not past decisions or motives that guided the self-reported behaviour. According to Fishbein and Ajzen (1975), there should be a minimum period between the measurement of intention and the measurement of behaviour to allow for precise situational correspondence and continuity between intention and behaviour. Given the difficulty in measuring waste prevention intentions as defined in the TPB, this construct was excluded from the integrated model.

In the empirical study conducted by Bortoleto *et al.* (2012), neither affective evaluation nor ascription of responsibility showed any significant effect on waste prevention behaviour. In the case of affective evaluation, individuals may engage in WPB regardless of their positive or negative feelings. Ascription of responsibility, according to Schwartz (1977), is the individual tendency to accept rationales for denying responsibility for the consequences of one's behaviour. In other words, individuals who feel that their behaviour is effective and that they are personally responsible for achieving the consequences of that behaviour are likely to place a higher priority on achieving it. For example, when a person anticipates costs for an action that he feels obligated to perform, he may employ various defences against this obligation, depending upon the personality and situational factors available to support such defences. It is a defensive tendency, not a spontaneous tendency to see the self as responsible for events initially. The absence of a significant effect of ascription of responsibility in the study conducted by Bortoleto *et al.* (2012) suggests that individuals engage in waste prevention

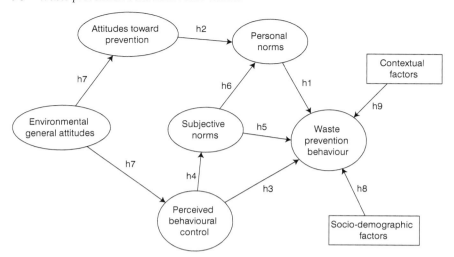

Figure 6.4 The framework model for waste prevention behaviour

behaviour regardless of whom they think is responsible for solving the problem. However, individuals who feel that their behaviour is effective consequently think that they are personally responsible for achieving the consequences of that behaviour. Thus, individuals may also judge their behaviour not to be effective in reducing waste. In waste prevention, it is difficult for individuals to evaluate the consequences of what is absent (i.e. waste not generated). As far as recycling is concerned, individuals can make the causal connection between their actions and the environment or direct responsibility towards others like the government and industry. Unlike recycling, waste prevention deals with changes in various activities before the waste is generated, thus it is more difficult to evaluate who is responsible for it and the consequences of engaging in WPB. For those reasons, the framework-model does not consider effects from affective evaluation and ascription of responsibility.

As shown in Figure 6.4, the framework-model is composed of an integrated model of waste prevention behaviour and two external variables, context-situation factors and demographics, with direct influence on the behaviour. Personal norms and perceived behaviour control (PBC) form the central point of the integrated model, as the most significant influence on waste prevention behaviour (WPB). General environmental values, attitudes towards prevention and subjective norms are indirect predictors of the behaviour. All these factors form the structural model to be applied in a given study field. Context-situation factors have a direct effect on the behaviour, and are interpreted through a qualitative method. Meanwhile, demographic variables, also with a direct effect on WPB, are quantified through statistical analysis. All the relationships within the framework-model are supported by a solid theoretical background as well as by an empirical data analysis. The framework-model provides a flexible and loose structure that permits not only variables but also areas of influence to be added or omitted. For instance, if additional variables are considered to be important in future studies, the model can be potentially improved by including them. This approach also allows for a combination of quantitative and qualitative methods. Each hypothesis, which composed the framework-model, is described as follows.

Hypothesis 1: Personal norms have a significant and direct effect on WPB.

Hypothesis 2: The individual's attitudes toward WPB have a positive and direct effect on personal norms having its effect on WPB mediated by them.

The Schwartz's model is recognised as a more predictive model than TPB because it considers the perceived moral obligation or personal norms. In previous studies, the inclusion of personal norms has increased the predictability of the TPB (Davies *et al.* 2002). Yet, Davies *et al.* (2002) state that personal norms have a direct influence on the behaviour rather than mediated by ascription of responsibility as suggested by Schwartz (1977). Personal norms take account of the individual's personal beliefs about what is right or wrong to do. The key distinguishing factor between householders who engage in WPB and those who do not lies in this concept of moral correctness of the behaviour. Those who engage in WPB perceive the behaviour to be morally correct and voluntary because personal costs are required yet the benefits are shared by the society. Results show that a sense of moral obligation to minimise waste is a primary motivator in the decision to engage in waste prevention behaviour (Bortoleto *et al.* 2012). Additionally, Schwartz's model states that the predictive effect of personal norms on behaviour is greater when an individual is more aware of the consequences of that behaviour (hypothesis 2). Within the WPB integrated model, this means that attitudes toward prevention have an indirect effect on WPB moderated by personal norms. Those who feel morally obligated to prevent (measured by personal norms) are more likely to perform the action if they believe in the positive consequences of preventing (measured by attitudes toward WPB). In a previous study, Hopper and Nielsen (1991) affirm that an attitude is a moderator between personal norms and recycling behaviour. This hypothesis was validated by the empirical analysis (Bortoleto *et al.* 2012) and incorporated into the framework-model.

Hypothesis 3: The individual's PBC has a positive and direct influence on WPB.

Hypothesis 4: PBC has a positive and direct effect on subjective norms and its effect on WPB is mediated by subjective norms.

PBC is defined as 'the person's belief as to how easy or difficult performance of the behaviour is likely to be' (Ajzen 1985). Hypothesis 2 measures the potential effect of PBC's direct influence to explain WPB. As in the original formulation of the TPB, PBC is composed by an individual's perceived ability to carry out certain actions (reflected by specific knowledge) and an individual's external conditions, which may encourage or discourage actual behaviour (represented by perceived convenience). Thus, it is expected that when an individual possesses greater awareness of the specific procedures involved in waste prevention and is satisfied with the external conditions to perform the action, the more likely s/he will understand the straightforwardness of the behaviour and the control of that behaviour. Hypothesis 4 measures the potential indirect effect of PBC mediated by subjective norms. According to Davies *et al.* (2002), having the specific knowledge and ability to perform the behaviour does not directly influence behaviour in question. Thus, PBC also has an indirect effect through subjective norms, referring to a combination of perceived control and social pressure to perform or not perform the behaviour. The integrated model therefore assumes that higher standards of waste prevention involvement can be found with household members possessing stronger PBC. Householders with higher PBC are those who (i) are aware of the opportunities to prevent solid waste in their daily life, so, they are more qualified to carry out WPB; and, (ii) have already adopted as routine some recycling activities, so they are more likely to adopt new environmental activities regarding waste prevention. That is, those attributing little importance to the obstacles of participating or those who are more aware of the importance of their own individual contribution, are the more likely to behave appropriately toward solid waste reduction.

> *Hypothesis 5*: Subjective norms have a direct influence on WPB.
>
> *Hypothesis 6*: Subjective norms have a positive and direct influence on personal norms. Through an internalisation process, personal norms mediate its effects, indicating an indirect influence of subjective norms on WPB.

Subjective norms are social factors that refer to the perceived social pressure to perform or not perform the behaviour, such as pressure from family, neighbours, peers, community and society at large. The empirical analysis of the integrated model has not found a significant direct influence of subjective norms in WPB. The results shows that individuals might not consider the opinion of family, peers and society as pressure to engage in WPB, supporting the premise of Schwartz's model that subjective norms have only an indirect effect on the behaviour (Bortoleto *et al.* 2012). In this way, individuals tend to internalise subjective norms as their own personal norms. In the case of WPB, as opposed to recycling behaviour, there are significantly fewer opportunities for social pressure to be exerted since the behaviour is mainly carried out in the privacy of the household. However, literature suggests that for positive norms to develop, prior examples must be present within the community, otherwise there is no one to catalyse the development of the norm (Everett & Peirce 1991). Oskamp *et al.* (1991) have found that social influences will only operate when the visibility of the behaviour is high, as it is for recycling schemes. Barr *et al.* (2001) also argued that the difference between recycling and waste prevention behaviours regarding the direct effect of subjective norms represent a less developed normative structure of WPB. It might therefore be expected that WPB would become more normative as time progresses, with the determinants of these actions bearing more resemblance to those of recycling (Barr *et al.* 2001). The integrated model for WPB underlines the importance of subjective norms in explaining WPB and its interaction with personal norms (internalisation process) to influence WPB rather than directly.

Hypothesis 7: General environmental attitudes have a positive and direct effect on attitudes toward prevention and perceived behaviour control.

The extension of the integrated model includes the direct influence of general environmental values (GEV) on both attitudes toward prevention and PBC, showing the indirect influence of general beliefs about the environment on WPB. The integrated model uses the new environmental paradigm (NEP) scale developed by Dunlap and Van Liere (1978) to measure GEV since Stern *et al.* (1995) show that broad beliefs regarding the environment are well captured on the NEP scale. Stern *et al.* (1995) state in their model of environmental concern that GEV has a direct positive and significant influence on attitudes toward the behaviour in question. Meanwhile, Grob (1995) has also found in his study that GEV has an indirect effect on the behaviour mediated by PBC. Barr *et al.* (2001) pointed out that environmental behaviour is not only directly determined by the general ideological position of consumers toward environmental issues, but is also extendable to the indirect relationship between these variables. Bortoleto *et al.* (2012) have found a relatively high magnitude of these two effects in their empirical test for the WPB integrated model. In this way, the framework-model supports these two hypotheses, providing comprehension of the potential indirect influence of GEV on WPB. This means that householders with strong environmental beliefs report a higher awareness level toward environmental degradation, greater sense of responsibility in preventing waste, and give less importance to difficulties associated with WPB.

Hypothesis 8: Determine whether the demographic profile influences WPB.
Hypothesis 9: Determine whether context-situational factors influence WPB.

A further structural set of variables that have been found to influence waste prevention behaviour are the personal circumstances and traits (demographics) of the individuals involved in such behaviour. They include age, gender, educational level, income level, household type and size of household. The use of socio-demographic predictors of environmental behaviours is still ambiguous and problematical. Indeed, as Berger (1997) has pointed out, researchers must be careful when assigning predictive value to such variables, since their actual relationship could be quite spurious. Hence, there is a need to be more specific in the analysis of such variables since they can vary according to each individual action (e.g. avoid, reuse, repair) of waste prevention behaviour. Besides, pro-environmental behaviours have become extensively diffused throughout our society so that demographic differences are progressively disappearing. Yet, both Tonglet *et al.* (2004) and Davies *et al.* (2002) state that demographics make a substantial improvement to the predictability of the pro-environmental behaviour in question.

According to Kaiser and Keller (2001), situational influences affect people's conduct, making some behaviours easier to perform than others. Our living environment, for instance, is among the more salient of these contextual factors. In the case of waste prevention, context-situational factors essentially concern the provision of public services, logistics, legislation and product availability to help householders prevent waste, and also the issue of cultural, climate and contextual differences that influence WPB. Berger (1997) gives a good example of the importance of public services for recycling behaviour. He found that when kerbside collection was added as a predictor for recycling behaviour, socio-demographic influence faded away. Scheuthle *et al.* (2005) found contrasting differences between two samples from different countries, related to climate, affluence and consumer goods. These examples demonstrate the importance of examining spatial and contextual differentiation in waste prevention provision as a crucial predictor of WPB (Chapter 5 has more information on this topic).

Applying the framework-model

The model of altruistic behaviour developed by Schwartz (1977) provides the basis for the framework-model. It also incorporates the TPB as well as the two pro-environmental models developed by Stern *et al.* (1995) and Grob (1995). The idea of combining these theories resulted from both sharing similar constructs. The main contribution from Schwartz's model relies on the introduction of personal norms as a mediator between subjective norms and WPB. The link between personal and subjective norms offers a useful basis on which to examine the normative internalisation process and its influence on WPB. The framework-model also shows that PBC has a marked influence on WPB. The extension of the proposed model to general environmental values and attitudes toward prevention show the importance of general beliefs about environmental protection to predict WPB. Examining context-situational factors is very useful to investigate previously cited relationships that are probably not valid or well-founded since these factors are clearly under-investigated. Despite poorly correlated socio-demographics variables in previous studies on pro-environmental behaviour, they are still an important source of data regarding WPB. Although based around the Schwartz's model and TPB, the framework-model is a significant step forward for those interested in understanding waste prevention behaviour. One of the most compelling and difficult questions to answer in recent decades has been the reasons for stated aspirations to protect the environment not being reflected in individual actions. This framework-model provides a means by which to conceptualise this relationship. Finally, it contributes in providing a way of understanding different variables within the context of each other and the 'value-action gap' problem.

References

Abrahamse, W., Steg, L., Gifford, R., & Vlek, C. (2009). Factors influencing car use for commuting and the intention to reduce it: A question of self-interest or morality? *Transportation Research Part F: Traffic Psychology and Behaviour, 12*(4), 317–324.

Abram, D. (1987). The perceptual implications of Gaia. *ReVISION, 9*, 2, 7–15.

Ajzen, I. (1985). *From intentions to actions: A theory of planned behavior* (pp. 11–39). Springer Berlin Heidelberg.

Ajzen, I. (1991). The theory of planned behavior. *Organizational Behavior and Human Decision Processes, 50*(2), 179–211.

Ajzen, I., & Madden, T. J. (1986). Prediction of goal-directed behavior: Attitudes, intentions, and perceived behavioral control. *Journal of Experimental Social Psychology, 22*(5), 453–474.

Bagozzi, R. P. (1992). The self-regulation of attitudes, intentions, and behavior. *Social Psychology Quarterly, 55*, 178–204.

Bagozzi, R. P., & Yi, Y. (1989). The degree of intention formation as a moderator of the attitude-behavior relationship. *Social Psychology Quarterly, 52*(4), 266–279.

Bamberg, S., Ajzen, I., & Schmidt, P. (2003). Choice of travel mode in the theory of planned behavior: The roles of past behavior, habit, and reasoned action. *Basic and Applied Social Psychology, 25*(3), 175–187.

Barr, S. W. (2007). Factors influencing environmental attitudes and behaviors: A UK case study of household waste management. *Environment and Behavior, 39*(4), 435–473.

Barr, S. W. (2008). *Environment and society: Sustainability, policy and the citizen.* Aldershot, Ashgate.

Barr, S. W., Gilg, A. W., & Ford, N. J. (2001). A conceptual framework for understanding and analysing attitudes towards household-waste management. *Environment and Planning A, 33*(11), 2025–2048.

Berger, I. E. (1997). The demographics of recycling and the structure of environmental behavior. *Environment and Behavior, 29*(4), 515–531.

Blamey, R. (1998). The activation of environmental norms. *Environment and Behaviour, 30*, 676–708.

Bortoleto, A. P., Kurisu, K. H., & Hanaki, K. (2012). Model development for household waste prevention behaviour. *Waste Management, 32*(12), 2195–2207.

Davies, J., Foxall, G. R. & Pallister, J. (2002). Beyond the intention–behaviour mythology: An integrated model of recycling. *Marketing Theory, 2*, 29–113.

Do Valle, P. O., Rebelo, E., Reis, E., & Menezes, J. (2005). Combining behavioural theories to predict recycling involvement. *Environment and Behaviour, 37*, 364–396.

Dunlap, R. E., & Van Liere, K. D. (1978). The new environmental paradigm. *Journal of Environmental Education, 9*, 10–19.

Eagly, A. H., & Chaiken, S. (1993). *The psychology of attitudes.* San Diego, CA: Harcourt Brace Jovanovich College Publishers.

Everett, J. W., & Peirce, J. J. (1991). Social networks, socioeconomic status, and environmental collective action: Residential curbside block leader recycling. *Journal of Environmental Systems, 21*(1), 65–84.

Fishbein, M., & Ajzen, I. (1975). *Belief, attitude, intention and behavior: An introduction to theory and research.* Reading, MA: Addison-Wesley.

Gamba, R. J. & Oskamp, S. (1994). Factors influencing community residents' participation in commingled curbside recycling programs. *Environment and Behaviour, 26*, 587–612.

Grob, A. (1995).A structural model of environmental attitudes and behaviour. *Journal of Environmental Psychology, 15*, 209–220.

Harland, P., Staats, H., & Wilke, H. A. (1999). Explaining proenvironmental intention and behavior by personal norms and the theory of planned behavior. *Journal of Applied Social Psychology, 29*(12), 2505–2528.

Hinds, J., & Sparks, P. (2008). Engaging with the natural environment: The role of affective connection and identity. *Journal of Environmental Psychology, 28*(2), 109–120

Hooper, J. & Nielsen, J. M. (1991). Recycling as altruistic behaviour: Normative and behavioural strategies to expand participation in a community recycling program. *Environment and Behaviour, 23*, 195–220.

Kaiser, F. G., & Fuhrer, U. (2003). Ecological behavior's dependency on different forms of knowledge. *Applied Psychology, 52*(4), 598–613.

Kaiser, F. G., & Keller, C. (2001). Disclosing situational constraints to ecological behavior: A confirmatory application of the mixed Rasch model. *European Journal of Psychological Assessment, 17*(3), 212.

Kaiser, F. G., & Wilson, M. (2004). Goal-directed conservation behavior: The specific composition of a general performance. *Personality and Individual Differences, 36*(7), 1531–1544.

Kaiser, F. G., Wölfing, S., & Fuhrer, U. (1999). Environmental attitude and ecological behaviour. *Journal of Environmental Psychology, 19*(1), 1–19.

Kals, E., Schumacher, D., & Montada, L. (1999). Emotional affinity toward nature as a motivational basis to protect nature. *Environment and Behavior, 31*(2), 178–202.

Kollmuss, A., & Agyeman, J. (2002). Mind the gap: Why do people act environmentally and what are the barriers to pro-environmental behavior? *Environmental Education Research, 8*(3), 239–260.

Nordlund, A. M., & Garvill, J. (2002). Value structures behind proenvironmental behavior. *Environment and Behavior, 34*(6), 740–756.

Oskamp, S., Harrington, M., Edwards, T., Sherwood, P. L., Okuda, S. M. & Swanson, D. L. (1991). Factors influencing household recycling behavior. *Environment and Behavior, 23*, 494–519.

Schahn, J., & Holzer, E. (1990). Studies of individual environmental concern: The role of knowledge, gender, and background variables. *Environment and Behavior, 22*(6), 767–786.

Scheuthle, H., Carabias-Hütter, V., & Kaiser, F. G. (2005). The motivational and instantaneous behavior effects of contexts: Steps toward a theory of goal-directed behavior. *Journal of Applied Social Psychology, 35*(10), 2076–2093.

Schwartz, S. H. (1977). Normative influences on altruism. In L. Berkowitz (Ed.), *Advances in experimental social psychology* (pp. 221–279). New York: Academic Press.

Sheeran, P. (2002). Intention–behavior relations: A conceptual and empirical review. *European Review of Social Psychology, 12*(1), 1–36.

Sparks, P., & Shepherd, R. (1992). Self-identity and the theory of planned behavior: Assessing the role of identification with 'green consumerism'. *Social Psychology Quarterly, 55*(4), 388–399.

Steg, L., & Vlek, C. (2009). Encouraging pro-environmental behaviour: An integrative review and research agenda. *Journal of Environmental Psychology, 29*, 309–317.

Stern, P. C., Aronson, E., Darley, J. M., Hill, D. H., Hirst, E., Kempton, W., & Wilbanks, T. J. (1986). The effectiveness of incentives for residential energy conservation. *Evaluation Review, 10*(2), 147–176.

Stern, P. C., Dietz, T., & Black, J. S. (1985). Support for environmental protection: The role of moral norms. *Population and Environment*, 8(3–4), 204–222.

Stern, P. C., Dietz, T., & Guagnano, G. A. (1995). The new ecological paradigm in social psychology context. *Environment and Behaviour*, 26, 723–743.

Swanson, J. (2001). *Communing with nature*. Corvallis, OR: Illahee Press.

Tonglet, M., Phillips, P. S., & Read, A. D. (2004). Using the theory of planned behaviour to investigate the determinants of recycling behaviour: a case study from Brixworth, UK. *Resources, Conservation and Recycling*, 41(3), 191–214.

Trumbo, C. W. and O'Keefe, G. J. (2005). Intention to conserve water: Environmental values, reasoned action, and information effects across time. *Society & Natural Resources*, 18, 573–585.

Vining, J., & Ebreo, A. (1992). Predicting recycling behavior from global and specific environmental attitudes and changes in recycling opportunities 1. *Journal of Applied Social Psychology*, 22(20), 1580–1607.

Vining, J., & Ebreo, A. (2002). Emerging theoretical and methodological perspectives on conservation behaviour. *Urbana*, 51, 61801 New York: John Wiley, 541–558.

Winter, D. D. N., & Koger, S. M. (2011). *The psychology of environmental problems: Psychology for sustainability*. Hove, UK: Psychology Press.

7 Applying the conceptual model
Waste prevention behaviour in São Paulo, Sheffield and Tokyo

Having described in the previous chapter how the waste prevention behaviour (WPB) framework-model is conceptualised and its possible determinants based on previous academic study (Bortoleto *et al.* 2012), this chapter describes (i) the three study areas, (ii) the instruments used to quantify statistically the cause and effect of WPB, and (iii) how far the influential factors of the framework-model could be conceptualised alongside individuals' engagement in solid waste reduction activities. In other words, this chapter demonstrates how the conceptual model presented in the preceding chapter was used to implement a series of studies of pro-environmental attitudes, WPB and linking variables. It outlines and explains all steps to develop and to implement the questionnaires as well as all statistical analysis of the collected data. Finally, the waste prevention framework-model is presented and evaluated accordingly to each study field (São Paulo, Sheffield, and Tokyo). As mentioned before, the specific example used here is waste prevention, but there is no constraint on adapting the methodology described here in order to study alternative pro-environmental behaviours (e.g. energy consumption, water conservation).

Study areas: the cities of São Paulo, Sheffield and Tokyo

São Paulo, Brazil

São Paulo Municipality is located in São Paulo State, Brazil, being considered one of the most developed and richest cities of Brazil with a Gross Domestic Product of US$ 18,181.03 per capita (IBGE 2014). This economic performance is accompanied by a high population density of 7,398.26 inhabitants per square kilometre, or 11,821,873 inhabitants in total, and several social-environmental problems characteristic of wealthy cities in developing countries. The negative social aspects could be summarised by the low performance in the Gini index of 0.45 (IBGE 2013), expressing a huge imbalance in income distribution, i.e. the largest fraction of economic resources is concentrated in the hands of a few people. Regarding environmental issues, one of several problems is related to the increasing amount of waste which reached about 5,205,374 tonnes in 2011 (14,261 tonnes per day or 1 kg per capita per day) (Abrelpe 2012). On average, a householder produces 365 kg per year in São Paulo.

The Department of Urban Cleansing is responsible for managing household waste in the city. However, since 2002, the entire waste management system (collection, treatment and disposal) has been outsourced to private companies for a period of two years. According to the local government, this was the best option to ensure the necessary investments in the system. In 2004, the local government closed down the last incineration plant in the city as well as the two composting plants due to inefficiency, technological obsolescence and air pollution. The two public landfills inside the city were also closed, one in 2007 and the other in 2009, and an energy recovery system to generate electricity was installed in both of them. The energy system can generate up to 200,000 MW per year through 16 units (Jacobi & Besen 2011). Currently, all general waste is sent to two private landfills, one in the city and the other in Caieiras, 40 km distant from São Paulo. In an attempt to minimise all potential problems associated with landfills, the municipality of São Paulo has implemented a Sorting and Composting Waste Treatment Plant (SCWTP) to recover inert materials and produce compost with organic materials present into USW. Although the SCWTP is considered a good alternative, the mere fact of adopting destinations other than landfill for USW is not enough to ensure that it is a better waste management option among several others available.

There are two types of kerbside collection, one for general waste and another for recyclable waste. In 2003, the city established a Solidary Selective Collection Programme to promote the social inclusion of waste pickers' cooperatives. These cooperatives are responsible for the separation of recyclable materials collected by a private company. Households are advised to separate only recyclable materials from general waste for kerbside collection. In 2012, the recycling rate in São Paulo was around 30 per cent for household waste (Cempre 2014). More than 1 tonnes of paper, cardboard, plastic, glass, steel and aluminium are mixed to general waste and buried at the landfill site. The unofficial collection is one of the main problems faced by the official collection. It is undertaken by waste pickers who are not affiliated to any cooperative. This unofficial collection takes place daily while the formal kerbside collection is weekly. And it reduces the production of the existing 20 sorting units (managed by former waste pickers) (Jacobi & Besen 2011). One of the reasons for this inefficiency is the lack of a formal municipal waste management strategy with prevention and recycling campaigns and policies. This absence of a policy has led the private sector to develop its own initiatives, such as the implementation of recycling dropping-off points at supermarkets in a partnership with waste pickers.

Sheffield, United Kingdom

Sheffield is a city and metropolitan area in South Yorkshire, United Kingdom. The city has a population of approximately 552,698 forming 229,928 households (Sheffield City Council 2014) and is the third largest English district by population. During the nineteenth century, Sheffield gained an international reputation for steel production. Many innovations were developed locally, including crucible and stainless steel, fuelling an almost tenfold increase in the population during the Industrial Revolution. The twenty-first century has seen extensive redevelopment in Sheffield along with other British cities. Currently, Sheffield is a major retail centre, and is home to many high-street department stores (Taylor *et al.* 1996) and in a 2012 survey of forecast expenditure at retail centres in the UK, Sheffield city centre was ranked twenty-eighth with a turnover of £670 million (CACI 2012).

Sheffield City Council is a unitary authority which means that it is responsible for both the collection and disposal of the waste generated by the population it serves. Sheffield has a long tradition of environmental activity. In 1989, it was the first 'recycling city' in the UK and played an important role in developing some of the recycling initiatives which have become a normal part of life in many UK cities. Sheffield was the first local authority to introduce blue boxes for kerbside collection of mixed recyclables in the UK and pioneered the use of a purpose-built vehicle similar to those being used in US kerbside schemes. As well as introducing the first recycling facilities for batteries and plastic bottles in the UK, Sheffield was also the first council to have the facility to sort plastic bottles for reprocessing (Coggins 2001).

The city currently has a good recycling rate of 30.87 per cent (October December 2013). The total household waste production in 2012 was 189,554 tonnes (552 kg per capita) of which only 3.21 per cent was sent to the landfill. In 2011, householders produced 200,066 tonnes (577 kg per capita). The city provides kerbside collection for recyclable materials and general waste. In 2013, due to cuts in government funding, the free garden waste collection was cancelled by the city council. There is a chargeable green bin collection service available to householders from May to November. Householders can also dispose of their garden waste for free at the recycling centres. The city council also encourages householders to compost their garden and food waste by offering a home compost bin with a discounted price for residents. The campaign also provides information and a community network based in Sheffield. As far as disposal of bulky waste is concerned, the city provides a special collection service for which householders pay between £18 and £54. The waste prevention programme in Sheffield consists of three main policies: home composting, reusable nappies and community group waste exchange. The community group waste exchange has its own website (Why Waste) which sources materials for groups' activities and provides a waste exchange platform for householders to advertise and sell their own unwanted goods.

Sheffield has a District Energy system that exploits the city's domestic waste, by incinerating it and converting the energy from it to thermal and electric energy. It provides heat and hot water for more than 140 buildings, which is distributed over 25 miles (40 km) of pipes under the city, via two networks. This system benefits not only cinemas, hospitals, shops, and offices but also universities (Sheffield Hallam University and the University of Sheffield), and residential properties. Currently the District Energy business is managed by

Veolia Environmental Services PLC, as part of one of the largest integrated waste management contracts in the UK (Veolia 2014a). The Energy Recovery Facility (ERF) can generate up to either 45MW of thermal energy for District Energy or 21MW of electrical energy for the National Grid (Veolia 2014b).

Tokyo, Japan

Tokyo is the capital of Japan, the centre of the Greater Tokyo Area, and the most populous metropolitan area in the world. It is located in the Kanto region on the south-eastern side of the main island, Honshu, and includes the Izu Islands and Ogasawara Islands. Tokyo is often referred to and thought of as a city, but is officially known as a metropolitan prefecture, which differs from a city. The Tokyo metropolitan government oversees Tokyo's 23 wards (each governed as an individual unit), which cover the area of the former city of Tokyo before it merged and became the subsequent metropolitan prefecture in 1943. In 2011, the estimated total population of Tokyo was 13 million or about 10 per cent of Japan's total population with a density of 6,029 persons per square kilometre. Tokyo has 6 million households with an average of 2.05 persons per household with a Gross Domestic Product of US$ 50,817 per capita (Tokyo Metropolitan Government 2012). The total amount of household waste generated in Tokyo in 2009 was 4.47 million tonnes (339 kg per capita) and the recycling rate in the 23 wards was 19.5 per cent (Tokyo Metropolitan Government 2011).

As an umbrella, the Japanese government developed different laws related to responsible consumption and recycling. However, the substantive measures are performed by local municipalities who manage their own collection and recycling systems. The metropolitan government formulated the Tokyo Metropolitan Waste Management Plan as a master plan for establishing a Sound Material-Cycle Society in Tokyo. The plan was renewed in June 2011 with the intention to reduce the final disposal amount of household waste to 0.25 million tons by the 2015 fiscal year. To achieve this, the plan promotes the 3Rs (reduce, reuse, recycle) through different policies, such as reduce and reuse initiatives, pay-as-you-throw programmes, recycling of packaging and containers, and recycling of used small electronic appliances. These policies ask citizens, businesses and local agencies to play their part in promoting waste reduction and recycling, sharing information and co-operating each other. In most municipalities (within the Tokyo area), combustible wastes, incombustible wastes, and recyclable materials are collected separately. Cans, glass bottles, PET bottles, and paper are usually collected as recyclable materials.

Some municipalities have introduced the collection of packaging plastics as recyclable materials to enforce citizens' separation and collection of packaging wastes based on the law for Promotion of Sorted Collection and Recycling of Containers and Packaging implemented in 1997. In some wards, only plastic trays are collected by the municipalities. The frequency of collection depends on local conditions; however, the most common combinations are twice a week for combustible wastes, twice a month for incombustible wastes, and once a week for recyclable materials. Some wards basically collect household wastes at kerbside collection points, whereas some wards and municipalities have introduced door-to-door collections (e.g. Shinagawa ward). Collection stations for paper packs and textiles are also found in many municipalities. In several Tokyo wards, waste oils are also collected at stations and elementary schools (e.g. Sumida and Chuo wards). There is a charge for waste bags in Tokyo (about 0.1 US$ per bag). The prices of waste bags are usually set by each city or town, whereas a common price is set in Tokyo's 23 wards. The actions and measures related to waste prevention in Tokyo include: charging for waste bags, subsidies for composting machines, charging for plastic shopping bags (at supermarkets and shops), a disposal system for glass and plastic bottles, a discount system, a used clothes collection (by clothing stores), and food waste campaigns. Household waste generated in Tokyo undergoes incineration and 100 per cent of the ash produced is disposed of in landfill sites within the Tokyo region, one of which is in Tokyo Bay and managed by the metropolitan government.

The questionnaire and its measurement instruments

Set out below is an explanation of the question content designed to measure the value of each individual construct. While the questionnaire was long, it was designed to enable respondents to complete it without difficulty (Oppenheim 1992), i.e. ticking scales or boxes. Computer-assisted web interviews (CAWI), using online questionnaires, were conducted to obtain the necessary data. People who register with a web research company are asked to complete a questionnaire and points are awarded corresponding to their answers. Respondents are chosen using randomised techniques. This method was deemed to be the most suitable data collection method for all three cities for the following reasons: the complexity of the concepts measured, the need for a high degree of standardisation, reduction of interviewing bias, maintaining respondents' anonymity, a cost efficient way of collecting a lot of data, an easily obtained large sample, time-efficiency, flexibility in displaying questions and ease of data entry and analysis. One of the principal shortcomings of online questionnaires is that they can be biased due to a narrow sample (Evans & Mathur 2005). For this reason, the quality of registered respondents was controlled by the research company to coincide with the age and sex distribution in the parent population. As stated by Fricker and Schonlau (2002), the differential between offline and online populations is narrowing fast and may be insignificant in the near future.

To ensure response rate, a covering letter was enclosed explaining the rationale behind the survey, and no incentive was given. A pilot study was also conducted to improve the face and content validity of the questionnaire. All survey data was treated as confidential, in the sense that only the researcher(s) had access to them, and steps were taken to ensure that no information was or will be published about identifiable persons without their permission. The following statement was written and highlighted in the covering letter: 'The contents of this questionnaire are absolutely confidential. Information identifying the respondent will not be disclosed under any circumstances'. The respondent's right to refuse to answer certain questions was respected and no undue pressure was brought to bear. The questionnaire consisted of four parts with questions relating to the framework-model: (i) personal factors associated with socio-demographics and situational factors; (ii) environmental values; (iii) practice of WPBs; and, (iv) psychological variables that assessed subjective and personal norms, perceived behavioural control and attitudes. At the end of the questionnaire, respondents were asked whether they had any further comment and were thanked for their participation in the survey.

The measurement of waste prevention behaviour – given the impossibility of observing and reporting waste prevention actions of the sample in this research, self-reported behaviour was used as a proxy in determining the dependent variable. Although these two measures are identical, Gamba and Oskamp (1994) have shown that their relationship is significant. These statements measured WPB over a range of activities: consumption, reusing, repairing, donation and home composting (see Table 7.1). These behaviours were selected based on the prevention activities that most of prevention programmes seek to encourage. The respondent scored each item according to the frequency with which that action was undertaken, using a 5-point Likert scale, from never (1) to always (5). All the statements were personalised and the use of emphasis in sentences (e.g., 'very', 'always') was avoided to reduce the amount of possible confusion between statements.

Table 7.1 Measurement statements for waste prevention behaviour

Measurement factor	Measurement statement*
WPB 1	Consciously buy products that have less packaging.
WPB 2	Take a reusable bag when shopping.
WPB 3	Consciously buy products that are designed to be reused.
WPB 4	Avoid buying single use items (e.g. plastic cups).
WPB 5	Repair something or have it repaired rather than buying a new one.
WPB 6	Reuse plastic or glass containers.
WPB 7	Use dishcloths rather than paper towels.
WPB 8	Buy refillable products to save packaging.
WPB 9	Donate unwanted used items/products to charity.
WPB 10	Buy returnable products (e.g. glass bottles).
WPB 11	Place food or garden waste in a home composter.
WPB 12	Refuse needless packaging when shopping.
WPB 13	Avoid buying bottled water

*São Paulo's Model: WPB1, WPB2, WPB6, WPB9; Sheffield's Model: WPB1, WPB2, WPB7, WPB9; Tokyo's Model: WPB1, WPB2, WPB7, WPB8

The measurement of attitudes toward waste prevention behaviour – in general terms, attitudes toward a particular behaviour determine whether the individual is in favour or against behaving in a specific manner. In this questionnaire, this latent variable was measured by using individuals' beliefs regarding the consequences of the behaviour, using a 5-point Likert scale ranging from strongly agree to strongly disagree. Negative items were re-coded as necessary so that all values indicated a pro-waste prevention stance. The benefits assessed included: protection of the environment, reduction of landfill waste, saving costs, health, and a better environment for future generations.

The measurement of subjective norms – in the manner suggested by Cheung *et al.* (1999), a global measure of subjective norms was derived by using a direct approach. Cheung *et al.* (1999) showed that the correlation between the composite approach proposed by Ajzen and Fishbein (1980) and the global measure method is high and statistically significant. The awareness of others' behaviour, along with the acceptance of that behaviour, was measured by asking respondents' beliefs about whether certain others thought waste prevention was important. This was assessed for internal referents, i.e. family members, and external referents, i.e. friends and neighbours. Each statement was measured using a 5-point Likert scale ranging from strongly agree to strongly disagree.

The measurement of personal norms – these items reflect respondents' beliefs about what is right or wrong to do. Accounting for an individual's personal beliefs regarding how they should behave forms an integral part of predicting moral behaviour. Because personal norms are built through a process of internalisation of social norms, they depend on both social norms and frequencies of behaviours. When individuals act in accordance with their personal norms, they experience a strong sense of pride. If, however, personal norms are violated, individuals experience feelings of guilt. In line with this general idea, personal norms were measured by the personal obligation to prevent waste, and by the feeling of guilt experienced when the behaviour is neglected. All measures were reported on a 5-point scale from strongly agree to strongly disagree.

The measurement of perceived behavioural control – there does not appear to be a generally preferred way of measuring perceived behaviour control (PBC). PBC has typically been operationalised directly by asking respondents how much control they have over the behaviour in question or how easy or difficult they feel it would be to perform the behaviour (Madden *et al.* 1992). Cheung *et al.* (1999) demonstrated that the product of control beliefs by the perceived power (which included situations that would facilitate or inhibit the behaviour) showed a significant correlation with a direct measure of PBC, which is representative of both perceived control and perceived difficulty. In this study, PBC was directly measured combining the perceived controllability of prevention and the perceived difficulty in preventing. Again, all measures were reported on a 5-point scale from strongly agree to strongly disagree.

The measurement of general environmental attitudes – to measure this latent variable, this study was built on the statements based on the new environmental paradigm (NEP) scale developed by Dunlap and Van Liere (1978). Stern *et al.* (1995) showed that broad concerns regarding the relationship between human beings and the environment are well captured by the NEP scale. As shown by Albrecht and Carpenter (1976), the statements gauged three constructs: balance of nature, limits to growth and humankind over nature. These constructs represented visions of environmental protection, sustainable development and indifference towards environmental matters, respectively. Each statement was measured using a 5-point Likert scale ranging from strongly agree to strongly disagree. Before applying these items in the structural analysis of the framework-model, an exploratory factor analysis was conducted because of their greater degree of internal consistency.

The measurement of personal factors – this part of the questionnaire asked respondents their age (only respondents over 18 years old were allowed to answer the questionnaire), gender, marital status, annual income, educational level, household composition and type. Age was categorised with five possible responses. Gender was a tick male/female question. Household composition comprised a range of family sizes. Education was considered if respondents had completed compulsory education and they were asked to tick the level they had reached post-16. Occupational status was assessed to verify the nature of the income data. Situational factors regarding recycling were also asked to establish whether participants (particularly from São Paulo) had access to the recycling scheme. Respondents were also asked if they took part in any sort of non-governmental organisation related to waste management, whether they participated in any informal selective collection programme and to whom they delivered recyclable materials.

Sample response and contributions of socio-demographic values

Sample profiles

The Brazilian study was undertaken in January 2012 and adults aged over 18 living in the city of São Paulo took part. The sample consisted of 700 respondents who were responsible for managing their household waste. In terms of representativeness of the wider parent population, the sample was on the whole acceptable. Using the technique adopted by Oskamp (1995), the demographic breakdowns were compared to the latest 2010 National Census from IBGE (2013). In all cases, age, gender, household members, education and income level were within 10 per cent of the census data. Socio-demographic characteristics of the respondents (one individual per household), along with some features of the households, are summarised in Table 7.2.

The British study was undertaken in November 2012 and adults aged over 18 living in the city of Sheffield participated. The sample consisted of 700 respondents who were responsible for managing their household waste. In terms of representativeness of the wider parent population, the sample was also examined compared to the latest 2011 National Census (Office for National Statistics

Table 7.2 Sample profile for São Paulo, Brazil

Variable	Research sample	
Age	18–24 yrs	6.3%
	25–39 yrs	37.4%
	40–54 yrs	38.1%
	55–74 yrs	18.1%
Gender	Male	42.3%
	Female	57.7%
Education	Middle school diploma	5.1%
	High school diploma	30.1%
	Undergraduate degree	49.9%
	Postgraduate degree	4.4%
	Other	10.4%
Marital status	Single	30.6%
	Married	50.0%
	Divorced	17.0%
	Widowed	2.4%
Income	Up to R$ 600	4.9%
	R$ 601–R$ 1,200	20.9%
	R$ 1,201–R$1800	14.7%
	R$ 1,801–R$ 2,400	12.3%
	R$ 2,401–R$ 3,000	9.6%
	Over R$ 3,001	25.6%
	Rather not say	12.1%
Household composition	One	9.6%
	Two	27.4%
	Three	28.1%
	Four	20.7%
	Five	9.4%
	Six or more	4.7%
Dwelling type	Flat/apartment	36.1%
	Detached house	63.9%

2012). In all cases, age, gender, household members, education and income level were within 10 per cent of the census data. Socio-demographic characteristics of the respondents (one individual per household), along with some features of the households, are summarised in Table 7.3.

The Japanese study was undertaken in February 2010 and adults aged over 20 living in the city of Tokyo took part. The sample consisted of 3,000 respondents who were responsible for managing their household waste. In terms of representativeness of the wider parent population, the sample was also examined compared to the latest 2010 National Census (Statistical Bureau 2010). In all cases, age, gender, household members, education and income level were within 10 per cent of the census data. Socio-demographic characteristics of the respondents (one individual per household), along with some features of the households, are summarised in Table 7.4.

Table 7.3 Sample profile for Sheffield, United Kingdom

Variable	Research sample	
Age	18–24 yrs	13.1%
	25–39 yrs	30.4%
	40–54 yrs	31.1%
	55–74 yrs	23.9%
	75 yrs and over	1.4%
Gender	Male	42.7%
	Female	57.3%
Education	Middle school diploma	10.4%
	High school diploma	28.9%
	Undergraduate degree	31.3%
	Postgraduate degree	16.6%
	Other	12.9%
Marital status	Single	38.7%
	Married	50.1%
	Divorced	9.3%
	Widowed	1.9%
Income	Up to £ 9,999	6.6%
	£10,000–£19,999	18.3%
	£20,000–£34,999	26.6%
	£35,000–£49,999	17.1%
	£50,000–£74,999	10.0%
	over £75,000	4.9%
	Rather not say	16.6%
Household composition	One	16.3%
	Two	36.9%
	Three	21.1%
	Four	17.3%
	Five	6.6%
	Six or more	1.9%
Dwelling type	Detached house	19.4%
	Semi-detached	39.1%
	Terraced	27.7%
	Flat/apartment	13.7%

Effects of socio-demographics values on waste prevention behaviour

One-way analysis of variance (ANOVA) was used to determine whether specific subgroups within the three samples held significantly different views regarding WPBs. The mean scores for each WPB statement were compared with the demographic variables of age, gender, marital status, family members, income, and educational level. One-way ANOVA tests the null hypothesis that two or more samples drawn from the same population will have equal means. The procedure is based on the F-test, which compares the between-groups variance with the within-groups variance, the larger the value of F, the more likely that the differences between groups are statistically significant. Where the p of F is less

Table 7.4 Sample profile for Tokyo, Japan

Variable	Research sample	
Age	20 yrs	20.8%
	30 yrs	24.3%
	40 yrs	18.3%
	50 yrs	19.3%
	60 yrs	17.2%
Gender	Male	49.8%
	Female	50.2%
Education	Middle school diploma	1.1%
	High school diploma	25.0%
	Undergraduate degree	53.6%
	Postgraduate diploma	6.0%
	Other	14.2%
Marital status	Single	41.9%
	Married	58.1%
Income	Up to 2 million yen	7.2%
	2 million–4 million yen	18.2%
	4 million–6 million yen	19.0%
	6 million–8 million yen	14.6%
	8 million–10 million yen	12.3%
	10 million– 12 million yen	6.6%
	12 million –15 million yen	4.8%
	more than 15 million yen	4.3%
	I don't want to answer	12.9%
Household composition	One	24.1%
	Two	26.1%
	Three	24.0%
	Four	17.7%
	Five	5.7%
	Six	1.8%
	Seven or more	0.6%
Household type	Detached house	35.6%
	Apartment	53.4%
	Public housing	7.1%
	Hostel, other	3.9%

than 0.05, the null hypothesis is rejected, the alternative hypothesis, that at least one group is statistically different from the others is accepted (Brace *et al.* 2006).

In the case of São Paulo, results suggest that individuals who engage in waste prevention tend to be female and over 40 years old. Similarly, for Sheffield, results also indicate that those who prevent waste are over 55 years old, female and living on their own. For Tokyo, results show that older respondents have higher practice rates as well as females and those living alone in houses. Education and income levels have not shown any statistical significance for any sample. Moreover, in both Sheffield and Tokyo, age (Sheffield: over 55, $p = 0.006$; Tokyo: over 50s, $p = 0.000$), marital status (Sheffield: married, $p = 0.048$; Tokyo: married,

p = 0.000), house composition (Sheffield: 3, p = 0.004; Tokyo: 5, p = 0.001), and house type (Sheffield: detached house, p = 0.006; Tokyo: detached house, p = 0.000) show significant effect on home composting engagement. While, in São Paulo, only the type of house was significant (detached house, p = 0.000). In case of 'I consciously buy products that have less packaging', only age (55–74 yrs, p = 0.014) had a significant effect in São Paulo, while in Sheffield and Tokyo, age (Sheffield: 55–74 yrs, p = 0.000; Tokyo: over 50s, p = 0.000), gender (Sheffield: female, p = 0.001; Tokyo: female, p = 0.000) and marital status (Sheffield: widowed, p = 0.000; Tokyo: married, p = 0.000) showed significant effect. Also household composition (3, p = 0.000) and type (detached house, p = 0.001) had significant effect in Tokyo. For 'I consciously buy products that are designed to be reused', only gender (female, p = 0.040) and household composition (5, p = 0.017) had a significant effect in São Paulo, while in Sheffield and Tokyo, age (Sheffield: 55–74 yrs, p = 0.000; Tokyo: 40s, p = 0.000) and marital status (Sheffield: married/widowed, p = 0.000; Tokyo: married, p = 0.000) showed significant effect. Also gender (female, p = 0.000), household composition (2, p = 0.000) and type (detached house, p = 0.001) had significant effect in Tokyo.

Cox *et al.* (2010) reviewed previous waste prevention studies in the UK, and revealed socio-demographic factors affecting waste prevention. They described that WPBs are more prevalent among individuals who are older, with middle to high incomes, female, living in detached properties, not living with children at home, and more concerned about the environment. Tonglet *et al.* (2004) concluded that people over 65, retired and living without children are significantly more likely to engage in waste minimization behaviours. Except for the effect of children and income, the same tendency shown in these previous studies was also observed in the results of all three samples; however, all WPBs did not show the same tendency. As previously pointed out, socio-demographic factors cannot completely predict pro-environmental behaviours (Hines *et al.* 1987). The different magnitudes and different significances among the samples and behaviours have also been found in previous studies, where socio-demographic effects on pro-environmental behaviours were analysed. As found by Tucker and Douglas (2007), demographic differences in pro-environmental behaviour are observed and, where seen, they appear to be quite intuitively plausible. Overall they are very poor predictors of WPB, with no universal relationship emerging between demographics and behaviour. Thus, the effect of other psychological factors (e.g. attitude, personal and subjective norms, and perceived behavioural control) have to be included to analyse correctly the influences on WPB.

Statistical data-analysis methodology

The integrated model was empirically analysed through structural equation modelling (SEM). The most commonly used estimation technique in SEM is the maximum likelihood method which assumes multivariate normality of the observed variables. This method, available in the software AMOS (Byrne 2013), was used in analysing the data since the observed variables showed multivariate

Table 7.5 Structural equation modelling fitness criteria

Model fit criteria	Interpretation and recommended acceptance levels
χ^2(chi-square)	Tests H_0: $\Sigma(\Theta)$ against H_a: $S \neq \Sigma(\Theta)$ $p >$ (considered significance level) 0.05
GFI	Ranges from 0 (no fit) to 1 (perfect fit) Values higher than 0.9 suggest a good fit
CFI	Ranges from 0 (no fit) to 1 (perfect fit) Values higher than 0.9 suggest a good fit
RMSEA	Values lower than 0.08 indicate adequate model fit Values lower than 0.05 indicate good model fit
AGFI	Ranges from 0 (no fit) to 1 (perfect fit) Values higher than 0.8 suggest a good fit

normality. To evaluate the model fit, we adopted the approach suggested by Ohtomo and Hirose (2007). The overall model fitness was assessed initially, and then the measurement and structural models were evaluated individually. Measures of overall model fit included absolute, incremental, and parsimonious indices of fit. The best-known index of absolute fit is the chi-square (χ^2) goodness-of-fit tests. However, the χ^2 test is quite sensitive to the sample size in indicating significant differences between the covariance matrices in any specified model. Besides the χ^2 test, two indices were used to evaluate the overall absolute fit of the proposed model: the goodness-of-fit index (GFI) and the comparative fit index (CFI). For incremental fit measures, the adjusted goodness-of-fit index (AGFI) index was used to evaluate the fit of the proposed model. Finally, the root-mean-square error of approximation (RMSEA), and the normed χ^2 (CMIN/DF) were used to evaluate the parsimonious fitness of the integrated model. Table 7.5 shows the minimum acceptance levels for these indices.

In evaluating the measurement model, the latent variables were assessed for reliability and validity. Reliability is concerned with the internal consistency of a construct, that is, whether the observed variables selected to indicate the construct do in fact measure the same (unobserved) concept. Before the estimation of the model, reliability was assessed after an exploratory factor analysis by computing Cronbach's alpha coefficients for each latent variable by using the Statistical Package for Social Sciences (SPSS) software (Brace *et al.* 2006). Reliability was also assessed by calculating the composite reliability coefficient from the sum of the standardised estimates and measurement errors for each latent variable by using the result from SEM (Hair *et al.* 1984). Kline (1998) suggests that reliability coefficients of around 0.9 should be classified as excellent, those around 0.8 as very good, those between 0.7 and 0.6 as adequate, and those below 0.5 as unreliable. Validity refers to whether one observed variable truly measures the construct that the researcher intends it to measure. Observed variables will be valid if they load significantly, or at least moderately, on their hypothesised latent variables. A confirmatory factor analysis was also conducted to verify the validity of the latent variables comprising each item. The number of measurement items (observed variables) for each latent variable was determined by an exploratory analysis of factors, by a reliability test, and according to the sample size to guarantee over-identification of the hypothetical model (see Table 7.6).

In analysing the fit of the structural model, it was examined whether parameter estimates possessed the correct sign and were statistically significant. All the integrated model's hypotheses were tested by observing the statistical significance of the corresponding direct paths in the structural model. Furthermore, we computed the reliability coefficient of the structural equation that models the latent variable of WPB. This coefficient is similar to the overall coefficient of determination in multiple regressions, and it shows how well the proposed relationship is represented. The data analysis concluded with an assessment of the total and indirect effects of each predictor latent variable on the WPB construct, based on its accordance with the theoretical background adopted in this study.

Results for São Paulo, Sheffield and Tokyo

São Paulo

Structural equation modelling was used to examine the causal model for São Paulo by using the maximum likelihood estimation method. Table 7.7 shows the correlation, mean values, and standards deviations for measures of waste prevention behaviour and the measured variables. The observed value for the χ^2 statistic is high and statistically significant, suggesting that the observed and predicted covariance matrices are not equal. Thus, the model ($p < 0.05$) should be rejected. However, in considering the dependence of the χ^2 test on the sample size ($n = 700$), the evaluation of the absolute fit of the model relied on two other adjunct measures. Both GFI and CFI exceed the recommended level of 0.9. According to these indexes, the model is classified as good. The RMSEA of less than 0.05 also indicates a good model fit. AGFI (higher than 0.8) also indicates that the model has a good fit. Overall, the integrated model exceeded the recommended highest acceptance levels, with an exception for the χ^2 test, suggesting a good incremental and parsimonious fit. Overall fit indices are reported in Table 7.8. Having developed a model with a good overall fit, a detailed analysis of the integrated model was conducted. Table 7.9 shows that all the latent variables are reliable, presenting adequate levels of Cronbach's alpha. A confirmatory factor analysis (using the maximum likelihood estimation method) was also conducted to verify the validity of the latent variables comprising each item. The results of the confirmatory factor analysis showed that all the factor loadings were significant and the fit was good, χ^2 (25, $n = 700$) = 46.297, $p = 0.006$; GFI = 0.987; RMSEA = 0.035; CFI = 0.991, verifying the validity of the latent variables composing each item. Table 7.10 presents the correlations among the latent variables derived from the confirmatory factor analysis.

Figure 7.1 shows the estimated standardised path coefficients, or the overall influence of each latent variable on the construct, on the integrated model itself. All proposed direct relationships are significant, and the corresponding

Table 7.6 Measurement instruments for the latent variables of the integrated model

Latent variable	Measurement instrument*
Personal norms	PN1: I am willing to change my habits to reduce waste at my house. PN2: I feel a strong personal obligation to reduce the amount of waste my household generates. PN3: I would feel guilty if I threw things away that still had a use. PN4: I would feel guilty if I bought products with excess packaging.
Subjective norms	SN1: Most famous people contribute to preserving the environment. SN2: Most people that I know contribute to preserve the environment.
Attitudes toward prevention	Att1: Each person's behaviour can have a positive effect on the environment. Att2: Environmental pollution can affect my family's health. Att3: Waste prevention practices make economic sense. Att4: Waste prevention can save natural resources.
General Environmental Attitudes	Envatt1: The balance of nature is very delicate and easily disturbed by human activities. Envatt2: Humans must live in harmony with nature in order to survive. Envatt3: If natural resources are over-exploited, human development may be harmed for future generations. Envatt4: Reducing waste is a good option to help solving waste problems.
Perceived behavioural control	PBC1: I know how to reduce waste in my house. PBC 2: I have plenty of opportunities to reduce waste in my daily life. *PBC3: Reducing waste requires significant lifestyle change and it is difficult for me to do this.* *PBC4: It is too complicated and inconvenient to act in ways that help the environment.*

*São Paulo's and Sheffield's Models: PN1, PN2, SN1, SN2, Att1, Att2, Envatt1, Envatt2, PBC1, PBC2; Tokyo's Model: PN3, PN4, SN1, SN2, Att1, Att3, Att4, Envatt1, Envatt3, Envatt4, PBC3, PBC4.

Note: Statements in italics indicate that the item is not pro-environmental. Scores were reversed for these items so that a higher score indicated increased willingness to engage in waste prevention behaviour.

Table 7.7 São Paulo integrated model: means, standard deviation, and correlation among the measured variables

	WPB6	WPB9	WPB1	WPB2	ENVATT1	ENVATT2	PN1	PN2	SN1	SN2	ATT1	ATT2	PBC2	PBC1
WPB6	1													
WPB9	.293**	1												
WPB1	.327**	.258**	1											
WPB2	.275**	.282**	.429**	1										
ENVATT1	.212**	.162**	.123**	.168**	1									
ENVATT2	.181**	.092*	.092*	.132**	.518**	1								
PN1	.225**	.165**	.281**	.313**	.294**	.330**	1							
PN2	.265**	.192**	.324**	.334**	.273**	.345**	.611**	1						
SN1	.194**	.066	.251**	.232**	.169**	.158**	.369**	.336**	1					
SN2	.122**	.036	.196**	.214**	.025	.041	.183**	.167**	.491**	1				
ATT1	.230**	.157**	.191**	.220**	.398**	.442**	.405**	.399**	.189**	.013	1			
ATT2	.227**	.174**	.208**	.200**	.407**	.472**	.381**	.395**	.207**	-.002	.675**	1		
PBC2	.249**	.129**	.224**	.253**	.210**	.224**	.359**	.408**	.443**	.372**	.253**	.255**	1	
PBC1	.218**	.143**	.255**	.247**	.208**	.234**	.394**	.414**	.505**	.349**	.254**	.278**	.631**	1
M	3.511	3.476	3.339	3.786	4.596	4.690	4.277	4.189	3.586	3.103	4.574	4.569	3.703	3.923
SD	1.420	1.066	1.163	1.177	0.618	0.529	0.689	0.776	0.958	1.010	0.597	0.598	0.924	0.859

**. Correlation is significant at the 0.01 level (2-tailed).
*. Correlation is significant at the 0.05 level (2-tailed).

Table 7.8 Overall fit indices for the São Paulo integrated model

Model fit criterion	Observed value	comment
χ^2(chi-square)	143.023, p=0.000, df=68	The model is rejected
GFI	0.972	Good model fit
CFI	0.975	Good model fit
RMSEA	0.039	Good model fit
AGFI	0.959	Good model fit

Table 7.9 São Paulo integrated model: evaluation of the latent variables' reliability

Latent variable	Cronbach's alpha (α)	Comment
Personal norms	0.755	Very good
Subjective norms	0.658	Adequate
Attitudes toward prevention	0.806	Very good
General environmental attitudes	0.682	Adequate
Perceived behavioural control	0.773	Very good
Waste prevention behaviour	0.638	Adequate

Note: According to Kline (1998) the reliability coefficients around 0.9 should be classified as excellent, around 0.8 as very good, between 0.7 and 0.6 as adequate and below 0.5 as unreliable measures

Table 7.10 São Paulo integrated model: correlations among the latent variables

	PN	SN	ATT	Envatt	PBC
Personal norms (PN)	–				
Subjective norms (SN)	0.511*	–			
Attitudes toward prevention (ATT)	0.614*	0.235*	–		
General environmental attitudes (Envatt)	0.552*	0.230*	0.725*	–	
Perceived behavioural control (PBC)	0.633*	0.732*	0.397*	0.379*	–

* $p<0.001$

hypotheses are accepted. The findings show that all specified paths are statistically significant, except for that between subjective norms and WPB. The indirect path from subjective norms to WPB through personal norms is statistically significant, and the hypothesis that the effect of subjective norms on WPB is mediated by personal norms is supported by the data (p < 0.05). The squared multiple correlation (R^2) for WPB is relatively high (0.405), suggesting that 40.5 per cent of the variability in this latent variable can be explained by the combined effects of the remaining five latent variables. Estimations of the standardised and

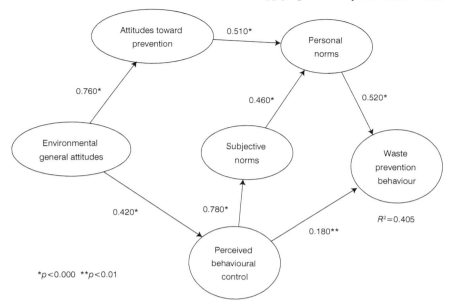

Figure 7.1 The standardised estimates for the São Paulo integrated model

indirect effects of each latent variable on the behaviour permit the estimation of the relative contribution of each predictor variable. If we take into account the absolute size of the standardised effects, the WPB is affected in the following order: personal norms (0.524), PBC (0.368), general environmental attitudes (0.359), attitudes toward prevention (0.270), and subjective norms (0.243). In the case of PBC and WPB, the total effect is the sum of the indirect (0.190) and direct (0.178) effects.

Sheffield

Structural equation modelling was used to examine the causal model for Sheffield by using the maximum likelihood estimation method. Table 7.11 shows the correlation, mean values, and standards deviations for measures of waste prevention behaviour and the measured variables. The observed value for the χ^2 statistic is high and statistically significant, suggesting that the observed and predicted covariance matrices are not equal. Thus, the model (p < 0.05) should be rejected. However, in considering the dependence of the χ^2 test on the sample size (n = 700), the evaluation of the absolute fit of the model relied on two other adjunct measures. Both GFI and CFI exceed the recommended level of 0.9. According to these indexes, the model is classified as good. The RMSEA of 0.071 indicates an acceptable model fit. AGFI (higher than 0.8) also indicates that the model has a good fit. Overall, the integrated model exceeded the highest recommended acceptance levels, with an exception to the χ^2 test, suggesting

Table 7.11 Sheffield integrated model: means, standard deviation, and correlation among the measured variables

	WPB1	WPB2	WPB7	WPB9	ENVATT1	ENVATT2	SN1	SN2	PBC2	PBC1	PN1	PN2	ATT1	ATT2
WPB1	1													
WPB2	.448**	1												
WPB7	.358**	.305**	1											
WPB9	.556**	.362**	.429**	1										
ENVATT1	.257**	.205**	.184**	.162**	1									
ENVATT2	.265**	.241**	.242**	.193**	.637**	1								
SN1	.219**	.172**	.111**	.218**	.173**	.193**	1							
SN2	.262**	.173**	.138**	.161**	.149**	.175**	.485**	1						
PBC2	.347**	.386**	.277**	.269**	.314**	.315**	.365**	.295**	1					
PBC1	.350**	.348**	.301**	.360**	.314**	.294**	.506**	.367**	.562**	1				
PN1	.451**	.358**	.300**	.369**	.375**	.398**	.358**	.327**	.472**	.519**	1			
PN2	.409**	.329**	.291**	.304**	.339**	.375**	.422**	.421**	.522**	.536**	.599**	1		
ATT1	.370**	.345**	.246**	.262**	.457**	.500**	.328**	.321**	.453**	.443**	.584**	.531**	1	
ATT2	.404**	.341**	.228**	.296**	.450**	.421**	.339**	.314**	.385**	.438**	.573**	.493**	.713**	1
M	3.176	3.863	3.713	3.294	3.984	4.007	3.134	3.017	3.850	3.584	3.777	3.646	4.029	3.787
SD	.918	1.057	.934	.944	.841	.852	.970	1.005	.878	.908	.899	.988	.920	.958

**. Correlation is significant at the 0.01 level (2-tailed).

a good incremental and an acceptable parsimonious fit. Overall fit indices are reported in Table 7.12. Following the same evaluation procedure, after developing a model with a good overall fit, a detailed analysis of the integrated model was conducted. Table 7.13 shows that all the latent variables are reliable, presenting adequate levels of Cronbach's alpha. A confirmatory factor analysis (using the maximum likelihood estimation method) was also conducted to verify the validity of the latent variables composing each item. The results of the confirmatory factor analysis showed that all the factor loadings were significant and the fit was good, χ^2 (25, n = 700) = 70.776, p = 0.000; GFI = 0.981; RMSEA = 0.049; CFI = 0.985, verifying the validity of the latent variables comprising each item. Table 7.14 presents the correlations among the latent variables derived from the confirmatory factor analysis.

Figure 7.2 shows the estimated standardised path coefficients, or the overall influence of each latent variable on the construct, on the integrated model itself. All proposed direct relationships are significant, and the corresponding hypotheses are accepted. The findings show that all specified paths are statistically significant. The indirect path from subjective norms to WPB through personal norms is statistically significant, and the hypothesis that the effect of subjective norms on WPB is mediated by personal norms is supported by the data ($p < 0.05$). The squared multiple correlation (R^2) for WPB is relatively high (0.552), suggesting that 55.2 per cent of the variability in this latent variable can be explained by the combined effects of the remaining five latent variables. Estimations of the standardised and indirect effects of each latent variable on the behaviour permit the estimation of the relative contribution of each predictor variable. If we take into account the absolute size of the standardised effects, the WPB is affected in the following order: personal norms (0.636), general environmental attitudes (0.516), PBC (0.423), attitudes toward prevention (0.349), and subjective norms (–0.139). In the case of PBC and WPB, the total effect is the sum of the indirect (–0.119) and direct (0.542) effects; as well as for subjective norm and WPB which total effect is the sum of the indirect (0.351) and direct (–0.490) effects.

Tokyo

Structural equation modelling was used to examine the causal model for Tokyo by using the maximum likelihood estimation method. Table 7.15 shows the correlation, mean values, and standards deviations for measures of waste prevention behaviour and the measured variables. The observed value for the χ^2 statistic is high and statistically significant, suggesting that the observed and predicted covariance matrices are not equal. Thus, the model ($p < 0.05$) should be rejected. However, in considering the dependence of the χ^2 test on the sample size (n = 3000; the larger the sample size, the more likely the rejection of the model), the evaluation of the absolute fit of the model relied on two other adjunct measures. Both GFI and CFI exceed the recommended level of 0.9. According to these indexes, the model is classified as good. The RMSEA of 0.054 indicates an acceptable model fit. AGFI (higher than 0.8) also indicates that the model has a good fit. Overall,

Table 7.12 Overall fit indices for the Sheffield integrated model

Model fit criterion	Observed value	Comment
χ^2(chi-square)	310.488, p=0.000, df=69	The model is rejected
GFI	0.941	Good model fit
CFI	0.938	Good model fit
RMSEA	0.071	Acceptable model fit
AGFI	0.910	Good model fit

Table 7.13 Sheffield integrated model: evaluation of the latent variables' reliability

Latent variable	Cronbach's alpha (α)	Comment
Personal norms	0.699	Adequate
Subjective norms	0.689	Adequate
Attitudes toward prevention	0.620	Adequate
General environmental attitudes	0.566	Adequate
Perceived behavioural control	0.607	Adequate
Waste prevention behaviour	0.713	Adequate

Note: According to Kline (1998) the reliability coefficients around 0.9 should be classified as excellent, around 0.8 as very good, between 0.7 and 0.6 as adequate and below 0.5 as unreliable measures

Table 7.14 Sheffield integrated model: correlations among the latent variables

	PN	SN	ATT	Envatt	PBC
Personal norms (PN)	–				
Subjective norms (SN)	0.693*	–			
Attitudes toward prevention (ATT)	0.833*	0.539*	–		
General environmental attitudes (Envatt)	0.604*	0.308*	0.680*	–	
Perceived behavioural control (PBC)	0.876*	0.751*	0.673*	0.507*	–

* p<0.001

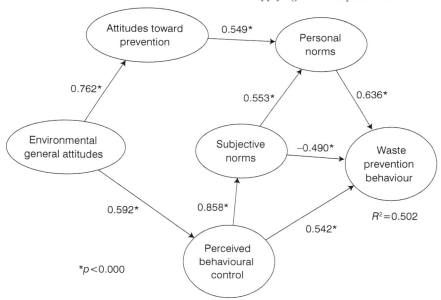

Figure 7.2 The standardised estimates for the Sheffield integrated model

the integrated model exceeded the highest recommended acceptance levels, with an exception for the χ^2 test, suggesting a good incremental and an acceptable parsimonious fit. Overall fit indices are reported in Table 7.16. Following the previous evaluation procedures, after developing a model with a good overall fit, a detailed analysis of the integrated model was conducted. Table 7.17 shows that all the latent variables are reliable, presenting adequate levels of Cronbach's alpha. A confirmatory factor analysis (using the maximum likelihood estimation method) was also conducted to verify the validity of the latent variables comprising each item. The results of the confirmatory factor analysis showed that all the factor loadings were significant and the fit was good, χ^2 (25, n = 3000) = 228.170, $p = 0.000$; GFI = 0.985; RMSEA = 0.050; CFI = 0.965, verifying the validity of the latent variables composing each item. Table 7.18 presents the correlations among the latent variables derived from the confirmatory factor analysis.

Figure 7.3 shows the estimated standardised path coefficients, or the overall influence of each latent variable on the construct, on the integrated model itself. All proposed direct relationships are significant, and the corresponding hypotheses are accepted. The findings show that all specified paths are statistically significant. The indirect path from subjective norms to WPB through personal norms is statistically significant, and the hypothesis that the effect of subjective norms on WPB is mediated by personal norms is supported by the data (p<0.05). The squared multiple correlation (R^2) for WPB is relatively high (0.518), suggesting that 51.8 per cent of the variability in this latent variable can be explained by the combined effects of the remaining five latent variables. Estimations of the standardised and

Table 7.15 Tokyo integrated model: means, standard deviation, and correlation among the measured variables

	ENVATT4	ENVATT1	ENVATT3	WPB1	WPB2	WPB7	WPB8	SN1	SN2	PBC3	PBC4	PN3	PN4	ATT4	ATT1	ATT3
ENVATT4	1															
ENVATT1	.395**	1														
ENVATT3	.334**	.283**	1													
WPB1	.162**	.174**	.221**	1												
WPB2	.140**	.145**	.182**	.494**	1											
WPB7	.177**	.185**	.225**	.440**	.407**	1										
WPB8	.131**	.131**	.149**	.327**	.263**	.409**	1									
SN1	.091**	.088**	.160**	.363**	.272**	.275**	.196**	1								
SN2	-.004	.015	.103**	.310**	.214**	.210**	.185**	.526**	1							
PBC3	.072**	.073**	.125**	.189**	.182**	.130**	.135**	.151**	.116**	1						
PBC4	.187**	.210**	.247**	.281**	.245**	.226**	.207**	.189**	.085**	.438**	1					
PN3	.166**	.159**	.233**	.280**	.215**	.276**	.205**	.353**	.327**	.076**	.159**	1				
PN4	.183**	.151**	.242**	.405**	.262**	.290**	.220**	.341**	.303**	.139**	.218**	.538**	1			
ATT4	.249**	.245**	.319**	.293**	.243**	.231**	.185**	.305**	.227**	.195**	.298**	.337**	.318**	1		
ATT1	.298**	.308**	.338**	.264**	.222**	.236**	.179**	.239**	.133**	.161**	.350**	.296**	.316**	.388**	1	
ATT3	.256**	.220**	.350**	.149**	.158**	.151**	.126**	.096**	.015	.093**	.239**	.124**	.193**	.272**	.402**	1
M	1.82	1.91	2.03	2.71	2.40	2.62	2.76	3.03	3.29	2.96	2.49	3.01	2.77	2.38	2.18	2.11
SD	.860	.899	.814	.980	1.212	.981	1.091	.865	.857	.946	.863	.942	.983	.857	.800	.802

**. Correlation is significant at the 0.01 level (2-tailed)

Table 7.16 Overall fit indices for the Tokyo integrated model

Model fit criterion	Observed value	Comment
χ^2(chi-square)	942.670, df=96, p=0.000	The model is rejected
GFI	0.962	Good model fit
CFI	0.925	Good model fit
RMSEA	0.054	Acceptable model fit
AGFI	0.947	Good model fit

Table 7.17 Tokyo integrated model: evaluation of the latent variables' reliability

Latent variable	Cronbach's alpha (α)	Comment
Personal norms	0.747	Adequate
Subjective norms	0.653	Adequate
Attitudes toward prevention	0.832	Very good
Environmental general attitudes	0.778	Very good
Perceived behavioural control	0.720	Adequate
Waste prevention behaviour	0.731	Adequate

Note: According to Kline (1998) the reliability coefficients around 0.9 should be classified as excellent, around 0.8 as very good, between 0.7 and 0.6 as adequate and below 0.5 as unreliable measures

Table 7.18 Tokyo integrated model: correlations among the latent variables

	PN	SN	ATT	Envatt	PBC
Personal norms (PN)	–				
Subjective norms (SN)	0.614*	–			
Attitudes toward prevention (ATT)	0.618*	0.424*	–		
Environmental general attitudes (Envatt)	0.450*	0.202*	0.821*	–	
Perceived behavioural control (PBC)	0.283*	0.231*	0.544*	0.401*	–

* $p<0.001$

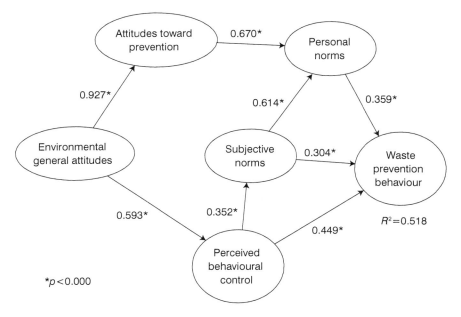

Figure 7.3 The standardised estimates for the Tokyo integrated model

indirect effects of each latent variable on the behaviour permit the estimation of the relative contribution of each predictor variable. If we take into account the absolute size of the standardised effects, the WPB is affected in the following order: PBC (0.435), subjective norms (0.424), general environmental attitudes (0.400), personal norms (0.362), and attitudes toward prevention (0.165). In the case of PBC and WPB, the total effect is the sum of the indirect (0.127) and direct (0.362) effects; and for subjective norm and WPB the total effect is the sum of the indirect (0.178) and direct (0.246) effects.

Analysis of the results and conclusions

A preliminary conclusion of this study is that the model of altruistic behaviour developed by Schwartz (1977) indeed provides the basis for the integrated model and which suggests that WPB is directly governed by the belief that individuals are personally responsible for the waste they generate and that they believe in the positive consequence of prevention. The framework-model suggests that the probability of a respondent engaging in WPB is greater if s/he believes that nothing should be wasted if it might be reused, and that wasting something goes against her/his principles. A key distinction between those who engage in WPB and those who do not is that the decision to engage is a function of the belief that it is the right thing to do. As proposed by *h1* (personal norms direct influence on WPB), individuals who engage in WPB perceived the task of minimising waste to be an integral part of who they are and how they live their lives. Results from the three samples show that a sense of moral obligation to prevent waste is a primary influence in the decision to engage in WPB. It is linked to an individual's self-concept; it would go against her/his principle not to prevent. The integration of the theory of planned behaviour (TPB) with the Schwartz model led from a reduced effect of attitudes toward prevention on WPB to an indirect one, supporting the *h2* (attitudes toward prevention has an indirect effect on WPB mediated by personal norms). This means that those who feel morally obligated to prevent are more likely to perform the action if they believe in the positive consequences of preventing. This hypothesis was validated on all three samples and it reiterates the action-attitude gap showing that attitudes on their own still remain relatively poor direct predictors of pro-environmental behaviour.

In accordance with *h3* (PBC direct influence on WPB), it can be stated that higher standards of waste prevention involvement can be found for household members possessing a stronger PBC. That is, those who attach little importance to obstacles to participating and those who are more aware of the importance of their own individual contribution are more likely to show behaviour associated with waste prevention. Accordingly, the individuals with greater PBCs are those who (i) are aware of the opportunities to prevent waste in their daily life and, therefore, more qualified to carry out WPB; and, (ii) are satisfied with the external conditions to perform the action. They are thus more likely to adopt new environmental activities regarding waste prevention. All three studies have also supported *h4* which assumes the potential indirect effect of PBC mediated by subjective norms referring to a combination of perceived control and social pressure to perform or not perform the behaviour (Davies *et al.* 2002). The predictability of WPB increases when the individual is influenced by others.

The inclusion of a moral element (i.e. personal norm) into the integrated model results in subjective norms having a direct influence on WPB. Both Sheffield and Tokyo WPB's model supports *h5* which assumes a direct influence of subjective norms on WPB. However, the São Paulo model has not supported this hypothesis replicating a previous result from Bortoleto *et al.* (2012). This model's results show that individuals might not consider the opinions of family, peers, and society as a pressure to engage in WPB. Previous studies have pointed out that subjective norms are an important influential factor in the engagement of individuals in recycling behaviour. However, particularly in São Paulo, waste prevention is significantly less attractive than recycling because of social pressure. This is because recycling is mainly undertaken in the privacy of the individual's home. Oskamp *et al.* (1991) have found that social pressure will only operate when the visibility of the behaviour is high, as in the case of recycling schemes. As supported by Sheffield's and Tokyo's models, WPB has become more normative as their waste management systems have been in place longer than São Paulo's, with the determinants of waste prevention actions bearing more resemblance to those of recycling. These results underline the importance of subjective norms in explaining WPB. All three models also support *h6* which assumes the indirect effect of subjective norms on WPB through an internalisation process (personal norms).

The last hypothesis of the integrated model, *h7*, assumes that general environmental attitudes have a direct effect on attitudes toward prevention and PBC. The results of all three models show that general environmental attitudes, as hypothesised by Stern *et al.* (1995), have a direct positive and significant effect on specific attitudes towards prevention. On the other hand, the hypothesis that general environmental attitudes may be associated with the WPB through PBC was also significant and, the total or indirect effect of general environmental attitudes on WPB was also statistically significant on all models. Strength of environmental values can be shown to be important in shaping WPB meaning that individuals with strong environmental beliefs demonstrate a higher awareness level toward environmental problems and attach less importance to difficulties associated with WPB.

The effectiveness of socio-demographics in the framework-model to increase the model's predictability is still uncertain. This study suggests that the predictability of WPB increases substantially if the respondent is female, over 50 years and lives in a detached house. This may not be surprising if it is seen that although men may have positive attitudes toward waste prevention, they are not actually the ones who do it, as suggested by Barr *et al.* (2001). It is therefore likely that gender depends on contextual factors, i.e. household lifestyle, more than a significant difference between men and women regarding WPB. Age seems the most significant socio-demographic factor involved in shaping WPB. It appears that those who are older are more likely to prevent waste, probably, through habit. This finding is consistent with other studies (Bowman *et al.* 1998) with similar results on recycling behaviour. This study has not found positive effects of educational level on WPB. This is at odds with Lansana's study (1992) which shows significant correlations with time spent in education and recycling behaviour. In addition, there are no statistically significant effects on WPB according to respondents' income level either. Household type shows a weak positive effect with WPB being more relevant in the context of home composting. It appears that size of house is important for some waste prevention actions as suggested by Oskamp *et al.* (1991) for other pro-environmental behaviour. The findings are important since they demonstrate the lack of efficacy in certain socio-demographic factors that have been previously significant in other researches. As pointed out by others, socio-demographic factors can be misleading when considered as part of the structural integrated model, since they may in fact form spurious rather than true correlations with behaviour (Tarrant & Cordell 1997). That is why this study analysed socio-demographics apart from the structural equation model. Nevertheless, socio-demographics can be an important variable to understand the relationship between contextual factors and the behaviour in question.

Various contextual conditions differentially constrain and facilitate individuals' engagement in WPB by making some actions easier to perform under one condition than under another. Consider the following statement: 'if I am offered a plastic bag in a store, I would take it'. The majority of respondents in São Paulo answered positively (32 per cent always, 25.9 per cent often) while in Sheffield 37 per cent indicated that they would accept it occasionally and 26 per cent rarely. The difference is probably due to two reasons: (i) Brazilians are used to discarding their general waste in supermarket plastic bags instead of regular black plastic bags, since they do not have to pay for them; (ii) in Sheffield two major supermarket chains charge consumers for plastic bags while others control how many bags a consumer can take. The lack of a regulation on this matter in São Paulo has greatly impacted individuals' decisions on whether to accept plastic bags or not. On the contrary, in Sheffield, the enforcement of the plastic bag charge has change individuals' use of plastic bags in supermarkets. Accordingly, contextual factors can also explain why subject norms have a direct influence on WPB in mature schemes rather than less mature waste prevention programmes. Contexts shape people's performance as a main effect by immediately constraining or facilitating behaviour; but at the same time, they also affect people's motivation to act in a certain way as an interaction effect by confronting individuals with differentially appealing opportunities and differentially daunting obstacles (Scheuthle *et al.* 2005).

The framework-model proposed in this study accounts for a different number of variables that impact on waste prevention behaviour which have been carefully categorised and grouped. It gives a logical theoretical framework-model updating the understanding of the determinants of waste prevention behaviour. Through the process outlined above, including the qualitative analysis of contextual factors, a framework-model for waste prevention behaviour has been conceived (see Figure 7.4). It offers a valuable contribution to the debate concerning individuals' engagement in waste prevention programmes and a primer for waste managers for organising waste management strategies. Finally, the

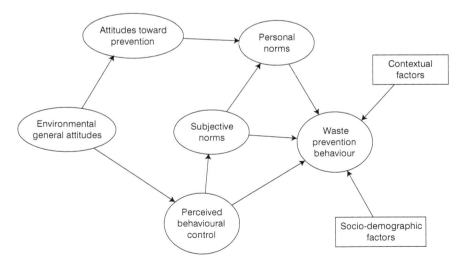

Figure 7.4 The framework-model for waste prevention behaviour

framework-model proposed in this study can explain individuals' waste prevention behaviour with a degree of sufficiency and accuracy that is lacking from the standard models (TPB, Schwartz' model) tested in previously studies.

References

Abrelpe (2012). Panorama dos resíduos sólidos no Brasil, 2011 Available at http://www.abrelpe.org.br/Panorama/panorama2011.pdf

Ajzen, I., & Fishbein, M. (1980). *Understanding attitudes and predicting social behaviour.* Englewood Cliffs, NJ: Prentice Hall.

Albrecht, S. L., & Carpenter, K. E. (1976). Attitudes as predictors of behavior versus behavior intentions: A convergence of research traditions. *Sociometry, 39*, 1–10.

Barr, S. W., Gilg, A. W., & Ford, N. J. (2001). A conceptual framework for understanding and analysing attitudes towards household-waste management. *Environment and Planning A, 33*(11), 2025–2048.

Bortoleto, A. P., Kurisu, K. H., & Hanaki, K. (2012). Model development for household waste prevention behaviour. *Waste Management, 32*(12), 2195–2207.

Bowman, N., Goodwin, J., Jones, P., & Weaver, N. (1998). Sustaining recycling: identification and application of limiting factors in kerbside recycling areas. *The International Journal of Sustainable Development & World Ecology, 5*(4), 263–276.

Brace, N., Kemp, R., & Snelgar, R. (2006). *SPSS for psychologists: A guide to data analysis using SPSS for Windows, versions 12 and 13.* Hillsdale, NJ: Erlbaum.

Byrne, B. M. (2013). *Structural equation modeling with AMOS: Basic concepts, applications, and programming.* Abingdon, UK: Routledge.

CACI (2012). *Retail dimensions report 2012.* London, UK.

Cempre (2014). CempreCicloSoft 2012. Cempre, São Paulo, Brazil. Retrieved from http://www.cempre.org.br/ciclosoft_2012.php

Cheung, S. F., Chan, D. K. S., & Wong, Z. S. Y. (1999). Reexamining the theory of planned behavior in understanding wastepaper recycling. *Environment and Behavior, 31*(5), 587–612.

Coggins, P. C. (2001). *Municipal waste management strategy, Sheffield city council.* Sheffield: WAMTEC and MEL Research Ltd.

Cox, J., Giorgi, S., Sharp, V., Strange, K., Wilson, D. C., & Blakey, N. (2010). Household waste prevention – a review of evidence. *Waste Management & Research, 28*(3), 193–219.

Davies, J., Foxall, G. R., & Pallister, J. (2002). Beyond the intention–behaviour mythology: An integrated model of recycling. *Marketing Theory, 2*, 29–113.

Dunlap, R. E., & Van Liere, K. D. (1978). The new environmental paradigm. *Journal of Environmental Education, 9*, 10–19.

Evans, J. R., & Mathur, A. (2005). The value of online surveys. *Internet Research, 15*(2), 195–219.

Fricker, R. D., & Schonlau, M. (2002). Advantages and disadvantages of Internet research surveys: Evidence from the literature. *Field Methods, 14*(4), 347–367.

Gamba, R. J., & Oskamp, S. (1994). Factors influencing community residents' participation in commingled curbside recycling programs. *Environment and Behaviour, 26*, 587–612.

Hair, J. F., Anderson, R. E., Tatham, R. L., & Black, W. C. (1984). *Multivariate data analysis with readings, 1995.* NewYork: Macmillan.

Hines, J. M., Hungerford, H. R., & Tomera, A. N. (1987). Analysis and synthesis of research on responsible environmental behavior: A meta-analysis. *The Journal of Environmental Education*, 18(2), 1–8.

IBGE. (2013). *Atlas do censo demográfico 2010*. Rio de Janeiro: IBGE.

IBGE, (2014). Cidades@database. Retrieved from from http://cod.ibge.gov.br/235J4.

Jacobi, P. R., & Besen, G. R. (2011). Gestão de resíduos sólidos em São Paulo: Desafios da sustentabilidade. *Estudos Avançados*, 25(71), 135–158.

Kline, R. B. (1998). Software review: Software programs for structural equation modeling: Amos, EQS, and LISREL. *Journal of Psychoeducational Assessment*, 16(4), 343–364.

Lansana, F. M. (1992). Distinguishing potential recyclers from nonrecyclers: A basis for developing recycling strategies. *The Journal of Environmental Education*, 23(2), 16–23.

Madden, T. J., Ellen, P. S., & Ajzen, I. (1992). A comparison of the theory of planned behavior and the theory of reasoned action. *Personality and Social Psychology Bulletin*, 18(1), 3–9.

Office for National Statistics. (2012). *2011 census: Statistical bulletin*. London, UK. Retrieved from http://www.ons.gov.uk/ons/guide-method/census/2011/census-data/index.html

Ohtomo, S., & Hirose, Y. (2007). The dual-process of reactive and intentional decision-making involved in eco-friendly behavior. *Journal of Environmental Psychology*, 27(2), 117–125.

Oppenheim, A. N. (1992). *Questionnaire design, interviewing and attitude measurement*. New York: Continuum.

Oskamp, S. (1995). Resource conservation and recycling: Behavior and policy. *Journal of Social Issues*, 51(4), 157–177.

Oskamp, S., Harrington, M., Edwards, T., Sherwood, P. L., Okuda, S. M. & Swanson, D. L. (1991). Factors influencing household recycling behavior. *Environment and Behavior*, 23, 494–519.

Scheuthle, H., Carabias-Hütter, V., & Kaiser, F. G. (2005). The motivational and instantaneous behavior effects of contexts: Steps toward a theory of goal-directed behavior. *Journal of Applied Social Psychology*, 35(10), 2076–2093.

Schwartz, S. H. (1977). Normative influences on altruism. In L. Berkowitz (Ed.), *Advances in experimental social psychology* (pp. 221–279). New York: Academic Press.

Sheffield City Council. (2014). 2011 Census: key statistics. Retrieved from https://www.sheffield.gov.uk/your-city-council/sheffield-profile/population-and-health/2011-census/key-statistics.html

Statistical Bureau, Ministry of Internal Affairs and Communications. (2010). Population census, 2009 in Japan. Retrieved from http://www.stat.go.jp/english/data/kokusei/

Stern, P. C., Dietz, T., & Guagnano, G. A. (1995). The new ecological paradigm in social psychology context. *Environment and Behaviour*, 26, 723–743.

Tarrant, M. A., & Cordell, H. K. (1997). The effect of respondent characteristics on general environmental attitude-behavior correspondence. *Environment and Behavior*, 29(5), 618–637.

Taylor, I. R., Evans, K., & Fraser, P. (1996). *A tale of two cities: Global change, local feeling and everyday life in the north of England: A study in Manchester and Sheffield*. London: Taylor & Francis.

Tokyo Metropolitan Government. (2011). Waste management and resource recovery – the environment of Tokyo 2011. Tokyo, Japan. Retrieved from http://www.kankyo.metro.tokyo.jp/en/attachement/waste.pdf

Tokyo Metropolitan Government. (2012). Overview of Tokyo – Tokyo's history, geography, and population. Tokyo, Japan. Retrieved from http://www.metro.tokyo.jp/english/profile/img/2012_en.pdf.

Tonglet, M., Phillips, P. S., & Bates, M. P. (2004). Determining the drivers for householder pro-environmental behaviour: waste minimisation compared to recycling. *Resources, Conservation and Recycling, 42*(1), 27–48.

Tucker, P., & Douglas, P. (2007). *Understanding household waste prevention behaviour* (final report). WR0112. London: Defra. Available from: http://randd.defra.gov.uk

Veolia. (2014a). District energy – history. Retrieved from http://www.veoliaenvironmentalservices.co.uk/Sheffield/What-happens-to-your-waste/District-Energy/History/

Veolia. (2014b). District energy network FAQs. Retrieved from http://www.veoliaenvironmentalservices.co.uk/Sheffield/Collections/FAQs/District-Energy-Network/

8 Goal-directed conservation behaviour and waste prevention behaviour

Waste management policy has many shapes. While end-of-pipe approaches have been dominant in the past, information based campaigns have gained ground. The idea is that increasing environmental awareness will result in changing people's behaviour towards a more environmentally benign direction, i.e. less waste generation. Have these efforts brought results? Most policies to foster waste prevention behaviour (WPB) (see Chapter 3) rely upon large-scale information campaigns. These campaigns often assume that changes in behaviour are a consequence of increasing public awareness about the issue, for example, of waste generation and fostering attitudes that are supportive of waste prevention (e.g. home composting). They provide information through media advertising, website, distribution of brochures and flyers. However, as mentioned on Chapter 5, information campaigns have little or no effect upon pro-environmental behaviour.

As a consequence, programmes that make use of information intensive approaches are less likely to foster behavioural change. But why would information not be a strong influence in changing individuals' behaviour? Consider the following situation. When I was living in Tokyo, I used to walk to the supermarket near my apartment during the weekend. There I could always find refill packages for most products (e.g. shampoo, soap, detergent) that I used, until the day the manager decided not sell refill packages any more for economic reasons. It was a small supermarket but close to my home, but the other option was 25 minutes away. While the exercise would have been good to me, I would rather have spent that time doing something else. From that day on, I would only buy refill packages when I was on my way home from the university and I remembered to do it. I am relatively knowledgeable about the importance of waste prevention in mitigating environmental problems and I have a strong sense of responsibility that I should protect the environment. However, in this situation, there was a factor (distance) that increased the difficulty of buying refill packages. Before, it was easier to perform the action. To sum up, a variety of barriers can make the behaviour apparently more difficult to the individual. For example my friend and neighbour, decided to walk to the biggest supermarket despite the distance to buy a shampoo refill. So, what did influence our decision to be different? According to Kaiser *et al.* (2010), 'the more obstacles a person overcomes and the more effort that person expends to implement his or her attitude, the more evident that person's commitment to the particular goal implied by the attitude'. Thus, when a slight difficulty was enough to stop me from taking a further step toward waste prevention, my motivation to the attitudinal goal (preserve the environment) was lower than my friend's.

Another approach, very commonly used in waste prevention policies (e.g. real nappies campaigns in the UK), assumes that individuals systematically evaluate choices and then act in accordance with their economic self-interest. This perspective suggests that in order to affect these decisions, local governments need only provide information to the public that is in their financial best interest and consequently the public will behave accordingly. In Sheffield, the real nappies campaign advertises 'Did you know that by the time your baby is potty trained you will have gone through 5,000 nappy changes? (…) The total cost of using real nappies can be less than half that of using disposables' (Sheffield City Council 2014). These campaigns also use economic incentives to increase behaviour change, such as in Sheffield where a £10 contribution, from the city council is available for residents who purchase real nappies through the Sheffield Real Nappy Network. Other types of incentives include rebates (subsides) on purchasing pro-environmental appliances or equipment (e.g. durable bags). However, efforts that have concentrated on underscoring the financial advantages of a waste prevention action have also been largely unsuccessful. Why is this? In general, they assume that householders would overcome any difficulty for their financial benefit. As pointed by Costanzo *et al.* (1986), the failure of mass media campaigns is due to an underestimation of the difficulty of changing behaviour. While these information and economic based campaigns do consider the human side of WPB, they do so in a very simplistic way. First and foremost, waste prevention policies involve not only specifics of the behaviour, but also the cultural practices, social interactions and the individual's environmental motivation. Thus, the diversity of barriers perceived by individuals with different levels of environmental motivation means that information campaigns alone will rarely result in behaviour change.

Unfortunately, to date psychologists apply by and large two rather suboptimal measures to deal with contextual influences on pro-environmental behaviour. They either cancel them out by aggregating behaviour cross-situationally, or they try to assess them subjectively by means of perceived control (Kaiser & Keller 2001). In Chapter 7, the framework-model for WPB has accounted separately for contextual influences on the behaviour since these factors influence WPB systematically rather than incidentally. The present chapter aims to test an alternative behaviour measure proposed by Kaiser and Wilson (2004) that addresses contextual differences more rigorously and systematically and consists of a combination of various conservation behaviours (i.e. general ecological behaviour scale). With this purpose, data collection was undertaken in two different cities, São Paulo and Sheffield, in order to assess the immediate impacts of context on people's WPB. The objective was to test the previous hypothesis (Kaiser & Keller 2001) that contextual conditions in the southern and northern hemispheres (i.e. Brazil and the UK) result in patterns of country-specific constrained or facilitated behaviours. These differences should become obvious in country-specific orderings of behaviour difficulties. Such differential behaviour difficulties may reflect effective situational influences and, at best, useful political actions that are potentially transferable from one sociocultural context to another (Kaiser & Biel 2000).

The concept of goal-directed behaviour and its unidimensional measurement

A goal-directed behaviour simply means that a person acts to achieve a certain goal. According to Greve (2001), it constitutes a special class of human conduct, which logically links a person's intention to achieve a particular goal with his or her performance. Consider the following situation: a person aims to contribute to decrease environmental impacts from her/his actions. To achieve the goal, s/he decides to participate in the recycling programme provided by the local government, and so, s/he decides to only buy products made with recyclable materials and also to buy a green container to store all recyclable waste for the kerbside collection. In other words, if a person intends to achieve a goal, a series of behavioural steps must be taken, such as sorting recyclable waste into categories for the kerbside collection. Such a combination of behaviours implies that people can select from various alternatives to fulfil their individual aspiration level, which leaves them with choices (Kaiser & Byrka 2011). Furthermore, a person's dedication to achieve a certain goal is most obvious in the face of increasingly demanding hurdles or progressively intolerable sacrifices (Scheuthle *et al.* 2005). And as far as pro-environmental behaviour is concerned, this goal is more visible when the involved activities are continuously more demanding of personal sacrifice (e.g. less consumption). Consequently, the more obstacles a person overcomes and the more effort a person expends along the way to the goal, the clearer is her/his commitment to the particular goal. Why bother with recycling, home composting and reusing product packages if s/he is not committed to protect the environment? On the contrary, going back to the initial example, that person realises that the kerbside collection is not door-to-door and s/he needs to drop-off the recyclable materials at the supermarket, and because of this tiny inconvenience s/he decides not to recycle. In this case, s/he does not, presumably, seriously intend to take part in the recycling programme. Any behaviour, such as WPB, involves costs as it requires personal resources such as time, money and effort. Of course, individuals usually prefer the more convenient and socially acceptable behaviours over the more difficult, stressful and costly ones. Thus, Kaiser and Byrka (2011) assume that people prefer less demanding actions to more demanding ones.

In their model, Kaiser and Wilson (2004) establish that behaviour can be characterised by the personal effort (i.e. one's commitment) and the behavioural costs involved in its fulfilment. Buying products made with recyclable material costs time and money, while getting up early to put the recyclable waste bin outside the house for kerbside collection requires commitment. 'Commitment and behavioural costs, which represent the difficulty people face in the realisation of an act, jointly result in a probability that a given person will behave in a certain way' (Kaiser & Wilson 2004). The difficulty, as mentioned earlier, is determined by the contextual conditions (i.e. sociocultural) in which individuals' behaviour takes place. Obviously, the economic incentives in the real nappies campaign in Sheffield created circumstances that facilitated people's attraction regardless of their motivation to act.

Environmental protection within contemporary societies requires that individuals undertake a broad range of actions that will result in less pollution and less resource and energy consumption, consequently, fewer environmental impacts. This diversity of possible actions implies that, in the absence of barriers, a person can select from different behavioural alternatives to achieve her/his goal. For example, instead of composting at home, an individual can start to buy less food and use it more efficiently to avoid food waste. However, as you can see, each of these behaviours involves costs, requires effort and other personal resources (e.g. time, money). If the goal can be accomplished with a variety of different activities, Kaiser *et al.* (2008) argue that 'a person will make a prudent selection of the behavioural means'. Traditionally, individuals choose the more convenient instead of the more complicated ones, and, because of that, householders usually choose the less demanding actions (e.g. reuse containers) instead of more difficult ones (e.g. less consumption) in waste prevention programmes. This becomes visible in the relative popularity of various WPBs as shown by Kurisu and Bortoleto (2011) in their study in Japan. According to Kaiser and Byrka (2011), this behaviour's popularity is, in turn, anticipated to be a function of two components: (i) people's overall environmental engagement, and (ii) the composition of all the figurative costs of a particular behaviour.

The Rasch model mathematically describes this functional relationship adequately (Kaiser & Wilson 2004). The classical Rasch model and, thus, the functional link between a person's overall engagement and his or her probability to act in a certain way is depicted in the following formula (Bond & Fox 2013): The mathematical formula for the Rasch Model is:

$$p\left(x = 1 \mid \theta, \delta\right) = \frac{e^{\theta_n - \delta_i}}{1 + e^{\theta_n - \delta_i}}$$

where the natural logarithm of the ratio of the probability (*pki*) of person *k* to take on a specific behaviour *i* relative to the probability of non-action (1 − *pki*) is given by the difference between *k*'s overall environmental engagement (Θ_k) and the composite of all the figurative costs of this behaviour (δ_i). Note that in this mathematical formalization, people are distinguishable with respect to their overall levels of engagement, and behaviours are distinguishable by how 'costly' they are to fulfil. By applying the Rasch model, Kaiser and colleagues were additionally able to circumvent some well-known technical problems of conventional factor analytical approaches that can occur when behaviours are involved (Kaiser *et al.* 2007). Conceptualising goal-directed pro-environmental behaviour of individuals in this manner implies that seemingly diverse behaviours, such as reusing, recycling and home composting, form a uniform set of behaviours. This in turn means that different behaviours which are linked by one underlying goal (i.e. environmental protection) can be mapped on to one dimension. Along this dimension, the behaviours are distinct only in terms of their difficulties. Unlike other measures of pro-environmental behaviour, Kaiser *et al.*'s (2007) unidimensional measure represents as much a measure of a person's pro-environmental attitudes as well as their overall behaviour performance, thereby departing from traditional views of attitude-behaviour relationships which perceive attitudes and behaviours as distinct psychological concepts. Kaiser and Wilson (2004) developed a unidimensional measure of goal-directed pro-environmental behaviour and found that energy conservation, mobility, waste avoidance, consumerism, recycling and vicarious behaviour can indeed be mapped onto one dimension.

Participants and procedure

Both samples consisted of information from São Paulo in Brazil and Sheffield in the United Kingdom. See Chapter 7 for a description of both study fields and questionnaire implementation. The data for this study were collected from the same samples using the questionnaire described on Chapter 7 through computer-assisted web interviewing. The São Paulo sample consisted of 700 adults with Portuguese being the language used by these participants. The respondents ranged from 18 to 74 years with 57.7 per cent female. The Sheffield sample also consisted of 700 adults with English being the language used by these participants. The respondents ranged from 18 to 75 years with 57.3 per cent female. See Tables 7.2 and 7.3 for further details of both samples. For the purpose of the present study, it was sufficient that the participants from both samples reflected a wide range of diversity in socio-demographic factors. The quality of registered respondents was controlled on both samples by the research company to coincide with the age and sex distributions in the parent population. The response alternatives were a yes/no format and responses to negatively formulated items were recoded as yes responses and vice versa.

The general ecological behaviour measure

Contextual factors affect people's behaviours, making some easier to perform than others (Guagnano *et al.* 1995). Our *living environments*,[1] for example, are among the more salient of these contextual factors. For example, if recycling bins are readily accessible, recycling is easy to carry out. According to Kaiser (1998), traditional measures of pro-environmental behaviour (based on correlations) do not systematically consider contextual influences. Consequently, an individuals' pro-environmental behaviour does not appear to be the same across different domains (e.g. recycling, waste prevention). In other words, by engaging in one behaviour (e.g. home composting) it does not necessarily mean that the same person does or does not recycle waste. On the opposite side, the general ecological behaviour (GEB) measure aggregates across a range of behaviours with considerably contrasting degrees of difficulty to being performed.

The difficulty of a pro-environmental behaviour, such as refusing a plastic bag at the supermarket, is estimated by considering the number of people who behave accordingly. Behaviour difficulty is a function of the number of people who perform a particular pro-environmental behaviour and it relates to the likelihood that a person will behave correspondingly regardless of his or her general pro-environmental behaviour level. If only a few people behave in a certain way, we are dealing with a difficult behaviour. The probability is low that anyone would demonstrate this particular behaviour. The easier a behaviour is to perform, the fewer situational constraints have to be assumed and the more likely it is that people will indeed perform the behaviour. High values for behaviour difficulty represent low endorsement probabilities. The difficulties a person actually overcomes can, in turn, be used to measure a person's pro-environmental behaviour level. A person is more likely to behave more pro-environmentally if they undertake more difficult tasks. In other words, a person's pro-environmental behaviour level is a function of the contextual factors he or she actually ignores. If the barriers are greater and the difficulties more numerous to overcome, the person's level of behaviour is higher. Conversely, the level of a person's pro-environmental behaviour tends to be low when even the smallest of difficulties are enough to prevent him or her from action.

Pro-environmental engagement was measured using a composite of 50 self-reported behaviours from the GEB scale (Kaiser & Wilson 2004). These items are grouped by different domains of pro-environmental behaviour (energy conservation, mobility and transport, waste avoidance, consumerism, recycling, vicarious behaviours toward conservation). 'I use renewable energy sources' or 'I use a compost bin' are two examples of items. The original German version of the GEB scale items were adapted from a former 'Guttmanscale' and translated into English (e.g. Kaiser & Wilson 2004) for application in Sheffield, and a Portuguese version for São Paulo. Back translations of the Portuguese GEB scale into English revealed a high item similarity although, strictly speaking, no perfect match was achieved. Such a straight forward procedure was applicable, since, at least, the 'structural equivalence' (i.e. unidimensionality) of the two GEB versions would be controlled statistically and all estimates would be in comparable measurement units (for more information, see Van de Vijver & Tanzer 1997).

A yes/no response format was used ($i = 18$) or responses were recoded to a yes/no format ($i = 32$). 'No' responses to negatively formulated items were recoded as 'yes' responses and vice versa. In all items, 'not applicable' was a response alternative when an answer was not possible and they were coded as missing values. Missing values were handled as 'no' responses (assuming participants' doubts – represented by missing values – to be indicators of not behaving pro-environmentally in general). Kaiser (1998) provided evidence for the validity of the GEB measure and Kaiser *et al.* (1999) criterion related and discriminant validity and for construct validity.

All 50 pro-environmental behaviours and all participants (N = 700 for each city) were assessed on a general performance scale using the Rasch model (for item response theory details and formulas, see Wright and Masters (1982) and for computational details, see Adams and Khoo (1996)). As mentioned earlier, the Rasch model distinguishes between behaviours solely on the basis of their difficulty and assumes that all behaviours are equally discriminating. Hence, within item response theory the Rasch model represents the one-parameter model. The GEB scale has an item response theory-based reliability of rel = 0.99 for the São Paulo sample and rel = 1.00 for Sheffield sample. Its internal consistency is $\alpha = 0.79$ for São Paulo and $\alpha = 0.75$ for Sheffield. One of the behaviour items, 'For longer journeys (more than 6 hours), I take an aeroplane', did not fit the 50-item GEB scale (t-value (t) > 2.33; $p < .01$). The overall fit statistics for the 49 items in this scale are for São Paulo: mean of mean squares (M(MS)) = 1.0, standard deviation of mean squares (SD(MS)) = 0.08, mean of t-values [M(t)] = –0.12, standard deviation of t-values (SD(t)) = 2.28; and for Sheffield: mean of mean squares (M(MS)) = 0.99, standard deviation of mean squares (SD(MS)(= 0.06,mean of t-values (M(t)) = 0.12, standard deviation of t-values (SD(t)) = 1.64. Ideally, M(MS) and SD(t) should be 1.0, whereas M(t) should be 0. For SD(MS) no general reference value can be given. Out of 700 participants in each sample, for São Paulo 29 (4.14 per cent) do not fit ($t > 2.33$; $p < .01$) while for Sheffield 41 (5.85 per cent) do not fit ($t > 2.33$; $p < .01$); the overall fit statistics for the participants for São Paulo are: M(MS) = 1.0, SD(MS) = 0.25, M(t) = –0.06, SD(t) = 1.25; and for Sheffield are: M(MS) = 1.0, SD(MS) = 0.29, M(t) = –0.05, SD(t) = 1.42. In summary, the fit statistics and reliability information of the extended version of the GEB scale are reasonable.

Comparing living environments

Since societies are rather complex aggregates of facilitating and constraining influences, the question arises as to which contextual factors account for the different behaviour imprints in São Paulo and in Sheffield. To investigate this, people's living environments were screened statistically for differential performance difficulties (i.e. applying a test of item parameter invariance, Embretson & Reise 2000). Note that aside from centring the behaviour difficulties at 0, no equality constraints were assumed for this statistical analysis. The exploratory search found 37 behaviours that differed significantly (χ^2 (1, n = 1400) > 7.88; $p < 0.005$). Table 8.1 points to five contextual factors that most likely result in the observed engagement dissimilarities in São Paulo and Sheffield. These five contextual origins of the both cities' typical behaviours are climate, affluence, quality and availability of local infrastructure, culture-specific beliefs and the implemented legislation.

Table 8.1 GEB scale: behaviours affected by city of origin

Behaviour	Imprint	Item	χ^2	pSP	pSH
In the winter, I leave the windows open for long periods of time to let in fresh air.	C	GEB 9	363.39	3.37	−0.44
I wash dirty clothes without prewashing.	B	GEB 10	304.01	0.46	−1.80
I use renewable energy sources.	C, B	GEB 45	257.32	−1.13	1.10
I kill insects with a chemical insecticide.	–	GEB 29	168.14	0.79	−0.78
I collect and recycle used paper.	I	GEB 14	154.65	−0.34	−2.02
I use fabric softener with my laundry.	B	GEB 34	131.40	2.53	0.71
I use an oven cleaning spray to clean my oven.	A, I	GEB 5	127.45	1.46	0.03
I drive my car in or into the city.	I	GEB 8	111.12	2.17	0.45
In hotels, I have the towels changed daily.	B	GEB 39	108.67	−0.31	−1.79
I buy drinks in cans.	I	GEB 4	108.45	1.84	0.43
I bring empty bottles to a recycling bin.	I	GEB 15	102.45	−0.56	−1.93
I read about environmental issues.	B	GEB 25	95.49	−0.30	0.92
I talk with friends about problems related to the environment.	B	GEB 26	90.67	0.12	1.38
I buy domestically produced wooden furniture.	I	GEB 6	72.28	0.76	2.38
I am a member of a car pool.	I	GEB 47	68.32	1.01	2.81
If I am offered a plastic bag in a store, I take it.	–	GEB 12	66.68	1.73	0.63
I do not own a car.	A	GEB 46	66.60	0.08	1.20
I buy bleached and coloured toilet paper.	B	GEB 19	61.60	−1.40	−0.38
I prefer a shower to a bath.	C	GEB 3	54.98	−3.49	−1.68
I boycott companies with an unecological background.	B	GEB 22	54.26	0.50	1.54
I have pointed out unecological behaviour to someone.	B	GEB 16	53.04	0.69	1.75
I buy products in refillable packages.	–	GEB 21	47.98	0.11	0.98
I keep the engine running when the traffic light is red.	A	GEB 28	45.38	0.81	2.00
I use a chemical air freshener in my bathroom.	A	GEB 37	44.44	−0.23	−1.02
I put used batteries in the rubbish.	–	GEB 35	40.29	−1.35	−0.53
I buy milk in returnable bottles.	I	GEB 18	29.06	0.93	1.73
In the winter, I keep the heating on so that I do not have to wear a sweater.	C	GEB 33	27.73	−2.39	−1.27
I buy convenience foods.	A	GEB 20	22.38	0.08	0.65
I use a clothes dryer.	C	GEB 24	20.42	−0.92	−0.26

Behaviour	Imprint	Item	χ^2	pSP	pSH
I have looked into the pros and cons having a private source of solar power.	A	GEB 43	19.06	0.78	0.18
I buy seasonal produce.	C, I	GEB 23	18.44	–1.56	–0.98
I buy meat and produce with eco-labels.	A,I	GEB 2	17.92	2.05	1.36
I drive to where I want to start my walks.	I	GEB 31	17.78	–0.11	0.54
I am a member of an environmental organisation.	–	GEB 38	14.30	3.20	2.34
I drive at speeds under 100kph (= 62.5 mph) on motorways.	–	GEB 11	12.90	–0.23	0.25
I drive in such a way as to keep my fuel consumption as low as possible.	A	GEB 48	9.70	–2.12	–1.57
Within a 30 km/20 mile radius, I use public transport or cycle.	I	GEB 13	9.04	–0.11	0.24
I have purchased solar panels to produce energy.	A	GEB 42	6.69*	3.09	2.47
I requested an estimate on having solar power installed.	A	GEB 44	6.12*	1.72	1.32
I own a fuel-efficient car (more than 33 miles per gallon).	–	GEB 49	5.42*	–0.17	–0.48
I own energy-efficient household devices.	A	GEB 40	5.35*	–2.22	–1.84
In winter, I turn down the heating when I leave my apartment for more than 4 hours.	C	GEB 30	2.72*	–1.75	–1.43
I keep the engine running while waiting at a level-crossing or in a traffic jam.	–	GEB 27	1.60*	0.81	0.63
I wait until I have a full load before doing my laundry.	–	GEB 7	1.01*	–2.46	–2.28
I ride a bicycle or use public transport to go to work or school.	–	GEB 1	0.80*	0.56	0.67
After meals, I dispose of leftovers in the toilet.	–	GEB 36	0.48*	–3.63	–3.42
I contribute financially to environmental organisations.	–	GEB 17	0.12*	2.87	2.79
I reuse my shopping bags.	–	GEB 32	0.04*	–3.78	–3.71
After a picnic, I leave the place as clean as it was originally.	–	GEB 41	0.04*	–3.94	–3.87

*$p > 0.005$, not significant
Reported differences are ordered by decreasingly significant χ^2–values ($p < 0.05$). The shading indicates that the item is not pro-environmental. It should be read as 'I refrain from…'.Differential behaviour difficulties are expressed in logits. A negative logit value indicates that the behaviour is easy to perform, while a positive value indicates that it is difficult to perform. pSP indicates the performance probability for the average São Paulo sample and pSH for the average Sheffield sample. Presumed contextual determinants are identified as C for Climate, A for Affluence, I for infrastructure, and B for Beliefs.

Climate

The annual average maximum temperature in São Paulo is 25°C with a minimum of 16°C (INMET 2014) compared to a relatively cold Sheffield with annual average maximum temperature of 13°C with a minimum of 6°C (Met Office 2014). Because of its predominantly sunny and warm weather, there is no need for a tumble dryer (GEB 24) in São Paulo, but there is, by contrast, an increased likelihood of using renewable energy sources (GEB 45). However, on the contrary, owning solar energy panels is not common (GEB 42, GEB 44). There is no need for heating due to the local climate (GEB 33). The warm weather also means that São Paulo residents do not need to purchase heaters or install central heating and most households do not have them. Additionally, climate facilitates a great variety of seasonal fruit and vegetables (GEB 23) and the preference for taking a shower rather than a bath (GEB 3).

Affluence

São Paulo's Gross Domestic Product (GDP) per capita is US$ 18,181.03 (IBGE 2014) and Sheffield's US$ 26,645.00 (OECD 2014). This more affluent way of life reflects naturally on some Sheffield householders' behaviours. In some cases, the relatively smaller budget of Brazilians compared to British householders seems, in some cases, to promote some environmentally friendly actions. For example, those living in São Paulo are less likely to use chemical cleaning products (GEB 5, GEB 37) or buy a car (GEB 46) or eat convenience food (GEB 20) but are more likely to use refill products (GEB 21) and to save fuel by not getting stuck in traffic jams or driving fast (GEB 28, GEB 48). However, affluence can also make it more difficult for householders to engage in pro-environmental behaviour. Solar panels are usually expensive for the average São Paulo householder in, so, as expected, there little likelihood of owing solar panels (GEB 42, GEB 43, GEB 44), despite the favourable climate when compared to Sheffield. Additionally, Brazilians are less likely to consume goods with eco-labels (GEB 2).

Infrastructure

The lack of a local infrastructure (e.g. recycling collection, public transport) seems to be another likely reason for not behaving in an environmentally responsible way. That is why United Kingdom residents recycle paper more often and bring bottles to recycling drop-offs (GEB 14, GEB 15) than those living in São Paulo who do not have a long-established recycling scheme. A less reliable public transport network is another factor which influences pro-environmental behaviour. Brazilians, for example, are more likely to belong to a car pool (GEB 47) and drive into the city (GEB 8). However, they are more likely to use the public transport for small distances (GEB 13, GEB 31). Availability of consumer goods is also an important factor related to environmentally friendly actions.

Brazilians more often purchase seasonal produce, wooden furniture made locally from native wood and milk in returnable bottles (GEB 23, GEB 6, GEB 18) while the British are more likely to buy products with eco-labels (GEB 2) or cleaning sprays (GEB 5) and canned drinks (GEB 4).

Culture-specific beliefs

In Sheffield, fabric softeners and tinted toilet paper have quite a bad reputation (GEB 34, GEB 19) as well as pre-washing (GEB 10). Repeated use of towels in hotels is also more likely to occur in Sheffield than in São Paulo, where the common knowledge encourages the behaviour (GEB 39). Environmental awareness is well distributed in São Paulo due to various issues concerning the natural forests and habitats. Not surprisingly, Brazilians are more likely to use renewable energy sources, to read and talk about environmental issues, to boycott companies with unecological reputations and complain about unecological behaviour (GEB 45, GEB 25, GEB 26, GEB 22, GEB 16).

The waste prevention measure

Kaiser and Wilson (2004) have tested a set of 50 behaviours by simultaneously applying a one- and a six-dimensional Rasch-type model. The study found that the multidimensional behaviour measure fits the data better than the general one. Yet, despite its statistical significance, its practical significance proved negligible as the unidimensional model was only marginally less able to predict the data compared to the six-dimensional one. According to them because the specific behaviours were highly correlated, a general measure is a reasonable alternative. Therefore, this part of the study empirically compared a WPB measure against the GEB scale to explore whether the more parsimonious model would be empirically similar in measuring a person's pro-environmental attitudes as well as their overall behaviour. Moreover, we aim to validate the WPB behaviour-based scale as an instrument for policy makers to implement waste prevention policies entirely based on evaluative statements.

When the 64 pro-environmental and waste prevention behaviours for São Paulo and Sheffield are calibrated together using the traditional Rasch model, the unidimensional model has a reliability of rel = 0.99 for São Paulo and rel = 0.99 for Sheffield, and a classical internal consistency of α = 0.86 for São Paulo α = 0.85 for Sheffield. Due to the relatively large sample size (n = 700 each sample), the study relies on the mean square (MS) statistics – weighted by the item variance – in the assessment of model fit (Bond & Fox 2013). This fit measure is independent of sample size and indicates the relative discrepancy in variation between model prediction and actual data. The overall fit statistics for the 64 items in this unidimensional model are for São Paulo: mean of mean squares (M(MS)) = 1.0, standard deviation of mean squares (SD(MS)) = 0.10, mean of t-values (M(t)) = –0.19, standard deviation of t-values (SD(t)) = 2.90; and for Sheffield: mean of mean squares (M(MS)) = 1.0, standard deviation of mean squares $(SD(MS)) = 0.10$, mean of t-values $(M(t)) = -0.12$, standard deviation of t-values $(SD(t)) = 2.86$. For São Paulo, seven items did not fit the 64 item scale with MS-values above 1.10 or below 0.90. For Sheffield, six items (9.37 per cent) did not fit the 64-item scale with the same criteria. In sum, the MS fit statistics for the 64 behaviours on this scale assessed both in São Paulo and Sheffield are very reasonable. Thus, assessing conservation behaviour based on a unidimensional model would be possible. When the 64-item scale is calibrated as a two-dimensional measure using the multidimensional random coefficients multinomial logic (MRCML) model, then the fit statistics of the behaviour items are as follows. This time, for São Paulo four items (9.3 per cent) had MS-values above 1.10 or below 0.90, namely, WPB 5, WPB 14, GEB 19, and GEB 49; and, for Sheffield four items (9.3 per cent) had MS-values above 1.10 or below 0.90 (WPB 1, WPB 3, WPB 4, and GEB 9). The two-dimensional model has a reliability of rel = 0.995. In the case of São Paulo, the correlation between both the GEB scale and the WPB scale considering the person's estimates of each is 0.892, while the correlation of each dimension of the two-dimensional measure is 0.768. For Sheffield, the correlation between both the the GEB scale and the WPB scale considering the person's estimates of each is 0.668, while the correlation of each dimension of the two-dimensional measure is 0.676. Generally, the fit statistics as well as the estimated behaviour difficulties for both solutions seem fairly comparable, for the one and the two-dimensional measure. This means that the more parsimonious WPB scale can be applied to measure a person's pro-environmental attitudes as well as their overall behaviour performance without a noteworthy loss of fit.

Waste prevention engagement was measured using a composite of 15 self-reported behaviours from the waste prevention behaviour (WPB) scale. These items are grouped by two main domains of WPB: reducing and reusing. 'I avoid buying bottled water' or 'I repair something or have it repaired rather than buying a new one' are two examples of items. The original Portuguese version of the WPB scale was developed based on a review of previous studies on waste prevention and pro-environmental behaviour (Bortoleto *et al.* 2012) and translated to an English version to be applied in Sheffield. Back translations of the Portuguese WPB scale into English revealed a high item similarity although, strictly speaking, no perfect match was achieved. Such a straightforward procedure was applicable, since, at least, the 'structural equivalence' (i.e., unidimensionality) of the two WPB versions will be controlled statistically and all estimates will be in comparable measurement units (Van de Vijver & Tanzer 1997).

A 5-point format response format was used for all 15 items. 'Always' and 'often' responses to negatively formulated items were recoded as 'never' and 'rarely' responses respectively. In sequence, positive responses (always, often) were recoded as 'yes' responses and negative responses (sometimes, rarely, never) were recoded to 'no' responses. Missing values were handled as 'no' responses (assuming participants' doubts – represented by missing values – to be indicators of not behaving pro-environmentally in general).

All 15 WPBs (see Table 8.2) and all participants ($n = 700$ for each city) were assessed on a general performance scale using the Rasch model as similar to the GEB scale. The WPB scale has an item response theory-based reliability of rel = 0.99 for the São Paulo sample and rel = 0.99 for Sheffield sample. Its internal consistency is $\alpha = 0.78$ for São Paulo and $\alpha = 0.81$ for Sheffield. All items fitted in the 15-item WPB scale (t-value (t) > 2.33; $p < .01$). The overall fit statistics for the 15 items in this scale are for São Paulo: mean of mean squares (M(MS)) = 0.99, standard deviation of mean squares (SD(MS)) = 0.14, mean of t-values (M(t)) = –0.32, standard deviation of t-values (SD(t)) = 3.08; and for Sheffield: mean of mean squares (M(MS)) = 1.01, standard deviation of mean squares (SD(MS)) = 0.17, mean of t-values (M(t)) = –0.46, standard deviation of t-values [SD(t)] = 3.07. Ideally, M(MS) and SD(t) should be 1.0, whereas M(t) should be 0. For SD(MS), no general reference value can be given. Out of 700 participants in each sample, for São Paulo 7 (1 per cent) do not fit (t > 2.33; $p < .01$) while for Sheffield 11 (1.57 per cent) do not fit (t > 2.33; $p < .01$); the overall fit statistics for the participants for São Paulo are: M(MS) = 0.99, SD(MS) = 0.30, M(t) = 0.00, SD(t) = 0.94; and for Sheffield are: M(MS) = 0.97, SD(MS) = 0.28, M(t) = –0.02, SD(t) = 0.99. In summary, the fit statistics and reliability information of the extended version of the WPB scale are reasonable.

Comparing contextual factors related to waste prevention behaviour

The WPB scale is relative smaller than the GEB scale focusing on reducing and reusing behaviours which are naturally less influenced by climate but highly related to affluence, available infrastructure and culture-specific beliefs. Table 8.2 shows that due to the lower GDP per capita in São Paulo, reusing plastic containers (WPB 7) and using plastic bags for waste disposal (WPB 2) are very common money-saving behaviours among Brazilians. In the case of Sheffield, higher affluence allows residents to refrain buying single-use items (WPB 4) giving preference to durable goods (usually more expensive). Affluence and culture-specific beliefs have had an influence on the bad reputation of Brazilians for wasting food (WPB 14) and, on the contrary, on their good reputation of donating unwanted used items (WPB 10). Home composting is strongly related to the availability of compost bins. In São Paulo, they are very difficult to obtain, but since they are easily available in Sheffield, Sheffield residents find it easier to compost their organic waste (WPB 12). Negative attitudes to the reliability of the water treatment system in São Paulo encourage residents to buy bottled water rather than drinking tap water (WPB 15).

Comparing living environments with latent classes

Both people's city of origin group and their corresponding latent class to which they are assigned statistically relate to a particular set of behavioural consequences and, as proposed, to situational influences which affect people's

Table 8.2 WPB scale: behaviours affected by city of origin

Behaviour	Imprint	Item	χ^2	pSP	pSH
Buy too much food and end up throwing some away.	B	WPB14	547.60	−1.44	2.80
Avoid buying single use items (e.g. plastic cups).	A	WPB4	151.47	0.98	−0.63
Place food or garden waste in a home composter.	I	WPB12	93.88	2.50	0.96
Refuse needless packaging when shopping.	−	WPB13	83.97	1.90	0.60
Donate unwanted used items/ products to charity.	B	WPB10	42.46	−1.90	−0.92
Use both sides of a piece of paper.	−	WPB6	28.86	−0.22	−0.92
Avoid buying bottled water.	B	WPB15	25.71	0.39	−0.25
Reuse plastic or glass containers.	A	WPB7	18.01	−1.35	−0.75
Take a durable reusable when shopping.	A	WPB2	14.21	−0.53	−1.04
Use dishcloths rather than paper towels.	−	WPB8	13.09	−2.07	−1.49
Repair something or have it repaired rather than buying a new one.	−	WPB5	12.77	−0.17	−0.63
Consciously buy products that are designed to be reused.	−	WPB3	6.61*	−0.01	0.32
Consciously buy products that have less packaging.	−	WPB1	1.75*	0.42	0.60
Buy refillable products to save packaging.	−	WPB9	0.16*	0.23	0.28
Buy returnable products (e.g. glass bottles).	−	WPB11	1.90*	1.26	1.07

*$p > 0.005$, not significant
Reported differences are ordered by decreasingly significant χ^2-values ($p < 0.05$). The shading indicates that the item is not pro-environmental. It should be read as 'I refrain from…'. Differential behaviour difficulties are expressed in logits. A negative logit value indicates that the behaviour is easy to perform, while a positive value indicates that it is hard to perform. pSP indicates the performance probability for the average São Paulo sample and pSH for the average Sheffield sample. Presumed contextual determinants are identified as C for Climate, A for Affluence, I for infrastructure, and B for Beliefs.

pro-environmental behaviours. In the case of the GEB scale, a comparison of the actual group with the latent class reveals a moderate but significant relationship between the two ($\chi^2(1) = 125.703$; $p < 0.000$; $n = 1400$). Yet, a look at Table 8.3 reveals that people living in São Paulo are mostly concentrated in class 2 (74.6 per cent) while those living in Sheffield are mostly in class 1 (84.1 per cent). In contrast, 178 out of 700 residents in São Paulo are also class 1 members while

Table 8.3 GEB scale: comparison of a person's residence group with her/his city of origin

Statistically derived class	City of origin group		Total
	São Paulo	Sheffield	
Class 1	178 (25.4%)	589 (84.1%)	767
Class 2	522 (74.6%)	111 (15.9%)	633
Total	700 (100%)	700 (100%)	1400

Note: The value in parentheses refers to the percentage of each city in the respective derived class.

Table 8.4 WPB scale: comparison of a person's residence group with her/his city of origin

Statistically derived class	City of origin group		Total
	São Paulo	Sheffield	
Class 1	160 (22.9%)	638 (91.1%)	798
Class 2	540 (77.1%)	62 (8.9%)	602
Total	700 (100%)	700 (100%)	1400

Note: The value in parentheses refers to the percentage of each city in the respective derived class.

111 out of 700 residents in Sheffield are also class 2 members. Both of these discrepancies between observed and expected counts are statistically significant ($p < .001$).

In the case of the WPB scale, a comparison of the actual group with the latent class reveals a moderate but significant relationship between the two ($\chi^2(1) = 8731.397$; $p < 0.000$; $n = 1400$). Yet, a look at Table 8.4 reveals that people living in São Paulo are mostly concentrated in class 2 (77.1 per cent) while those living in Sheffield are mostly in class 1 (91.1 per cent). In contrast, 160 out of 700 residents in São Paulo are also class 1 members while only 62 out of 700 residents in Sheffield are also class 2 members. Both of these discrepancies between observed and expected counts are statistically significant ($p < .001$).

Conclusions about contextual differences

This chapter shows that, on average, São Paulo residents performed 22 (out of 49) more pro-environmental acts than did Sheffield residents. Conversely, householders from Sheffield, on average, performed 7 (out of 15) more waste prevention acts than Brazilians. Evidently, contexts either discourage or encourage individuals by confronting them with subjective challenges or incentives. However, because different people undertake different things when they intend to achieve a particular (e.g. decrease waste generation) goal, it is not possible to predict deterministically which behaviours will be adopted. It is impossible to foresee whether people will limit their consumption, recycle paper, or take a reusable bag when shopping. Yet, people will favour relatively easy actions over more difficult ones in a given context. And given the average motivational level of a particular population, motivating people toward waste prevention (or any other pro-environmental behaviour) will inevitably fail unless it is made easy enough to engage in by providing structural changes, such as tax incentives or legal enforcement. One good example from this study is the item 'Place food or garden waste in a home composter' on the WPB scale. The lack of legislation on this matter in São Paulo has not encouraged local shops to sell home composters. While it is easy in Sheffield to find home composters at hardware stores, and they are even sold by the council at a discount, a highly motivated person would find it harder do home composting in São Paulo. On average, Sheffield residents performed better here than householders from São Paulo. Therefore, the results prove that obstacles and opportunities instantaneously affect a person's pro-environmental behaviour beyond one's subjective acknowledgment. Consequently, in the case of the GEB scale, 84.1 per cent of all people exposed to the same conditions (i.e. São Paulo, Sheffield) are assigned to the corresponding class (see Table 8.3). In the case of WPB, 91.1 per cent are assigned to the same class (see Table 8.4).

In fact, contextual conditions affect behaviour in two distinct ways. Contexts shape people's performance as a main effect by immediately constraining or facilitating behaviour; but at the same time, they also affect people's motivation to act in a certain way as an interaction effect by confronting individuals with differentially appealing opportunities and differentially daunting obstacles. As indicated by the framework-model for WPB, it is not possible to correctly compare individuals' pro-environmental behaviours without considering the contextual (or the living environment) influence. Although, Kaiser and Biel (2000) argue that strong behaviour measurement is possible within relatively similar sociocultural boundary conditions (i.e. within countries), this may not be applicable for countries, such as Brazil and USA. Contextual conditions differ within these countries and they play an important role in shaping individuals' pro-environmental behaviours. This chapter also provides evidence not only that differential endorsement probabilities disclose the behavioural consequences of certain *living environments* but also that a more parsimonious behaviour item scale (i.e. the WPB scale developed by Bortoleto *et al.* 2012) can be applied to measure a person's pro-environmental attitudes as well as their overall behaviour performance without a noteworthy loss of fit. This novel methodology to infer waste prevention behaviour can be an important instrument for policy makers to implement waste prevention policies entirely based on evaluative statements.

Note

1 As mentioned before in Chapter 5, the words *living environment* refer to the total physical, social, political, and economic situation in which a person lives.

References

Adams, R. J., & Khoo, S.-T. (1996). *QUEST: The interactive test analysis system.* Camberwell,Victoria, Australia: ACER.

Bond, T. G., & Fox, C. M. (2013). *Applying the Rasch model: Fundamental measurement in the human sciences.* Hove, UK: Psychology Press.

Bortoleto, A. P., Kurisu, K. H., & Hanaki, K. (2012). Model development for household waste prevention behaviour. *Waste Management, 32*(12), 2195–2207.

Costanzo, M., Archer, D., Aronson, E., & Pettigrew, T. (1986). Energy conservation behavior: The difficult path from information to action. *American Psychologist, 41*(5), 521.

Embretson, S. E., & Reise, S. P. (2000). *Item response theory for psychologists.* Mahwah, NJ: Erlbaum.

Greve, W. (2001). Traps and gaps in action explanation: Theoretical problems of a psychology of human action. *Psychological Review, 108*(2), 435–451.

Guagnano, G. A., Stern, P. C., & Dietz, T. (1995). Influences on attitude-behavior relationships: A natural experiment with curbside recycling. *Environment & Behavior, 27*, 699–718.

IBGE. (2014). Cidades@ database. Retrieved from http://cod.ibge.gov.br/235J4.

INMET. (2014). Climatologia, gráficos climatológicos. Retrieved from http://www.inmet.gov.br/html/clima.php

Kaiser, F. G. (1998). A general measure of ecological behavior. *Journal of Applied Social Psychology, 28*, 395–422

Kaiser, F. G., & Biel, A. (2000). Assessing general ecological behavior. *European Journal of Psychological Assessment, 16*(1), 44–52.

Kaiser, F. G., & Byrka, K. (2011). Environmentalism as a trait: gauging people's prosocial personality in terms of environmental engagement. *International Journal of Psychology: Journal International de Psychologie, 46*(1), 71–9.

Kaiser, F. G., Byrka, K., & Hartig, T. (2010). Reviving Campbell's paradigm for attitude research. *Personality and Social Psychology Review: An Official Journal of the Society for Personality and Social Psychology, Inc., 14*(4), 351–67.

Kaiser, F. G., & Keller, C. (2001). Disclosing situational constraints to ecological behavior: A confirmatory application of the mixed Rasch model. *European Journal of Psychological Assessment, 17*(3), 212–221.

Kaiser, F. G., Midden, C., & Cervinka, R. (2008). Evidence for a data-based environmental policy: Induction of a behavior-based decision support system. *Applied Psychology, 57*(1), 151–172.

Kaiser, F. G., Oerke, B., & Bogner, F. X. (2007). Behavior-based environmental attitude: Development of an instrument for adolescents. *Journal of Environmental Psychology, 27*(3), 242–251.

Kaiser, F. G., & Wilson, M. (2004). Goal-directed conservation behavior: the specific composition of a general performance. *Personality and Individual Differences, 36*(7), 1531–1544.

Kaiser, F. G., Wölfing, S., & Fuhrer, U. (1999). Environmental attitude and ecological behaviour. *Journal of Environmental Psychology, 19*, 1–19.

Kurisu, K. H., & Bortoleto, A. P. (2011). Comparison of waste prevention behaviors among three Japanese megacity regions in the context of local measures and socio-demographics. *Waste Management, 31*(7), 1441–1449.

Met Office. (2014). Sheffield 1981–2010 averages. Retrieved from http://www.metoffice.gov.uk/climate/uk/averages/19812010/sites/sheffield.html

OECD. (2014). OECD regions at a glance 2011, regional economic disparities. Retrieved from from http://www.oecd-ilibrary.org/sites/reg_glance-2011-en/03/06/index.html

Scheuthle, H., Carabias-Hütter, V., & Kaiser, F. G. (2005). The motivational and instantaneous behavior effects of contexts: Steps toward a theory of goal-directed behavior. *Journal of Applied Social Psychology, 35*(10), 2076–2093.

Sheffield City Council. (2014). Recycling and reducing, real nappies. Retrieved from https://www.sheffield.gov.uk/environment/waste/reducingrecycling/realnappies.html.

Van de Vijver, F., & Tanzer, N. K. (1997). Bias and equivalence in cross-cultural assessment: An overview. *European Review of Applied Psychology, 47,* 263–279

Wright, B., & Masters, G. N. (1982). *Rating scale analysis: Rasch measurement.* Chicago, IL: MESA.

Part IV
Conclusion

9 The effect of improved waste management

Material rebound and its causes

Ana Paula Bortoleto and Siegmar Otto

By now, we are quite aware of the false promise of the low-fat biscuit. For some time people jumped to the conclusion that 'low-fat' meant 'no consequences'. And because the biscuits seemed guilt-free to them, they tended to eat more of them than regular biscuits. However, after a while, the body would stay the same weight, if not bigger. But what has this obvious nutritional rebound in common with rebound in the case of the waste generation? Basically, the mechanism at the consumer end is the same: more consumption because of the reduced environmental impact (i.e. low-fat biscuits and eco-products) per consumption unit. The big difference, however, is the conspicuousness of the rebound. In the case of the low-fat biscuit you simply need a mirror or an honest friend to recognise the rebound and only a scale to measure its effect. In case of material consumption, the identification of rebound is complicated and a precise calculation of the actual effect is extremely difficult, if not impossible.

Rebound in economics was first discussed about 150 years ago by William Stanley Jevons, an economist, who was becoming concerned about the longer-term future for the UK coal industry (Greening & Greene 2000; Midden *et al.* 2007; Sorrell & Dimitropoulos 2008). He was concerned that this vital resource (which spurred the Industrial Revolution) would run out sooner than people anticipated. Subsequently, he came up with a theory when he suggested that, instead of reducing the total amount of coal used by the introduction of efficiency measures, these efficiency advances would, in reality, ultimately increase the amount of coal used by stimulating the demand for iron through a reduction in its unit price. Hence coal, a finite resource, would run out faster than was previously the case.

There is a similar phenomenon in waste management, and it is one that explains a great deal about individuals' waste management behaviours and why we cannot expect recycling or any other end-of-pipe technology to solve all our waste generation problems. In the twenty-first century, individuals have different reasons for throwing things away – reasons that, while not entirely new, operate on an exceptional scale. More often, we are discarding things simply because we do not want or need them anymore. Vast numbers of individuals judge their clothes and shoes old-fashioned because of changing tastes (Lipovetsky 2002). Our waste today is mostly composed of packaging designed to protect goods/

food and disposable products used to save washing. We buy technology intended to become obsolete after little use. Most of the time, technological innovation makes an expensive electronic appliance outdated even before it hits the market. This phenomenon promotes a veneration of newness which fills our rubbish bins with perfectly good stuff that is simply outmoded.

In most cities worldwide, recycling policies were put in force with the intention of involving householders in pro-environmental behaviour. Most of them easily recognised the satisfaction of doing 'something good for the environment', and because of that, waste managers thought that recycling would be a way of decreasing waste generation. However, despite the increase in recycling rates, the World Bank report states that by 2025 waste will likely increase to 4.3 billion urban residents generating about 1.42 kg/capita/day of municipal solid waste (2.2 billion tonnes per year) (Hoornweg & Bhada-Tata 2012). At the end, we are recycling more and wasting even more. Devoted recyclers buy more food in disposable containers than others as well as products made with recycled materials. The ugly side of recycling is the over-consumption and wasteful habits that produce waste to be recycled or discarded in the first instance (Ha 2005). Recycling is actually downcycling and it reduces the value of a product by lowering its quality and functionality. A clear example of downcycling is plastic recycling which fills supermarket shelves with cheap plastic cups, chairs, and office supplies. Overall it seems that recycling does not simply reduce the impact of waste. It also seems to foster consumption and, thus, rebound.

If we focus on understanding what waste is, instead of what is inside the rubbish bin, our attention will be concentrated on human behaviour. Everything that needs to be thrown away will require the householder to make a decision about its usefulness. So, this is a process of defining what waste is. This is a private process that happens within the household. The value or lack of value that we assign to products/food depends on who is making the decision. But, above all, it depends on economic status: more affluence = more waste.

But what really drives increased use of materials when efficient technology (including recycling) merely seems to enable it? All waste is basically generated through consumption. If no one bought and used smartphones or TVs, no company would produce and market them. Thus, consumption and waste generation must be driven by people's motives to consume. For the majority of people, those motives seem to be endless, as more money (more affluence) means more consumption to fulfil more personal goals and dreams. Thus, because efficient technology reduces the cost of products and services, money is saved and reinvested in additional consumption leading to rebound (Otto *et al.* in press). Later on this chapter we will discuss these psychological drivers of rebound and its implication in more detail.

Why more efficiency does not always benefit the environment

In many cases, and waste management is one of them, environmental policies deal with very complex systems. Complexity makes it difficult to understand the overall effect of individuals' behaviour and may lead to rebound effects. Owing to unforeseen behavioural change of users or consumers, a measure taken to improve environmental performance does not lead to any improvement or may even worsen the situation. For example, in big cities, traffic can become problematic. Let us imagine the government wants to reduce air pollution and formulates a policy stating that only cars with number plates ending in an even number can drive on Mondays, Wednesdays and Fridays. Those with number plates ending in odd numbers can drive on Tuesdays, Thursdays and Saturdays. Finally, on Sundays, cars with both types of number plate are allowed on the roads. The first effect could be that people buy a second car, with a specific request for certain number plates, so they can drive every day. The rebound effect is that, the days when all cars are allowed to drive, some inhabitants now use both cars (whereas they only had one car to use before the government implemented the policy). The policy did not obviously lead to environmental improvement but even made air pollution worse. This has already been observed in São Paulo, where the traffic jams and air pollution got worse since a similar legislation was approved. The CETESB report shows an interruption in the decrease in levels of air pollution since 2006. In addition, the study has found that levels of pollution in the city are stable; however, the innovations on automotive emission-control technologies are only sufficient to compensate for traffic congestion and increased car use (CETESB 2013).

The seemingly positive effect of efficiency increases is often related to the overall environmental impact through the IPAT identity (Ehrlich & Holdren 1971) (without accounting for rebound). This equation ($I=P*A*T$) represents the environment impact (I) as being the product of three factors, namely population (P), affluence (A) and technological performance or efficiency (T). The latter factor captures increased efficiency, which has the direct effect that it lowers I. For instance the IPCC (2007) uses the formula for its calculation of future scenarios. According to Ehrlich and Holdren (1971), their IPAT identity states that higher affluence and more people will increase human impact. Technology in this formula however, mediates the effect of people and their affluence on the environment. If, for instance, technology becomes twice as efficient in terms of resource consumption, which means that it uses only half the resources to produce the same output, then, environmental impact is halved. This fact, the pure multiplicative link between people, affluence and technology, is the basis on which proponents of the efficiency strategy base their arguments. For instance Oskamp (2000), by referring to the multiplicative character of the IPAT identity, claims that decreasing affluence is an unattractive option, while a gradual population decrease and a very strong increase in technological efficiency would be most desirable.

Indeed, efficiency improvements would help to conserve the environment as hoped for by many, if there were to be no complex interdependencies between the number of people, their affluence and the technology they use. However, such an assumption is a fatal flaw proponents of energy efficiency strategies make – with or without wrongly interpreting the IPAT identity. In 1971, when Ehrlich and Holdren (1971) developed their IPAT identity, they already and explicitly mentioned the complex interdependencies between P, A and T. Almost 30 years later, Holdren (2000) feels obliged to write a commentary because since their original publication, scientists (e.g. Oskamp 2000) misused their formula without reflecting on the complex web of underlying societal phenomena in which the formula is imbedded: 'relying exclusively on changes in technology to address the environmental challenges …, while neglecting the population and affluence components in the IPAT identity, would be folly' (Holdren 2000). Neither affluence, nor technology or people can be manipulated without unwanted side effects (Holdren 2000). And now we have to deal with one of those side effects: rebound!

Definition and measurement of rebound – a short overview

Relying on a combination of secondary analysis of case studies and original material from Norway, Ruud (1992) outlines and documents the crucial difference between 'eco-efficiency' and 'eco-effectiveness'. The study provides data that clearly shows that major industrial actors are willing to sign up to sustainable development in pursuit of greater eco-efficiency and he demonstrates that this does not always result in greater overall eco-effectiveness. That which proves 'efficient' in an isolated process or product characteristic, does not always prove 'effective' when assessed within a broader consequential framework. Rebound effects cannot only undermine 'green' efforts, but lead, on the aggregate and over time, to a worsening of the situation. Three types of rebound have so far been identified by previous researchers: direct, indirect, and economy-wide.

Direct Rebound is when the reduction in the price of ownership or in the use of a commodity such as energy occurs (i.e. a more fuel efficient car will do more miles to the gallon so you reduce the unit price of travelling each mile); you may then see an unanticipated increase in the purchase/use of that product or commodity. The most common example of this type of rebound is home insulation. Basically, this involves upgrading a poorly insulated house or an inefficient heating system to a better insulated house or more efficient heating system. If the householder does not change his/her heating patterns after the upgrading, modelled predictions expect a quantified energy and carbon saving. However, the increase in thermal efficiency results in people tending to leave their heating on for longer because it is cheaper to do so. Thus, by not accounting for the potential changes in householder behaviour, the energy saving does not occur at the levels predicted by the models.

Indirect Rebound occurs where one saves money (or time or resources) on one commodity, only to use that saved money (and/or time) to buy/do more of something else. And depending on what that extra activity or purchase ends up being, it might result in a net increase in energy and/or carbon consumed. Using the previous example again, after insulation has been installed, consider that the householder does not increase the thermostat or leaves the heating on for longer so s/he will benefit from the predicted reduction on her/his energy bill. It is what is done with the saved money that determines whether indirect rebound occurs or not. If the money is spent to buy an additional television, then this will increase the energy consumption and carbon emission from what was saved by the efficiency measure itself. The Indirect Rebound effect has previously proven very difficult to quantify, as it is more difficult to observe exact cause and effect than with direct rebound. However, there are many studies being carried out now on attempting to model this effect.

Both direct and indirect rebounds are defined as occurring on a microeconomic scale (i.e. at the individual level). *Economy-wide rebound* factors both have direct and indirect effects up to the macro-scale and models/calculates what impact they may have at a national level and over longer timescales. The nature of this effect entails that much is done at the modelling level. However there are now studies of industrial sectors, over longer timescales, showing the effect of economy-wide rebound (Sorrell 2007).

Psychological explanation of rebound

The paragraphs above deal with the description and measurement of rebound mainly at the economic level. Besides those definition and measurement attempts, explanations of the origin of rebound have been rare so far. The first step in order to search for the origin of rebound is still within the realm of the economy: in a functioning market, products and services (for whose production and provision materials are used) are finally utilised or consumed by people. Thus, the next step would be to ask why people use and consume products and services.

To identify the drivers of people's consumption, we have to answer the question: Why do people act and use technology. Basically we have to understand why people act from a psychological point of view; that is, we have to understand people's subjective reasons for acting. Traditionally in psychology, a rational choice logic is adopted in which the anticipation of personal utility makes a person choose certain behaviour (Ajzen & Fishbein 1980; Fishbein & Ajzen 1975) Correspondingly, the preference for using a particular technology is grounded in the same subjective rationality. From this perspective, using technology and switching to more efficient technology that reduces behavioural costs or increases obvious returns is rational. It is rational to use the most efficient technology because it increases personal affluence irrespective of its positive or negative environmental impact. But how does this connect to waste?

Take, for instance, the technological improvements (efficiency gains) in the storage, transportation and conservation of food. Recall how much time and manual labour it took to conserve and store food a few hundred years ago. Leaves or earthenware containers were used to store food for a few days, weeks and perhaps even months. Imagine how much work it took to produce earthenware manually and how often people had to go to get fresh food, because they could only store it for a few days. Today, with plastic bags or containers, tins and glass containers, insulation bags and boxes, packaging food is lightweight, cheap and inexpensive. Conservation technology (e.g. refrigerators, vacuum packaging) enables the preservation of many kinds of food and their instant availability. But also motorised transport enables the fast and/or cheap movement of huge quantities of food or its ingredients. All these technologies have one thing in common. They make food cheaper. Obviously cheaper food is less valued and more affordable leading to an increase also in food waste. In 2012, 7.0 million tonnes of food and drink waste were thrown away in the UK (enough waste to fill Wembley Stadium nine times over). From this amount, 4.2 million tonnes (or 60 per cent of the total) is avoidable, worth £12.5 billion; 1.2 million tonnes (17 per cent of the total) was considered 'possibly avoidable'; 1.6 million tonnes (23 per cent of the total) was unavoidable waste. The reasons for disposal vary considerably by food group, but most was wasted because it was not used in time, or too much was prepared, cooked or served (WRAP 2012).

All technologies have been developed to fulfil a plethora of specific individual needs and motives, which serve a certain individual goal. For instance, according to expectancy-value theory (Fishbein & Ajzen 1975), a person would favour pizza delivery or heat a frozen pizza[1] when he is quite sure about a number of positively valued outcomes (e.g. free time to watch a film), leading to a positive attitude – a reason to prefer fast food. In other words, people choose behaviour with the maximum net gain that is behaviour with higher benefits and reduced costs to fulfil their goals. The net gain of consuming fast food instead of spending time on a home-made dish is based on the different characteristics of the two dishes. For a person who prefers fast food, time savings and other positive sides of it obviously outweigh positive aspects of home-made food. Each person attributes subjective value to the relevant aspects of an option; therefore, our behaviour is motivated by a multitude of subjective utilities. Only if a person sees a chance to increase overall subjective utility does the person switch to the behaviour with the higher utility, because it is rational to do so.

To further understand preference for ever more efficient technology, we have to understand behaviour and its link to costs in its biological functionality. From such an evolutionary perspective (Dawkins 2006), we argue that the struggle for survival and reproduction induces behavioural costs to the individual and that any reduction in these costs leads to an advantage through saved resources now available to any other behaviour, but especially reproduction. Hence, the fewer individual resources (e.g. time) are spent on behaviour which is needed to survive (e.g. the acquisition of food and water) the more resources are left to foster other behaviour with further positive effects on survival and reproduction (e.g. attract mates or invest in the offspring). Hence, reduction of behavioural costs – which basically boils down to efficiency improvements – can be regarded as the essence of evolution, which has brought forward an extreme variety of tools and strategies. For instance a woodpecker's bill makes it highly efficient in picking insects and their grubs from a tree or, as a strategy, the cuckoo uses other birds to breed its eggs and feed its chicks. This functional basis of biological evolution also underlies human behaviour and the human disposition to seek behaviours with ultimate utility and to substitute less efficient behaviour with more efficient behaviour (e.g. to grow one's own vegetables and cook a meal opposed to fast food). Humans obviously brought this game to a new level. With the biface, or even more symbolically, with the leverage, the first technology to amplify, or to increase the efficiency of human behaviour was invented and since then the magnitudes of behaviour amplification through technology have reached impressive heights.

Furthermore, efficiency improvements in any domain can be used to fulfil one's goals in any other domain through the generic value of time and money which is freed through efficiency improvements. Thus, for instance, money which is saved though a more efficient production and provision of food can be used to buy more elaborate clothes in order to look fashionable and impress potential mates, adding to the waste problem. But also products made from downcycled materials are often cheaper and, thus, enable people to afford more things (e.g., to own a large set of chairs and tables made from downcycled materials for parties – instead of borrowing them once or twice a year).

The bottom line is that technology is not used because it is just sitting there and waiting or because people wish to do something for the environment (i.e. use green(er) technology). From a psychological perspective, people act and use technology because they are motivated to meet their personal ends. From a biological perspective, technology is functional in the struggle for survival and reproduction and used to increase the efficiency of behaviour, which means reducing behavioural costs. Overall, new, more efficient technology usually is a better means to personal ends than antecedent technology and people will always switch to better, more efficient technology because it increases their overall utility.

With each switch to more efficient technology (e.g. from packaging food with leaves to earthenware, tins, glass containers and plastic vacuum packaging) people get closer to their goals and or reduce their behavioural costs (e.g. more and secure food in less time). Through reduced behavioural costs, people save money or time, which they can invest in the fulfilment of any other of the less satisfied motives. Thus, saved money and time will be reinvested again, hence, leading to more utility in the domain it is invested in and to rebound.

How significant is the rebound effect in waste management?

A way of promoting eco-efficiency is related to the strategy of enhancing resource efficiency. This can be approached through the redesign of products, finding new ways of meeting customers' needs with an eco-sensitive framework. To a large extent this can be further related to initiatives aimed at more holistic and integrated sustainable production and consumption. The recycling of aluminium, for example, has impacts on both the consumption and production patterns of aluminium. Despite criticisms of the industry that refer to aluminium as 'frozen electricity' (Young 1992), it remains a fact that the energy requirements of re-melting aluminium is only 5 per cent of what is required to produce virgin metal. Efforts to close the material aluminium loop through intense recycling will consequently influence current production and consumption patterns.

Table 9.1 Evolution of primary production and consumption, domestic and per capita consumption, and recycling rates of aluminium for the period of 2007 to 2010

Items	2007	2008	2009*	2010
Domestic production (000 t)				
Annual production of primary aluminium from the major producers.	1,660	1,661	1,536	1,540
Consumption of primary aluminium (000 t)	–	931	–	995
Domestic consumption (000 t)				
It includes raw materials production, recycled materials and imported raw materials	918.90	1,027.00	1,008.3	1,299.60
Per capita consumption (kg/person)	4.9	5.9	5.3	6.7
Recycling rate (%)	96.5	91.5	98.2	97.6

* 2009 data reflects the impacts from the economic crisis in 2008.

Source: Abrelpe (2011) and Cardoso et al. (2011)

Recycled aluminium is thereby not only providing a reduction in raw material intensity, but the energy intensity associated with the aluminium production. It generally produces significant cost savings over the production of new aluminium even when the costs of collection, separation and recycling are taken into account. Over the long term, even larger national savings are made when the reduction in the capital costs associated with landfills; mines and, international shipping of raw aluminium are considered. In this context, the European Aluminium Association states that: 'Its unique recycling potential and intrinsic value means that aluminium is the most cost-effective material to recycle. The market for used aluminium is steadily growing. The more aluminium there is in a product, the more chance it has of being recycled'. And not only producers but also consumers now recognise aluminium as an ideal 'green material'. In an informal effort of street collectors' cooperatives and the population, Brazil currently recycles around 98 per cent of its aluminium can production, equivalent to 14.7 billion drink cans per year, ranking first in the world (Campos 2013). Data from Brazil has shown that despite the increase of aluminium recycling rates, production of aluminium has not fallen (see Table 9.1).

Currently, aluminium has been used not only for drink cans but also for many other purposes, including car manufacturing. Through research and development auto manufacturers are seeking materials solutions that enable lighter versions of automobiles with reduced maintenance to be produced. This is a central focus of the Sustainable Mobility Project of the World Business Council for Sustainable Development (WBCSD 2010). Again, aluminium is providing a reduction in energy intensity associated with the use of automobiles as a result of reduced fuel consumption related to less weight per vehicle. As a consequence, the number of vehicles would most probably increase, and the net total result will be a growth in CO_2 emissions rather than the expected reduction. In order to avoid such rebound effects, the focus would have to be extended from eco-efficient solutions for individual vehicles to eco-effective solutions for total mobility.

It will not be possible to introduce new efficiency technologies in recycling processes and change the makeup of waste management systems (moving it away from landfill disposal and towards recycling) solely by converting existing production facilities and redesigning products. Instead, new capacity and infrastructure will need to be developed on a large scale. In other words, entirely new markets are required. In this way, it is possible to identify another rebound effect at implementation level that can be termed the new market effect.

For instance, depending on how the recycling infrastructure is built, the large-scale introduction of recycling may indeed lead to efficiency gains per kilogram recycled. But to understand the implications of the rebound effect for society at large it is important to consider not only the lifecycle analysis of the recycling processes, use and disposal of recycled products but also the construction of the new infrastructure made necessary by the implementation of recycling systems – from the industries involved in producing recyclable goods to the use of secondary raw materials. Even the salaries that the workers of the new recycling stations use to pay for their own needs can produce rebound effects – for example, if their income is now higher than it used to be or if more people are now in work overall. In sum, the new markets effect encompasses all the material rebound effects that are not included in the life cycle analysis of individual products.

As mentioned before, green consumerism can also stimulate rebound effects through the design of the so called eco-products. Its starting point is the fact that consumption of recycled products, more environmentally friendly products often does not decrease but increases the overall consumption. For example, the rate of printed documents increases when bleached paper is replaced by recycled paper. Also, more environmentally friendly products often do not replace but instead supplement conventional products. For example, when a very important document needs to be printed, the recycled paper, less environmentally harmful, is replaced by the more energy-intensive white paper. In terms of the lifecycle analysis of the recycled product or the resource use of an individual consumer, resource consumption may indeed fall, but for society as a whole the combined use of recycled and non-environmental products produces a material rebound effect. That is why investments in recycling efficiency measures cannot only increase the demand for energy and/or materials for the production of the associated goods but also increase the consumption of these products and, consequently, waste generation.

For waste prevention research, rebound effects could be defined in a similar manner. If individuals change their consumption patterns to avoid waste generation, the new expenditure total is different from the old one. Thus, individuals spend the leftover on other durable goods or services, which might cause an increase in emission loads. This is also a consequence of rebound effects. Researchers call effects of this type *income rebound effects* to emphasise that they cover only some part of the direct rebound effects in *price rebound effects*. This is why, as pointed out by many researchers (e.g. Hertwich 2003), rebound effects should be considered in the analysis of sustainable consumption and also in waste prevention policies.

Discussion on the impacts of rebound

Are the waste management policies in question designed, for example, to take into account and reduce rebound effects? Do they promote a decoupling to such an extent that sectorial businesses actually stand forth as progressive partners for sustainable development? Such a dilemma indicates that waste generation challenges call for integrated technological, economic and cultural solutions at the global and local level: 'solutions that tolerate more comprehensive and holistic scrutiny as to their overall impact' (Moors 2000). Rebound evaluation should be an essential part of planning a sustainable integrated waste management system in the sense that system-wide effects must always be considered before judging any strategy or policy.

In its broadest sense the rebound effect occurs when some pro-environmental activity results, directly or indirectly, in some environmental harm which partly or wholly cancels out the initial environmental benefit. For example, by purchasing a product refill and reusing its packaging, a householder will reduce her/his carbon emissions and expenses. However, s/he will spend the saved money on something else and this act will have associated environmental impacts. Even if s/he saves the money and put it in her/his savings account, the bank will lend it to someone else who will spend it. As we said previously, rebound effects from pro-environmental activities (e.g. recycling, reusing) can occur inside or outside the household boundaries.

The rebound effect is of growing interest as a number of waste prevention policies promote material efficiency in order to reduce waste generation and the effectiveness of these policies depends on how big the rebound effect is. Clearly some of these policies will deliver savings for householders that could be redistributed to other product groups. There is considerable uncertainty associated with which products or services householders might buy with this additional money. There is some speculation regarding the durability of products, if its improvement would change their final price. It would be made to a higher standard and to maintain profitability in the sector the price would increase.

The packaging reuse example presented above stresses how waste prevention is not immune to the rebound effect. The WRAP report on resource efficiency (Scott *et al.* 2009) shows the analysis of the rebound effects on GHG savings through allocating household savings to a range of service sectors. The result of reducing food waste strategies reveals the potential reduction around 200,000 CO_2e (000 t) if the rebound effect is at its strongest. In this worst case scenario, the additional money has been allocated to a range of service related products that are rising most sharply in terms of consumption from now until 2050. On average this equates to a 50 per cent reduction in the potential savings of the strategies. It is still difficult to be certain about these effects, however the

WRAP report acknowledges the importance of taking account of some rebound consequences to waste reduction policies and that mechanisms are required to ensure the lessening of these effects.

So we pose the question: what should we spend the saved money on to minimise the rebound effect? As revealed earlier, spending money on complimentary goods and services will not solve the problem, because most of them are not free of emissions. For example, recreation, at the first sight, is a low-carbon activity; but it might be necessary to travel to the recreation site, and travel is relatively carbon intensive. In contrast, there will be a limit to the amount of switching householders will be willing to do (e.g. how much recreation someone will want). Some waste prevention actions are relatively expensive (e.g. durable goods) and their consumption takes money away from other things, thereby creating an additional reduction in emissions. Regulatory systems can offer a structural solution by regulating prices to compensate for technological efficiency gains in order to prevent increasing affluence, and consequently, rebound effects. Even though this is the quickest way to reduce economic activity, it seems a rather unfeasible way within the present economic system. On the other hand, until now, nobody has yet been forced to pay the real costs for products and services because current pricing does not account for resource depletion, pollution, and poverty caused by the production of these goods.

From a psychological perspective, an increase in intrinsic environmental motivation would probably be the only way beyond regulation. It has been shown that education (knowledge) and appreciation for nature are two psychological aspects which are linked positively to intrinsic environmental motivation and thus are two potential levers (Frick *et al.* 2004; Brügger *et al.* 2011). Additionally, it has been shown that intrinsic environmental motivation increases over time, if people are exposed to environmentally relevant threads such as climate change (Otto & Kaiser submitted). Even though, a quick fix increasing environmental motivation would not persuade people to accept a certain standard of living (i.e. certain level of affluence) and make them abstain from consuming ever more natural resources. At the end, waste will always be produced. So there is a need to reduce the carbon intensity of the waste management processes and policies any city needs, as well as create behavioural intervention policies to allow householders to put their own interests aside to do what is best for society by perceiving more value on the things they own and decreasing their desire to buy more. As Aldous Huxley once wrote 'Technological progress has merely provided us with more efficient means for going backwards' (Huxley 1937).

Note

1 Fast food, such as pizza delivery or frozen pizza, is only available because of the constant technological innovation at the food industry (e.g. mechanised agriculture, logistics improvement, new types of packaging). With this increasing efficiency, the dependent product or service also becomes more efficient (i.e. faster and/or cheaper). Consequently, the behaviour becomes more efficient too.

References

Abrelpe (2011). *Panorama dos residuos solidos no Brasil 2011.* São Paulo. Associação Brasileira de Empresas de Limpeza Pública e Resíduos Especiais.

Ajzen, I., & Fishbein, M. (1980). *Understanding attitudes and predicting social behavior.* Upper Saddle River, NJ: Prentice Hall.

Brügger, A., Kaiser, F. G., & Roczen, N. (2011). One for all? Connectedness to nature, inclusion of nature, environmental identity, and implicit association with nature. *European Psychologist, 16,* 324–333.

Campos, H. K. T. (2013). Recycling in Brazil: Challenges and prospects. *Resources, Conservation and Recycling, 85,* 130–138.

Cardoso, J. G. R. C., Carvalho, P. S. L. C., Fonseca, S. M., da Silva, M. M., & Rocio, M. A. R. (2011). *A indústria do alumínio: Estrutura e tendências.* Brasilia: BNDES.

CETESB. (2013). *Qualidade do ar no estado de São Paulo 2012* (série relatórios). São Paulo: Governo do Estado de São Paulo, Companhia Ambiental do Estado de São Paulo.

Dawkins, R. (2006). *The selfish gene* (30th Anniversary ed.). New York: Oxford University Press.

Ehrlich, P. R., & Holdren, J. P. (1971). Impact of population growth. *Science, 171,* 1212–1217.

Fishbein, M., & Ajzen, I. (1975). *Belief, attitude, intention, and behavior: An introduction to theory and research.* Reading, MA: Addison-Wesley.

Frick, J., Kaiser, F. G., & Wilson, M. (2004). Environmental knowledge and conservation behavior: Exploring prevalence and structure in a representative sample. *Personality and Individual Differences, 37,* 1597–1613.

Greening, L. A., & Greene, D. L. (2000). Energy efficiency and consumption – the rebound effect – a survey. *Energy Policy, 28,* 389–401.

Ha, T. (2005). 10 Years of recycling: The good, the bad and the ugly. Report by Planet Ark for National Recycling Week 2005. Sydney, Australia.

Hertwich, E. (2003). The seeds of sustainable consumption patterns. *Proceedings of the 1st International Workshop on Sustainable Consumption.* Society for Non-Traditional Technology, Tokyo. Available at http://www.score-network.org/files/808_5.pdf.

Holdren, J. P. (2000). Environmental degradation: Population, affluence, technology, and sociopolitical factors. *Environment, 42*(6), 4–5.

Hoornweg, D., & Bhada-Tata, P. (2012). *What a waste: A global review of solid waste management.* Urban development series: Knowledge papers no. 15. Washington, DC: World Bank.

Huxley, A. (1937). *Ends and means: An inquiry into the nature of ideals and into the methods employed for their realization.* New Brunswick:NJ,Transaction Publishers.

IPCC. (2007). *Fourth assessment report. Climate change 2007: Mitigation of climate change.* Bern: Intergovernmental Panel on Climate Change.

Lipovetsky, G. (2002). *The empire of fashion: Dressing modern democracy.* Princeton, NJ: Princeton University Press.

Midden, C. J. H., Kaiser, F. G., & McCalley, L. T. (2007). Technology's four roles in understanding individuals' conservation of natural resources. *Journal of Social Issues, 63,* 155–174.

Moors, E. H. M. (2000). *Metal making in motion. Technology choices for sustainable metals production.* Delft: Delft University Press.

Oskamp, S. (2000). A sustainable future for humanity? How can psychology help? *American Psychologist, 55,* 496–508.

Otto, S., & Kaiser, F. G. (submitted). Ecological behavior across the lifetime of individuals: Why environmentalism increases as people grow older.

Otto, S., Kaiser, F. G., & Arnold, O. (in press). The critical challenge of climate change for psychology: Preventing rebound and promoting more individual irrationality. *European Psychologist*.

Ruud, A. (1992). Does Norwegian industry have different environmental considerations at home than in developing countries? *Norwegian Journal of Geography*, 46(4):183–191.

Scott, K., Barrett, J. Baiocchi, G., & Minx, J. (2009) *Meeting the UK climate change challenge: The contribution of resource efficiency*, Waste Resources Action Programme (WRAP).

Sorrell, S. (2007). *The rebound effect: An assessment of the evidence for economy-wide energy savings from improved energy efficiency*. London: UK Energy Research Centre.

Sorrell, S., & Dimitropoulos, J. (2008). The rebound effect: Microeconomic definitions, limitations and extensions. *Ecological Economics*, 65, 636–649.

WBCSD. (2010). *Vision 2050 – The new agenda for business*. Full Report.

WRAP. (2012). Household food and drink waste in the United Kingdom 2012. CFP2012. Retrieved from http://www.wrap.org.uk/sites/files/wrap/hhfdw-2012-main.pdf

Young, J. E. (1992). Aluminum's real tab. *World Watch* (United States), 5(2), 26–33.

10 Waste prevention behaviour and fast and frugal heuristics

Ana Paula Bortoleto, Astrid Kause and Konstantinos Katsikopoulos

Waste prevention encompasses both theoretical and applied research. Applied, because a primary goal is to address and ameliorate solid waste impacts and, consequently, environmental degradation. Theoretically, environmental psychology research has yielded some broad conclusions that have important relevance for urban issues, particularly waste generation. They include the idea that behaviour is strongly affected by the intrinsic motivation that follows that behaviour, that people learn not only behaviours but also values and norms from those around them and that people in different environments respond differently to different kinds of messages, policies and interventions. As a result, a relative homogeneity is expected within a context for pro-environmental behaviour, and somewhat larger differences across different contexts (e.g. countries). The effect of specific experiences and environmental knowledge may have an impact on developing individuals' intrinsic motivation. These arguments are clearly relevant to understanding the interdependence between people's engagement in waste prevention public policies and their perception of environmental protection.

Despite all the progress on waste prevention behaviour research presented in this book, two core aspects are still worth deeper investigation. One is that intrinsic motivation to act towards environmental protection seems to be influenced by different causes (e.g. appreciation of nature, knowledge). This means that most environmental policies currently in force are only lowering difficulties and not actually influencing people to overcome them. They are essentially based on extrinsic motivation, for example, in London where parents receive an incentive of £25 to use cloth nappies instead of the disposable ones. A second, and even more urgent motivation, is that human behaviour is adapted to host a function of multiple causes, many of which are at odds with each other. Thus, the heuristics people use can have undesirable consequences if applied in inappropriate situations.

Our starting point in this chapter is that we can greatly benefit from theories which do not assume that people decide as a rational *Homo economicus*. In other words, no one decides completely rationally by including all available information.

The social and behavioural sciences, such as behavioural economics, have accumulated a lot of knowledge about people's bounded rationality. To our knowledge, there are few studies on pro-environmental behaviour so far, which deliberately incorporate the latest knowledge on bounded rationality. Instead, research on pro-environmental decision making seems to assume that there is knowledge deficit which can and should be closed by knowledge proliferation in general (Schultz 2002). By acknowledging the importance of fast and frugal heuristics, research on pro-environmental decision making might increase the effectiveness of waste prevention information interventions significantly.

Waste prevention behaviour and the decision-making process

A great deal of research has examined perceptions of environmental threats. In general, people have been shown to assess risks inaccurately, inflating the probabilities of some events and underestimating others (Slovic *et al.* 1980). For instance, individuals show higher sensitivity to dread risks (e.g. nuclear power plant accidents) that kill many people at once, compared with continuous risks (e.g. the slow increase in average global temperature), relatively frequent events that kill many people over a longer period of time. The different reaction to dread risks is often regarded as a bias since continuous risk should not be perceived as less dreadful. The human perception of threats is highly dependent on framing or the nature of the risk.

Many researchers have previously attempted to explain why people fear dread risks more than continuous risks and different hypotheses have been proposed. Slovic (1987) introduced the psychometric paradigm where he suggests that high lack of control, high catastrophic potential, and severe consequences account for the increased risk perception and anxiety associated with dread risks. Gigerenzer *et al.* (2009) argue that people lack knowledge about the statistical information underlying risks, particularly when questioned about the large number of fatalities caused by continuous risks. The mass media and people's social circle can also frame the issue by overvaluing relatively rare but dramatic risks and undervaluing frequent and less dramatic risks (Leiserowitz 2005). And, along with the preparedness hypothesis, people are prone to fear events that have been particularly threatening to the survival of the human race. Based on this hypothesis, Galesic and Garcia-Retamero (2012) found that people's fear peaks for risks killing around 100 people and does not increase if larger groups are killed.

One of the reasons that people may not take action to avoid waste production and mitigate its environmental impacts is that they lack first-hand experience of its potential consequences. In many situations, environmental degradation is still considered distant for a large part of population and they tend to feel that environmental threats will have a greater impact on the global environment rather on their own local environment. However, major extremes in weather, and ecosystem changes, are already being experienced across multiple geographical regions (e.g. Brazil, the UK, USA) and are expected to increase in frequency and severity as a result of greenhouse emissions and local pollution. Previous psychological research (Spence *et al.* 2011) shows that those who report experience of flooding in the UK express more concern over climate change and feel more confident that their actions will have an effect on greenhouse emissions. From this perspective, individuals who have direct experience of an environmental disaster that may be linked to human actions would be more likely to be concerned by the issue and thus more inclined to undertake sustainable behaviours.

Recognising a threat does not always mean understanding that threat. Past research, for example, found that many Americans confuse global climate change with ozone depletion (Bord *et al.* 2000). Bord *et al.* (2000) found that an accurate understanding of the cause of global warming was not related to a belief that global warming exists. Misinformation was just as predictive of a belief in global warming. In contrast, accurate information was the best predictor of an intention to do something about it. Additionally, lay people tend to perceive areas that are vulnerable to environmental impacts as geographically distant, at least in Western countries (Lorenzoni & Pidgeon 2006). For this reason, most decision makers may believe they simply need to impart their knowledge to the public. However, discussion about risk threats is about more than information; they include other factors that might have not been featured into the scientific and economic assessments.

In fact, research seems to suggest that there are negative effects of bombarding the public with pro-environmental information. Research suggests that information campaigns are not particularly effective in promoting pro-environmental behaviour (Abrahamse *et al.* 2005). For example, what Gifford (2011) calls 'environmental numbness' can occur when people are provided with a lot of information about imminent environmental dangers such as climate change which seem quite distant because they are not causing any direct personal difficulties (Belch 1982; Burke & Edell 1986). Hoggan and Littlemore (2009) argue that oversimplified scientific messages or mixed messages (e.g. presenting both the positive and negative effects of a pro-environmental policy) also instil confusion and lack of engagement. Laboratory research on resource dilemmas, which mimic the pro-environmental decisions policy-makers have to make, found that when people are confronted with real or perceived uncertainty, pro-environmental behaviour is reduced (de Kwaadsteniet 2007; Artinger *et al.* 2012). As a result, there is a subtle point: it is clear that there are limits to how much uncertainty should be communicated to the general public.

Information can also be obtained from the mass media (e.g. TV, newspapers, radio, internet). Over the past decade, the media have paid increasing attention to environmental issues, so it is not surprising that most people are familiar with environmental problems. In spite of this, the media does not necessarily represent a balanced view of the scientific evidence, but can be biased in one or the other direction. Boykoff and Boykoff (2004) found significant difference between the scientific community discourse and the US quality-press discourse regarding the existence of anthropogenic contributions to global warming, and decisions regarding action on global warming. What led to a biased coverage of global warming creating both discursive and real political space for the US government to shirk responsibility and delay action regarding the Kyoto Protocol? Again, recognising an environmental issue does not mean understanding the issue.

Today's daily life provides too much information for anyone to attend to, let alone integrate and apply. Psychologist Herbert A. Simon has won a Nobel Prize for identifying the limits on human rationality and describing some of the shortcuts, or heuristics, people use to cope with information overload as well as information scarcity. He argued that due to time constraints and cognitive limitations, it is not possible for humans to consider all existing decision outcomes and then make fully reasoned, purely rational, choices. He suggested that humans operate rationally within practical boundaries, or within the limits of bounded rationality (Simon 1955, 1956). Information, according to him, is anything that might inform a person about something or provide knowledge about it. Information sources may be observations, people, speeches, documents, pictures, organisations, media, experiences, etc.

There are two common interpretations of bounded rationality: cognitive limitations and optimisation under constraints (Gigerenzer & Selten 2002). At a first approximation, the research programme on cognitive limitations (Kahneman *et al.* 1982) studies how people are not able to memorise and remember all relevant facts or fail to reason and make decisions according to the abstract laws of logic or probability theory. Optimisation under constraints (Sargent 1993) may accept that people's memories and perceptions are flawed but holds that, given this flawed input, people are able to perform accurately the computations of logic, probability and utility theory.

In this chapter, we focus on a less well-known approach to bounded rationality that takes seriously and provides detail on how people process different kinds of information. More specifically, we outline the basics of a theory of bounded rationality that is based on fast and frugal heuristics. These heuristics are inspired by Simon's approach to bounded rationality and flesh his ideas out. While these heuristics share some common ground with the heuristics studied in the cognitive-limitations programme of Tversky and Kahneman (such as using as foundations what is known about the psychology of memory) there are some key differences.

At the centre is the observation that heuristics are not necessarily second best; instead, as we emphasise here, they can lead to good decisions, sometimes even better than models considered more rational. In this chapter, we put special emphasis in showing under what conditions this holds. Additionally, fast and frugal heuristics are modelled by precise mathematical models rather than by verbal labels such as availability. This is important because it can aid theory development for not only waste prevention behaviour, but also for pro-environmental behaviour research.

The potential of fast and frugal heuristics

People often have to make decisions in the face of limited time, information, and computational resources facing a situation with inherent uncertainty. Specifying the decision processes that people use under these conditions is at the heart of the research programme on fast and frugal heuristics (Gigerenzer *et al.* 1999).

These heuristics are rules of thumb that can be formulated as simple algorithms. The objective is thereby not to fulfil logical requirements such as transitivity or consistency and neither to find a solution to an optimisation problem, all of which are principles on which the decision making of *Homo economicus* are grounded. Rather, the fast and frugal research programme focuses on the performance of the decision algorithm in a given context-situation, judging the results by criteria such as speed, frugality, accuracy, and robustness (Gigerenzer & Brighton 2009).

A good illustration to understand the principal approach taken is to use a Darwinian perspective. Evolution can be characterised as proceeding step-wise. Instead of a grand plan on which everything is built, as for instance embodied in the principles of rational choice theory, the result is like a toolbox where adaption has given rise to a solution for a particular context. Thus, fast and frugal heuristics are neither good nor bad, neither rational nor irrational, per se but have to be evaluated with respect to their performance in a given environment-situation. In doing so, heuristics exploit both core psychological capacities (e.g. recognition, visual tracking, memory, social imitation) and the structure of the context (e.g. non-compensatory cue validities or the trade-off between an algorithm's bias and variance, both of which we will deal with in detail later). Already Herbert Simon stressed that mind and context-situation are like the two blades of a pair of scissors; accounting for both is necessary to understand decision making.

Ignorance-based decision making

Imagine you have the once in a life-time chance participating in a game show and are faced with the final question which wins 1 million dollars. You are asked which city has more inhabitants, Milwaukee or Detroit. What is your answer?

If you are American, then the chances that you answer correctly are fairly good; 60 per cent of undergraduate students at the University of Chicago stated Detroit, which is the correct answer. However, if you are an average German, you most likely have never heard of Milwaukee and know little about Detroit. How many correct inferences did the less knowledgeable Germans achieve? Ninety per cent responded correctly and picked Detroit (Goldstein & Gigerenzer 2002). The same condition can be faced if you are asked which city (Detroit or Milwaukee) would produce more CO_2 emissions. Yet, how is it possible that people know less but make more correct inferences? The answer seems to be that the Germans used a heuristic, whereby they picked the city they recognised, making the inference that this also has the larger population. The Americans could not rely on this heuristic as they had heard of both.

This already indicates in what conditions the recognition heuristic can be used well: if subjects have only partial knowledge in combination with the cue value strongly correlating with the criterion value. In the above example, the likelihood that the city is larger correlates positively with whether Germans have heard about it or not. More generally, the heuristic can be stated as follows:

Recognition heuristic: if one of two objects is recognised and the other is not, then infer that the recognised object has the higher value with respect to the criterion.

The heuristic builds on the core capacity of recognition – such as face, voice, and name recognition. Good performance of the recognition heuristic is given when ignorance is systematic rather than random, i.e., when recognition is strongly correlated with the criterion. Such a situation is given in competitive contexts for instance between name recognition and the output of a researcher. It has been applied to the domain of sports giving rise to such astounding results that the heuristic predicted the results of the tennis matches at Wimbledon 2003 and 2005 with equal or higher accuracy than the ATP rankings and the seeding of the Wimbledon experts (Scheibehenne & Bröder 2007; Serwe & Frings 2006). Results even indicate that, in the financial domain, recognition-based portfolios (the set of most-recognised options), on average, outperform professionally managed funds, the market (Dow and Dax), chance portfolios, and experts (Ortmann *et al.* 2008). Interestingly, the recognition heuristic mainly works in down-turning markets (Andersson & Rakow 2007). More generally it has been found that where the accuracy of the recognition heuristic is substantial (where the correlation exceeds .7) people use it in about 90 per cent of all cases (Pachur & Hertwig 2006).

Inherent to the recognition heuristic is that it is non-compensatory. In order to illustrate, it is helpful to contrast with compensatory models, such as expected utility models. Conventionally, in such a setting, the class of linear rules is employed such as multiple linear regressions. The linear rule is an analogy of the expected utility rule for making choices. The relevant pieces of information (cues) are weighted and added. The weighted sum of cue values for each object is computed, the object with the higher sum is inferred to have the higher criterion value, i.e., in the example this yields the prediction which of two cities is larger. The weight of a cue can be computed in a number of ways as, for example, by minimising the sum of squared differences between the real criterion values in the ecology and the criterion values estimated by the linear rule.

Non-compensatory models such as the recognition heuristic, rather than integrating all the available information – allowing a low value on one cue to be compensated for by a high value on another – rely only on part of the information. In the face of uncertainty, for instance due to limited information, this aids the performance of a non-compensatory decisions process. Reviewing 45 studies of peoples' choices, Ford, Schmitt, Schechtman, Hults, and Doherty reported that non-compensatory making is the dominant mode, particularly when the decision problem becomes more complex such as when the number of alternatives and dimensions are large (Ford *et al.* 1989).

The recognition heuristic makes the strong claim that decisions are based solely on whether the object is recognised or not, ignoring any potential other cues that are available. For instance, suppose a person (i) recognises Detroit and not Milwaukee and (ii) recalls that the automobile industry in Detroit has been hit for a long time by recession. The second cue implies that the population might have been declining over the recent years. Yet, the heuristic suggests that information on the potentially confounding cue, the automobile industry, is systematically ignored. In line with this, Pachur *et al.* report that an astounding 50 per cent of people consistently choose the recognised object in every single trial even though they had three other cues available that pointed in the other direction (Pachur *et al.* 2008).

The less-is-more effect

The recognition heuristic relies on the so called less-is-more effect, where less information can lead to more accuracy. This stands in sharp contrast to the proposition of the research programmes of cognitive limitations and optimisation under constraints. These are based on the premises that the way to make better decisions is to ensure that people have as much information as possible. Since information gathering is costly, this entails that it is optimal to terminate search in the world (Stigler 1961) and in memory (Anderson 1991) when the expected costs exceed the expected benefits. Taking into account these costs gives rise to the assumption that there is a trade-off between accuracy and effort. This trade-off is one central reason for the research programmes of cognitive limitations, and optimisation under constraints suggest why people use simple heuristics resulting in second-best decisions compared to strategies that use more information and computation.

The fast and frugal research programme contrasts this claim and makes the counterintuitive prediction that heuristics can be more accurate than strategies that use more information, computation, and time. It suggests that the accuracy-effort trade-off is not universal but that there are situations where higher accuracy is achieved with less information; this holds even when the information search is entirely free.

> *Less-is-more effect*: More information or computation can be detrimental to accuracy; humans therefore rely on fast and frugal heuristics in order to be more accurate than when using decision strategies that are more information, computation, and time intensive.

The less-is-more effect is intrinsically linked to the non-compensatory nature of the recognition heuristic. It is a further challenge to the conventional benchmark of rational choice models such as expected utility which uses a process of weighting and adding all the available information to reach a conclusion about which option to take.

Lexicographic heuristics

The recognition heuristic works when one object is recognised and the other not. When both objects are recognised, the decision maker might still be uncertain which of two objects has a higher value. This situation is addressed by the class of lexicographic heuristics. For instance, take two professors at a Midwestern college where you have to infer which of them gets a higher salary. A predictive cue in this setting is gender; however, a similar case can be made with a continuous cue such as years after finishing the doctorate (which also can be binarised). Or, consider two different types of apples in the organic-food section at the supermarket where you have to deduce which of them has a higher carbon footprint. In this case, as in the previous, a predictive cue is country of origin; conversely, a parallel cue can be described using price per kilo. In this setting, conventionally a compensatory analysis is performed adding and weighting all available information such as in a linear regression.

The class of lexicographic heuristics dispenses with adding, and instead orders cues by their validity. The validity of a cue is a conditional probability that it points to the object with the higher criterion value. The take-the-best heuristic (Gigerenzer & Goldstein 1996) orders cue by decreasing validity. After cues are ordered, take-the-best proceeds by comparing the value of the first cue for both objects. If this cue discriminates between the objects (i.e. the cue values differ), the inference is made that the higher cue value points to the object with the higher criterion value. An inspection of further cues is only undertaken if the first cue did not discriminate. This entails that all information that is ranked below the discriminating cue is ignored. If there is no cue that discriminates, an object is picked at random.

The take-the-best heuristic is a non-compensatory strategy just as the recognition heuristic. A low value on one cue is not compensated by a high value on another cue. Furthermore, unlike linear rules, lexicographic heuristics specify the processes by which people make inferences. For instance, take-the-best specifies how people search for information (by ordering cues by validity), how they decide to stop the search (as soon as one cue discriminates between the objects and allows a decision to be made), and how they decide based on the available information (by using the discriminating cue). The use of lexicographic heuristics like take-the-best depends on the decision context; the key for its use is for instance whether the decision has to be made under time pressure or how skewed the distribution of cue validities is (Bröder & Newell 2008).

The study of the conditions under which a model, such as take-the-best, achieves high predictive accuracy is the study of the ecological rationality of the model. Recent work has distinguished the mathematical conditions under which tallying and take-the-best are accurate (Baucells *et al.* 2008; Katsikopoulos & Fasolo 2006; Katsikopoulos & Martignon 2006; Martignon & Hoffrage 2002; Katsikopoulos 2011). For example, when cue validities are equal, tallying achieves maximum accuracy among all possible inference models; when some cues have much higher validities than others, take-the-best achieves maximum accuracy.

Lexicographic heuristics are not only applicable to paired comparisons but also to tasks such as risky choices. For instance, the priority heuristic (Brandstatter *et al.* 2006) specifies the decision process how people choose between lotteries which are the standard task to assess choice under risk (also see Hertwig & Erev 2009). For instance, a decision maker has to choose between option A which yields €200 with 50 per cent or option B that yields €90 for sure. As all lexicographic heuristics, the priority heuristics proceeds cue by cue. The cues in this case are the probabilities and outcomes of the two possible options.

Compared with the dominant theories of risky choice, such as cumulative prospect theory (Tversky & Kahneman 1992), an extension of expected utility models, Brandstatter *et al.* (2006) found that the priority heuristic overall predicts people's choices better. Katsikopoulos & Gigerenzer (2008) showed that the heuristic implies, rather than just being consistent with, a number of major empirical phenomena in risky choice, such as common consequence effects and the fourfold pattern of risk attitude reversals. In other words, phenomena such as the Allais paradox are implied by a simple heuristic that does not transform values and probabilities in complex non-linear fashion, as prospect theory and other modifications of expected utility theory need to do.

Tallying heuristics

Linear models weigh the cues and then add these up. Lexicographic strategies dispense with adding. A different approach is taken by tallying heuristics where cues are added but not weighted (Dawes 1979). That is, object A is inferred to have a higher criterion value than object B if the sum of cue values on A is higher than the sum of cue values on B.

Tallying can have a higher predictive accuracy than linear regressions (Dawes & Corrigan 1974) due to for instance the absence of sampling error in the estimation of weights (Einhorn & Hogarth 1975; Schmidt 1971). The findings were replicated by Czerlinski *et al.*, testing tallying heuristics in 20 different real-world, paired comparison tasks such as which Chicago high school has the higher student drop-out rate based on the socioeconomic and ethnic compositions of the student bodies, the sizes of the classes, and the scores of the students on various standardised tests (Czerlinski *et al.* 1999). Extending the original approach, they did not only fit the data but split the sample in half. Using the first half, they estimated the parameters of the model and predicted the outcome of the second half. Testing a number of different algorithms they found that on average the models successfully predicted as follows: regression 68 per cent, tallying 69 per cent, take-the-best with dichotomised cues 71 per cent, a simple Bayesian network called naive Bayes 73 per cent, regression with un-dichotomised cues 76 per cent, and take-the-best with un-dichotomised cues 76 per cent. One interpretation of these results is that using less complex computations and sophisticated information can lead to more predictive accuracy. That is, simplicity can, under some conditions, lead to robustness (yet, as the performance of tallying shows, there are limits to the benefits of simplicity).

In finance, tallying refers to a strategy where investors allocate an equal amount of money to each asset in their portfolio. This strategy has also been referred to as 1/N heuristic, where N is the number of assets or alternatives. Benartzi and Thaler show that people when deciding about saving plans or privatised Social Security plans divide their contributions evenly across the funds offered in the plan as the 1/N heuristic suggests (Benartzi & Thaler 2001). They suggest that people behave sub-optimally, calling it naive diversification. However, investigating the claim that 1/N heuristic is indeed sub-optimal, DeMiguel *et al.* used a comprehensive simulation analysing the performance of 1/N heuristic relative to 14 optimal asset allocation models (including sophisticated Bayesian and non-Bayesian models) in seven investment problems, such as how to allocate money across ten sector portfolios of the S&P 500 (DeMiguel *et al.* 2009). In order to estimate the parameters of the 14 optimal models, each was given 120 months data of asset returns. However, none of the models was able to consistently outperform tallying (1/N) on a number of established measures of financial performance. DeMiguel *et al.* (2009) estimated that for the optimisation models to be able to perform better than tallying the models would need input from 500 years of asset data.

A central component of the study of DeMiguel *et al.* 2009 is that the data was not simply fitted but rather that the decision algorithms were in competition with each other to see which one performs better in a sample testing. Fitting performs best in hindsight, yet, what is at stake in decision making often is foresight. This difference is a central component in explaining why and when a heuristic performs well. The research programme on cognitive limitations sets forth that the use of heuristics often leads to biased decision making. A bias thereby refers to the difference between the observed action and the optimal outcome. Yet, it is not only bias that shapes performance. The error that a decision strategy exhibits, which centrally shapes its performance, is driven by the bias-variance dilemma as thefollowing equation illustrates (Hastie *et al.* 2003):

Error = $(bias)^2$ + variance + noise

The error term depends on bias and variance plus a random term. To illustrate, assume that there are 100 individuals drawn from a limited random sample from the same population. Because of sampling error, the individuals do not obtain the same samples. Across samples, bias refers to the difference between the mean prediction and the true state of the population. Variance results from differences in the samples drawn, and is the expected squared deviation around the mean prediction. The performance of a decision strategy is shaped by how bias and variance change as more information becomes available. Fast and frugal heuristics rely on low variance at the cost of potentially incurring bias (Perlich *et al.* 2003). If information is limited or situations produce noisy data, fast and frugal heuristics can often outperform computationally more intensive algorithms. The bias-variance dilemma is thus a further central element shaping the success of a decision strategy. Decision making is often not done in isolation from others, peers but also strangers are an important factor influencing behaviour which we will look at in the next section (Hertwig *et al.* 2012).

Social heuristics

When the seventh and final volume of Harry Potter, J. K. Rowling's boy wizard, was released in the United States in 2007, it sold 8.3 million copies within the first 24 hours (CBS News, July 23, 2007). Is this book that brilliant? Is it entirely different from quality to the first book in the series which was rejected by eight publishers (Watts 2007)? Besides quality, what probably comes into play here is that people might like what they believe others like (Salganik *et al.* 2006). Social influence can lead to snowball effects and winner-take-all markets which even experts do not anticipate or least find difficult to predict.

The behaviour of others does not only shape our decisions when buying books, but also our decisions affecting environmental conservation. Goldstein *et al.* (2008) compare under what circumstance guests of a hotel are more willing to reuse towels. Appeals employing descriptive norms such as referring to the fact that the majority of hotel guests reuse their towels proved much more effective than the conventional method of only referring to environmental protection. The most effective proved not only to refer to what others did but specifically to the majority in the very same situation. The ability to imitate is elementary to human behaviour; for instance babies can already imitate the facial gestures of others (Meltzoff & Moore 1977). The simple heuristic that bets on the behaviour of others works as follows (Richerson & Boyd 2005):

> *Imitate-the-majority heuristic:* Determine the behaviour followed by the majority of those in your peer group and imitate it.

The imitate-the-majority heuristic tends to perform well when (i) the observer and the demonstrators of the behaviour are exposed to similar situations that (ii) are stable rather than changing, and (iii) noisy, that is, where it is hard to see what the immediate consequence of one's action is. However, what the majority does is not necessarily always beneficial to the individual. People for instance take up unhealthy behaviour from their social network such as overeating (Christakis & Fowler 2007) and the information they adopt from others might be unreliable or even outdated (Kendal *et al.* 2009). Under what circumstance individual learning is better than social learning goes to the heart of the study of ecological rationality (Todd *et al.* 2012). For instance, the higher the likelihood that a certain action is costly or even hazardous, the more people rely on social learning (Bandura 1977). For instance, taxi drivers in the United States experience the highest rate of deadly violent assaults than any other profession with the exception of the police force. Instead of individual learning, taxi drivers rather rely on social learning of the cues that indicate trustworthiness or the lack thereof of a potential customer (e.g., fully zipped, bulky coat) (Gambetta & Hamill 2005). Hence, particularly novice taxi drivers strongly rely on learning from experienced taxi drivers in order to cope with the dangers of their profession.

Social heuristics appear to guide many of our decisions, and imitate-the-majority is only one such heuristic in the adaptive toolbox of humans. Consider deciding about green versus grey energy. Assume you have moved into a new apartment, and you need to choose basic utility providers. In the United States, the United Kingdom, and many countries in Europe, 50 per cent to 90 per cent of the people asked said that they would favour a 'green' electricity provider and were even willing to pay a small premium for it. But, unfortunately, these statements do not reflect behaviour: The percentage of people who consume green electricity is marginal; for example, 2 per cent in Germany and 0.5 per cent in the United Kingdom; this discrepancy between what people say and what they do can be explained by the use of a social heuristic (Pichert & Katsikopoulos 2008). When one moves into a new apartment, there is typically an electricity carrier that provides a default (the carrier that was used by the previous tenant or the carrier that the landlord has chosen). The new tenants take no action, and the default is used.

Default heuristic: If a decision is set as the default, do not change it.

The default heuristic can explain a flurry of phenomena such as peoples' retirement plans and whether people are organ donors or not (Johnson & Goldstein 2003). Heuristics such as take-the-best can also be applied in a setting where the outcome does not only depend on the action of a decision maker but also on the behaviour of others involved, i.e. social settings. Garcia-Retamero & Dhami show that take-the-best captures the decision making of professional burglars in choosing which of two properties to rob. Among other things, they base their decision on social information such as whether the property is cared for (Garcia-Retamero & Dhami 2009).

Fast and frugal trees

An elderly man with chest pains is brought to hospital. The doctors have to decide under considerable time pressure whether the patient has low-risk ischemic heart disease and only needs regular care, or whether he is high risk and should be admitted to hospital. In such a situation, time, information, computational capacities are scarce, stakes are high, and yet doctors have to be accurate in their decisions. The fast and frugal heuristics research programme has provided some answers as to how professionals and laypeople make, or should make, accurate categorisations with limited resources, by using simple trees.

To model classification tasks one can use trees. A way to solve such a tree would involve Bayes' rule where n is the number of binary cues and the number of leaves is 2^n yet, as the number of cues grows, a fully-fledged tree becomes quickly computationally intractable or error prone as one has too little data to estimate the many possible leaves. A fast and frugal tree has only $n+1$ leaves which makes it tractable and more robust (Martignon *et al.* 2008). For example, Figure 10.1 shows such a tree for the ischemic heart-disease problem (Green & Mehr 1997).

Fast and frugal trees are 'minimal' in the sense of using the fewest number of question nodes and still involve all available cues, one at a time. They specify

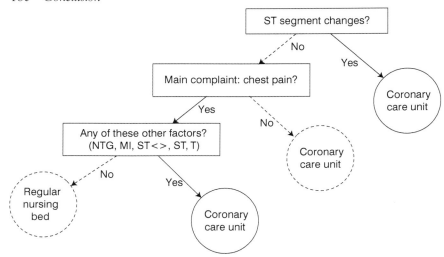

Figure 10.1 Fast and frugal tree for coronary care unit allocation

Adapted from Green and Mehr (1997)

how information is searched for, how the search is stopped, and how a decision is taken based on the obtained information. For example, a physician using the tree in Figure 10.1 first looks up the ST segment, then the chest pain, and finally other symptoms (Bandura 1977). Martignon *et al.* (2008) tested the accuracy of fast and frugal trees for 30 classification problems such as medicine, sports, and economics against a number of complex decision strategies. They report that logistic regression performs best in data fitting but in prediction, fast and frugal trees are close or identical to the best performing complex strategy.

Discussion on future research

The dominant paradigms for analysing decision making have been the research programmes dealing with cognitive limitations and optimisation under constraints. Yet, these assume that decisions taken are often only second best. Moreover, if there is a trade-off between information search and accuracy, people would be doomed to make sub-optimal decisions. Indeed, householders typically do not understand how or when environmental impacts occur, and even if they do, it is difficult for them to act upon them in daily life. However, there is an alternative to understand how householders make their decision, for example, to bring their own bag to the supermarket: fast and frugal heuristics. They correspond to natural intuitions, but they can have the accuracy of fancy statistical models (Gigerenzer & Kurzenhauser 2005). This line of research therefore invites a new approach for intervention policies in order to improve pro-environmental behaviour.

Pro-environmental decisions are often made under substantive uncertainty. Typically, environmental issues are characterised by complex causal processes (Pawlik 1991), leading to a general underestimation of distant and future risks on a large part of the population (Gifford *et al.* 2009). Slimak and Dietz (2006) surveyed risk professionals and the general public to find their ratings of 24 environmental threats. Overall, the public responded more to threats that were of low probability but high consequence whereas risk professionals responded to threats that were probable but had incremental impact. Even experts, whose work is based on science, must always cope with uncertainties when involved in decisions where not all the factors are necessarily knowable to them. Post-normal science argues that there must be an extended peer community consisting of all those affected by an issue (e.g. environmental accident) who are prepared to enter into dialogue on it as an extension of the franchise of science (Funtowicz & Ravetz 1992). Not surprisingly, a greater threat is perceived when people are aware of a risk and perceive the associated consequences as severe.

Yet, discussions of risk are about more than information; they also include a subtext about difficulties, social control, and motivations. Kaiser *et al.* describe pro-environmental behaviour using the Campbell paradigm, where engagement in a specific behaviour is a function of (i) the difficulty of behaviour and, (ii) his/ her motivation to support environmental policies (Kaiser *et al.* 2010); where (i) is a result of the context-situation and, (ii) is likely to be linked to environmental knowledge and appreciation of nature. This must be taken into account when investigating people's actual decision making but also when deriving normative solutions for how people should behave. We have outlined that in situations with uncertainty, heuristics can in fact perform at least as well or even outperform rational choice, the benchmark used by the research programmes of cognitive limitations and optimisation under constraints. This suggests that it is important to consider the domain under investigation and whether the applied programme is suitable. The fast and frugal research programme has quickly gained prominence over the last 15 years in a number of domains. This provides an extensive base on which researchers that seek to encourage pro-environmental behaviour can readily access.

According to Katsikopoulos (in press), there exist two distinct cultures of research on bounded rationality, the idealistic and the pragmatic, and they lead to two very different approaches to economic theory and policy. The empirical part of the idealistic story is that people systematically behave irrationally, which has also been suggested by Thaler and Sunstein (2009). They advocate 'nudging' people by setting up a choice architecture which alters people's behaviour in a predictable way in order to improve their lives. They stress that protecting the environment cannot only be achieved by government intervention as many regulatory efforts have been costly and wasteful but that it is necessary to build on an understanding of human decision making and how to shape it. Setting defaults such as for green or grey energy is an important element in this context. At the same time, Thaler argues that '*our ability to de-bias people is quite limited*' (Bond 2009) suggesting that people's ability to learn and reason frequently leads to the choice of the second best option even if they had the opportunity to learn.

As a result, this idealistic approach differs from the pragmatic approach which focuses on the impact of providing people with tools for boosting performance on tasks of practical importance. In other words, the main argument of the pragmatic approach is that people can indeed learn to behave rationally, which makes education its focal point. This highlights that the conventional normative standards we use to judge behaviour might not always fit. In contrast, the review above suggests that this is not necessarily the case, rather if behaviour has had the chance to adapt to a fundamentally uncertain environment, it performs in fact very well. Identifying the decision process people use may thus aid what has been labelled 'intuitive design' in the fast and frugal research programme where social engineering improves decision making. Engineering has provided us with many advances increasing technology efficiency and freeing up money and time. Yet, it has been found that increased efficiency does not by itself necessarily lead to pro-environmental behaviour. Individuals are motivated to reinvest their initial efficiency gains (time and money) on further consumption to maximise their personal efficiency. Resource use was diminished due to increased efficiency in one area, at the same time this gave rise to more consumption in another area eroding the initial savings, leading to the so called rebound effect (Sorrell & Dimitropoulos 2008). Otto *et al.* (in press) argue that extrinsic enticements (e.g. financial incentives, social pressure, social status) despite successfully promoting efficient technology, indirectly contribute to the rebound problem rather than to its effective solution (Otto *et al.* in press). Next to appreciation for nature, pro-environmental information seems promising to amend these subsequent actions. Yet, this information should be provided without overwhelming the individual and should be linked to a credible source (Bortoleto *et al.* 2012).

Given the significance and complexity of environmental impacts and the fact that many of them are due to human behaviour, it is important to study how ordinary people understand and evaluate such impacts. A lot of research has been done about the way people conceptualise environmental problems, but not much on the consequences of these perceptions for actual decisions on pro-environmental behaviour. Most, if not all, environmental problems before the most recent trends of climate change were rather well defined in terms of what a consumer or citizen could do to help solve it. For instance, to help saving the ozone layer, a consumer simply needed to buy CFC-free fridges and spray cans, which at that time were sufficiently labelled. But in order to help tackle climate change on the individual level, a person will have to reduce his/her greenhouse gas emissions. Hence, apart from a general intrinsic motivation to reduce one's overall emissions, a person has to know which alternative behaviour or product has a lower carbon emission. Such decisions are extremely complex and, even lifecycle studies can only give approximations of the CO_2 impacts for certain products or behaviours (Jungbluth *et al.* 2000). Again, even if risk perceptions are not a surrogate for motivation to engage, what people know about environmental impacts is likely to affect which behavioural options they take into consideration and which they consider to be environmentally friendly or harmful.

Since environmental problems entail such complex processes and substantial controversy in the media, we can expect people to have knowledge gaps or misconceptions. Denial still also remains as a wall for both social and natural scientists since behaviour change cannot occur as long as the problem is not seen as a problem by people. It functions as a justification for inaction or postponed action giving sufficient reason to act in favour of self-interests rather than for the environment. However, any attempt to apply a psychological approach to issues such as pro-environmental behaviour needs to confront the problem of how far societal phenomena can be explained by theories developed primarily to account for how people think and act as individuals. It may be unproductive to simply import the theoretical idea that people exhibit biased and irrational behaviours and thus the only solution is to nudge them. Instead, the conditions under which people make for or against environmental choices should be uncovered empirically and it should be considered how people can be educated.

Future research on waste prevention behaviour needs a renewal of the quest for theoretical principles of broad applicability. To understand the decision process of engaging in waste prevention behaviour, it is necessary to consider both the mind and the immediate social and non-social context/environment individuals act in. Promotion of any pro-environmental behaviour must be true to the science and to the decisions that ordinary individuals face. It must focus on the information most relevant to their decisions and present it in a way comparable with decision makers' information-processing strengths and weaknesses (Bostrom & Fischhoff 2001). Doing so requires an empirical understanding of the decision processes that people bring to this issue. In case of waste prevention behaviour, much research is still needed to find these significant links.

References

Abrahamse, W., Steg, L., Vlek, C., & Rothengatter, T. (2005). A review of intervention studies aimed at household energy conservation. *Journal of Environmental Psychology*, 25, 273–291.

Anderson, J. R. (1991). The adaptive nature of human categorization. *Psychological Review*, 98(3), 409–429.

Andersson, P., & Rakow, T. (2007). Now you see it now you don't: The effectiveness of the recognition heuristic for selecting stocks. *Judgment and Decision Making*, 2(1), 29–39.

Artinger, F., Fleischhut, N., Levati, V. M., & Stevens, J. R. (2012). Cooperation in Risky Environments: Decisions from Experience in a Stochastic Social Dilemma. In N. Miyake, D. Peebles, & R. P. Cooper (Eds.), *Proceedings of the 34th Annual Conference of the Cognitive Science Society*. Austin, TX: Cognitive Science Society.

Bandura, A. (1977). Self-efficacy: Toward a unifying theory of behavioral change. *Psychological Review*, 84(2), 191–215.

Baucells, M., Carrasco, J. A., & Hogarth, R. M. (2008). Cumulative dominance and heuristic performance in binary multiattribute choice. *Operations Research*, 56(5), 1289–1304.

Belch, G. E. (1982). The effects of television commercial repetition on cognitive response and message acceptance. *Journal of Consumer Research*, 9, 56–65.

Benartzi, S., & Thaler, R. H. (2001). Naive diversification strategies in defined contribution saving plans. *American Economic Review*, 91, 79–98.

Bond, M. (2009). Decision-making: Risk school. *Nature News*, 461(7268), 1189–1192.

Bord, R. J., O'Connor, R. E., & Fisher, A. (2000). In what sense does the public need to understand global climate change? *Public Understanding of Science, 9*(3), 205–218.

Bortoleto, A. P., Kurisu, K., & Hanaki, K. (2012). Model development for household waste prevention behaviour. *Waste Management, 32*(12), 2195–2207.

Bostrom, A., & Fischhoff, B. (2001). Communicating health risks of global climate change. In G. Böhm, J. Nerb, T. McDaniels, & H. Spada (Eds.), *Environmental risks: Perception, evaluation and management* (pp. 31–56). Amsterdam: JAI.

Boykoff, M. T., & Boykoff, J. M. (2004). Balance as bias: global warming and the US prestige press. *Global Environmental Change, 14*, 125–136.

Brandstatter, E., Gigerenzer, G., & Hertwig, R. (2006). The priority heuristic: Making choices without trade-offs. *Psychological Review, 113*(2), 409–432.

Bröder, A., & Newell, B. R. (2008). Challenging some common beliefs: Empirical work within the adaptive toolbox metaphor. *Judgment and Decision Making, 3*(3), 205–214.

Burke, M. C., & Edell, J. A. (1986). Ad reactions over time: Capturing changes over time. *Journal of Consumer Research, 13*, 114–118.

Christakis, N. A., & Fowler, J. H. (2007). The spread of obesity in a large social network over 32 years. *The New England Journal of Medicine, 357*(4), 370–379.

Czerlinski, J., Gigerenzer, G., & Goldstein, D. (1999). How good are simple heuristics? In G. Gigerenzer, P. Todd, & ABC Research Group (Eds.), *Simple heuristics that make us smart* (pp. 97–118). New York: Oxford University Press.

Dawes, R. M. (1979). The robust beauty of improper linear models in decision making. *American Psychologist, 34*(7), 571–582.

Dawes, R. M., & Corrigan, B. (1974). Linear models in decision making. *Psychological Bulletin, 81*(2), 95–106.

de Kwaadsteniet, E. W. (2007). *Uncertainty in social dilemmas* (Unpublished doctoral dissertation), Leiden University, The Netherlands.

DeMiguel, V., Garlappi, L., & Uppal, R. (2009). Optimal versus naive diversification: How inefficient is the 1/N portfolio strategy? *Review Of Financial Studies, 22*(5), 1915–1953.

Einhorn, H. J., & Hogarth, R. M. (1975). Unit weighting schemes for decision making. *Organizational Behavior and Human Performance, 13*(2), 171–192.

Ford, J. K., Schmitt, N., Schechtman, S. L., Hults, B. M., & Doherty, M. L. (1989). Process tracing methods: Contributions, problems, and neglected research questions. *Organizational Behavior and Human Decision Processes, 43*(1), 75–117.

Funtowicz, S. O., & Ravetz, J. R. (1992). Three types of risk assessment and the emergence of post-normal science. In S. Krimsky & D. Golding (Eds.) *Social theories of risk.* Westport, CT: Praeger.

Galesic, M., & Garcia-Retamero, R. (2012). The risks we dread: A social circle account. *Public Library of Science, 7*(4), e32837.

Gambetta, D., & Hamill, H. (2005). *Streetwise: How taxi drivers establish their customers' trustworthiness.* New York: Russell Sage Foundation.

Garcia-Retamero, R., & Dhami, M. (2009). Take-the-best in expert-novice decision strategies for residential burglary. *Psychonomic Bulletin & Review, 16*(1), 163–169.

Gifford, R. (2011). The dragons of inaction: Psychological barriers that limit climate change mitigation and adaptation. *American Psychologist, 66*(4), 290.

Gifford, R., Scannell, L., Kormos, C., Smolova, L., Biel, A., Boncu, S., Corral, V., Hanyu, K, Hine, D. W., Kaiser, F. G., Korpela, K., Lima, L., Mertig, A. G., Garcia Mira, R., Moser, G., Passafaro, P., Pinheiro, J. Q., Saini, S., Sako, T., Sautkina, E., Savina, Y., Schmuck, P., Schultz, P. W., Sobeck, K., Sundblad, K., & Uzzell, D. (2009). Temporal pessimism and spatial optimism in environmental assessments: An 18-nation study. *Journal of Environmental Psychology, 29,* 1–12.

Gigerenzer, G., & Brighton, H. (2009). Homo heuristicus: Why biased minds make better inferences. *Topics in Cognitive Science, 1*(1), 107–143.

Gigerenzer, G., & Goldstein, D. G. (1996). Reasoning the fast and frugal way: Models of bounded rationality. *Psychological Review, 103*(4), 650–669.

Gigerenzer, G., & Kurzenhauser, S. (2005). Fast and frugal heuristics in medical decision making. In R. Bibace,K. L. Laird, & J. Valsiner (Eds.), *Science and medicine in dialogue*. Westport, CT: Praeger.

Gigerenzer, G., Mata, J., & Frank, R. (2009). Public knowledge of benefits of breast and prostate cancer screening in Europe. *Journal of the National Cancer Institute, 101,* 1216–1220.

Gigerenzer, G., & Selten, R. (2002). *Bounded rationality: The adaptive toolbox*. Cambridge, MA: MIT Press.

Gigerenzer, G., Todd, P. M., & the ABC Research Group. (1999). *Simple heuristics that make us smart*. Oxford: Oxford University Press.

Goldstein, N. J., Cialdini, R. B., & Griskevicius, V. (2008). A room with a viewpoint: Using social norms to motivate environmental conservation in hotels. *Journal of Consumer Research, 35*(3), 472–482.

Goldstein, D. G., & Gigerenzer, G. (2002). Models of ecological rationality: The recognition heuristic. *Psychological Review, 109*(1), 75–90.

Green, L., & Mehr, D. (1997). What alters physicians' decisions to admit to the coronary care unit? *Journal of Family Practice, 45*(3), 219–226.

Hastie, T., Tibshirani, R., & Friedman, J. H. (2003). *The elements of statistical learning*. New York: Springer.

Hertwig, R., & Erev, I. (2009). The description-experience gap in risky choice. *Trends in Cognitive Sciences, 13*(12), 517–523.

Hertwig, R., Hoffrage, U., & the ABC Research Group. (2012). *Simple heuristics in a social world*. New York: Oxford University Press.

Hoggan, J., & Littlemore, R. (2009). *Climate cover-up: The crusade to deny global warming*. Vancouver: Greystone Books.

Johnson, E. J., & Goldstein, D. (2003). Do defaults save lives? *Science, 302*(5649), 1338–1339.

Jungbluth, N., Tietje, O., & Scholz, R. (2000). Food purchases: Impacts from the consumers' point of view investigated with a modular LCA. *International Journal of Life Cycle Assessment, 5,* 134–142.

Kahneman, D., Slovic, P., & Tversky, A. (Eds.). (1982). *Judgment under uncertainty: Heuristics and biases* (1st ed.). Cambridge: Cambridge University Press.

Kaiser, F. G., Byrka, K., & Hartig, T. (2010). Reviving Campbell's paradigm for attitude research. *Personality and Social Psychology Review, 14*(4), 351–67.

Katsikopoulos, K. V. (2011). Psychological heuristics for making inferences: definition, performance, and the emerging theory and practice. *Decision Analysis, 8,* 10–29.

Katsikopoulos, K. V. (in press). Bounded rationality: The two cultures. *Journal of Economic Methodology*

Katsikopoulos, K. V., & Fasolo, B. (2006). New tools for decision analysts. *IEEE Transactions on Systems, Man and Cybernetics, Part A: Systems and Humans, 36*(5), 960–967.

Katsikopoulos, K. V., & Gigerenzer, G. (2008). One-reason decision-making: Modeling violations of expected utility theory. *Journal of Risk and Uncertainty, 37*(1), 35–56.

Katsikopoulos, K. V., & Martignon, L. (2006). Naïve heuristics for paired comparisons: Some results on their relative accuracy. *Journal of Mathematical Psychology, 50*(5), 488–494.

Kendal, R. L., Coolen, I., & Laland, K. N. (2009). Adaptive trade-offs in the use of social and personal information. In R. Dukas & J. Ratcliffe (Eds.), *Cognitive Ecology II* (pp. 249–271). Chicago, IL: University of Chicago Press.

Leiserowitz, A. A. (2005). American risk perceptions: Is climate change dangerous? *Risk Analysis, 25*(6), 1433–1442.

Lorenzoni, I., & Pidgeon, N. F. (2006). Public views on climate change: European and USA perspectives. *Climate Change, 77*, 73–95.

Martignon, L., & Hoffrage, U. (2002). Fast, frugal, and fit: Simple heuristics for paired comparison. *Theory and Decision, 52*(1), 29–71.

Martignon, L., Katsikopoulos, K. V., & Woike, J. K. (2008). Categorization with limited resources: A family of simple heuristics. *Journal of Mathematical Psychology, 52*(6), 352–361.

Meltzoff, A. N., & Moore, M. K. (1977). Imitation of facial and manual gestures by human neonates. *Science, 198*(4312), 75–78.

Ortmann, A., Gigerenzer, G., Borges, B., & Goldstein, D. G. (2008). The Recognition Heuristic: A Fast and Frugal Way to Investment Choice? In C. R. Plott & V. L. Smith (Eds.), *Handbook of Experimental Economics Results* (Volume 1, pp. 993–1003). Amsterdam: North-Holland.

Otto, S., Kaiser, F. G., & Arnold, O. (in press). The critical challenge of climate change for psychology: Preventing rebound and promoting more individual irrationality. *European Psychologist*.

Pachur, T., Bröder, A., & Marewski, J. N. (2008). The recognition heuristic in memory-based inference: is recognition a non-compensatory cue? *Journal of Behavioral Decision Making, 21*(2), 183–210.

Pachur, T., & Hertwig, R. (2006). On the psychology of the recognition heuristic: Retrieval primacy as a key determinant of its use. *Journal of Experimental Psychology: Learning, Memory, and Cognition, 32*(5), 983–1002.

Pawlik, K (1991). The psychology of environmental change: Some basic data and an agenda for cooperative international research. *International Journal of Psychology, 26*(5), 547–563.

Perlich, C., Provost, F., & Simonoff, J. S. (2003). Tree induction vs. logistic regression: A learning-curve analysis. *Journal of Machine Learning Research, 4*, 211–255.

Pichert, D., & Katsikopoulos, K. V. (2008). Green defaults: Information presentation and pro-environmental behaviour. *Journal of Environmental Psychology, 28*(1), 63–73.

Richerson, P. J., & Boyd, R. (2005). *Not by genes alone: How culture transformed human evolution*. Chicago, IL: University of Chicago Press.

Salganik, M. J., Dodds, P. S., & Watts, D. J. (2006). Experimental study of inequality and unpredictability in an artificial cultural market. *Science, 311*(5762), 854–856.

Sargent, T. J. (1993). *Bounded rationality in macroeconomics: The Arne Ryde memorial lectures*. New York: Oxford University Press.

Scheibehenne, B., & Bröder, A. (2007). Predicting Wimbledon 2005 tennis results by mere player name recognition. *International Journal of Forecasting, 23*(3), 415–426.

Schmidt, F. L. (1971). The relative efficiency of regression and simple unit predictor weights in applied differential psychology. *Educational and Psychological Measurement, 31*(3), 699–714.

Schultz, P. W. (2002). Knowledge, education, and household recycling: Examining the knowledge-deficit model of behavior change. In T. Dietz & P. Stern (Eds.). *New tools for environmental protection*. Washington DC: National Academy of Sciences,

Serwe, S., & Frings, C. (2006). Who will win Wimbledon? The recognition heuristic in predicting sports events. *Journal of Behavioral Decision Making, 19*(4), 321–332.

Simon, H. A. (1955). A behavioral model of rational choice. *Quarterly Journal of Economics, 69*, 99–118.

Simon, H. A. (1956). Rational choice and the structure of the environment. *Psychological Review, 63*, 129–138.

Slimak, M. W., & Dietz, T. (2006). Personal values, beliefs, and ecological risk perception. *Risk Analysis, 26*(6) 1689–1705.

Slovic, P. (1987). Perception of risk. *Science, 236*, 280–285.

Slovic, P., Fischhoff, B., & Lichtenstein, S. (1980). Facts and fears: Understanding perceived risk. In R. Schwing & W. A. Albers, Jr. (Eds.), *Societal risk assessment: How safe is safe enough?* New York: Plenum.

Sorrell, S. & Dimitropoulos, J. (2008). The rebound effect: Microeconomic definitions, limitations and extensions. *Ecological Economics, 65*, 636–649.

Spence, A., Poortinga, W., Butler, C., & Pidgeon, N. F. (2011). Perceptions of climate change and willingness to save energy related to flood experience. *Nature Climate Change, 1*, 46–49.

Stigler, G. J. (1961). The economics of information. *Journal of Political Economy, 69*(3), 213–225.

Thaler, R. H., & Sunstein, C. R. (2009). *Nudge: Improving decisions about health, wealth, and happiness* (Updated). London: Penguin.

Todd, P. M., Gigerenzer, G., & the ABC Research Group. (2012). *Ecological rationality: Intelligence in the world*. Oxford: Oxford University Press.

Tversky, A., & Kahneman, D. (1992). Advances in prospect theory: Cumulative representation of uncertainty. *Journal of Risk and Uncertainty, 5*(4), 297–323.

Watts, D. J. (2007). Is Justin Timberlake a product of cumulative advantage? *The New York Times Magazine*, April 15. Available at http://www.nytimes.com/2007/04/15/magazine/15wwlnidealab.t.html

11 Concluding thoughts

Throughout this book, I have discussed the different aspects of waste prevention issues and argued that they are mostly behavioural problems, caused by the collective actions of individuals and their underlying beliefs and values. Technological innovation, mitigation and adaptation, and regulations concerning, not only waste generation issues but also, the diversity of environmental impacts are interconnected by human actions. By framing environmental research as exclusive to natural and applied sciences, the scientific community helps people to distance themselves from these problems, as well as their responsibility for them. Looking at human behaviour is crucial for solving environmental degradation (e.g. waste generation issues). Thus, central to this entire discussion of waste prevention behaviour is the recurring principle of interconnection. Just as the ecosystem of our planet is based on interactive relationships, so should environmental research be as well. Sustainable development depends on interdisciplinary research and mostly on researchers open enough to effectively interact and cooperate (not only collaborate) with others from different areas of knowledge. Environmental research is enormously complex and no one discipline can capture everything. It may be easier to immediately focus on natural science to explain the processes behind environmental problems and, consequently, to rely on applied science to solve them. However, when looking into the cause of these problems a simple phrase echoes 'Based on the scientific evidence, I am convinced that we are facing anthropogenic climate change brought about by the emission of greenhouse gases into the atmosphere' (von Storch 2006). Acknowledging human action as a cause of environmental degradation means that social science plays an important role not only to explain but also to change human behaviour regarding the environment. I believe that only by fostering a truly interdisciplinary research atmosphere, i.e. where different areas of knowledge co-exist as a function of a problem and not of a theory, environmental researchers will be able to eventually help not only to decrease environmental impacts but also to shift human behaviour toward a sustainable society. The inaction will ensure that environmental research remains fragmented as usual, yet 'research as usual' is already leading to several published articles which make little contribution to promote further insights on how to achieve a sustainable society. It is imperative. We need to organise our researches around effective 'tools' and concentrate on their contribution and utility to sustainable development. Our planet does not care if we spend centuries debating the merits of each area of knowledge and nor which theory is better. While we discuss, the planet will continue to deteriorate, causing more severe flooding, earthquakes, tsunamis and extreme variations on weather. By recognising the interconnectedness of different disciplines on environmental research, the scientific community will offer an intellectual coherence to a discipline increasingly fragmented by diverse competitive theories and by the great challenge of human behaviour.

Developing an effective waste prevention programme

Each of the different perspectives discussed on this book about waste prevention issues provides some understanding of the basis of waste prevention behaviour, and offers important insights to the development of an effective waste prevention programme. Waste generation issues can be attributed at least in part to our individualistic society which emphasises individual human beings' pursuit of wealth and happiness, and encourages the unrestricted consumption of products to achieve personal gain. Economists use the term depreciation to describe how high-quality products purchased from stores lose their value when transferred to the individual's property. In other words, a product enters the individual's home as a high-value object and leaves it as waste. Zygmunt Bauman (2013) affirms that 'principal among the consumerist ways of dealing with disaffection is disposal of the objects causing disaffection'. The value or lack of value that individuals assign to products/waste is essentially subjective and it is shown by the high rate of waste generation in most cities. Currently, our society devalues durability, associating old with outdated, unfit and destined for the waste bin. And it implies to individuals that a certain product, despite the fact that it is still well conserved and undamaged, is no longer good enough for them and stimulates their desire to buy a new (but not really improved) version of the same product. Nick Gregson, in her book *Living with Things* (2007), says 'At one level, the presence (and absence) of these objects in our homes enables the narration of the self we wish to be seen to be'. Disposability also involves the ideal of cleanliness without considerable effort or hired help, and became a selling point for disposable products. The definition of waste depends on consumption patterns and the sorting process that creates waste in the first place. It varies from person to person and it is more complex than the simplistic categorisation of waste (e.g. organic waste, plastic waste) usually implies. The categories of waste are related to the objects we use and throw out which are fluid and socially defined, as they move in and out of these classifications. Waste prevention deals with products and not with waste, since prevention means avoiding the existence of waste. Some individuals keep things because they are particularly sentimental or especially frugal, and some cultures value saving things more than others. Some groups have developed practices for reusing objects (e.g. waste pickers). As shown in Chapter 7, age matters too. Older people are more likely to preserve since new is normal for the young. These facts lead to the over-riding conclusion that only by looking into human behaviour and its relation to waste that waste prevention programmes will have the lasting and profound impact on waste generation that is so obviously needed.

Having presented the importance of social understanding of waste generation problems, there is also the issue of how to change householders' attitudes and behaviours towards waste prevention. This book has presented a lengthy analysis through two distinct (yet complementary) studies based on the understanding of waste prevention behaviour influences (Chapter 7) and construction (Chapter 8). There are two topics requiring further comments than those made in their respective chapters. The first refers to the altruistic nature of waste prevention behaviour (or any pro-environmental behaviour per se). Great interest has been devoted within psychological literature to altruism and pro-environmental behaviour. Altruistic individuals are characterised by intrinsic motivation which induces them to forgo commodities, convenience, and personal advantages for the collective good (Otto *et al.* in press), for instance, environmental protection. Jon Elster (2007) defines altruistic motivation as 'the desire to enhance the welfare of others even at a net welfare loss to oneself' and an altruistic action as 'an action for which an altruistic motivation provides a sufficient reason'. According to him, it is not possible to infer the existence of altruistic motivations from altruistic behaviour, simply because other motivations may mimic altruism. However, Kaiser *et al.* (2010), in their definition of the Campbell Paradigm, argue that an attitude can be defined by carving out a set of behaviours which is thought to represent the means people can use when implementing their personal levels of an attitude. Thus, an altruistic behaviour is not only dependent on altruistic motivation but also on the set of behaviours and their structure. In other words, a person's intrinsic motivation to protect the environment (e.g. reduce her/his waste generation) can be inferred directly from her/his lifestyle. That is why householders, who engage in waste prevention behaviour, often put their own interests aside to do what is best for the community (e.g. less consumption). Indeed, the studies presented in Chapter 7 support Schwartz's model of altruistic behaviour showing the direct influence of internalised norms on waste prevention behaviour. Van der Werff *et al.* (2013) argue that pro-environmental self-identity is related to one's obligation-based intrinsic motivation (i.e. feelings of moral obligation) to act pro-environmentally, which in turn affects pro-environmental actions. This means that the obligation-based intrinsic motivation mediates the relationship between environmental self-identity and pro-environmental behaviour. Essentially, individuals who engage in waste prevention differ from recyclers in terms of motivation levels and behaviour difficulties. While both intrinsic and extrinsic motivations may encourage recycling, mainly intrinsic motivations are relevant in waste prevention. Chapter 8 makes this fact plain by showing that recycling (GEB 14) is an easy task when compared to waste prevention (GEB 12) in both São Paulo and Sheffield. In addition, Abbott *et al.* (2013) argues that intrinsic motivation detached from strictly economic incentives may well support waste reduction behaviour. Therefore, waste prevention policies should not rely on economic incentives or social status but instead should enforce altruistic behaviour. One example is the voluntary simplicity movement[1] in which people have voluntarily chosen to downscale their material possessions in order to live without 'being distracted by consumer culture'. This movement teaches different methods, so that people learn to appreciate and experience more from less. Some studies have shown that this movement is enhancing pro-environmental behaviours and decreasing impulsive buying and energy consumption (Alexander & Ussher 2012). Voluntary simplicity implies the principle of responsible consumption, which is, not only reducing how much one consumes, but choosing environmentally friendly products whenever possible. And, for that, comes the second point for this section, contextual factors.

In fact, one of the biggest challenges regarding waste prevention programmes is how far legislation or policy guidelines may or may not go. Skinner *et al.* (1977) extensively argued that what people do is largely shaped by the previous consequences of their behaviour. Context-specific constraints can make it difficult (costly, inconvenient) for individuals to act pro-environmentally, a critical problem not only for waste prevention but for any environmental policy. Lejano and Fernandez de Castro (2013) argue that society is ridden with institutions that prevent individuals from action upon intrinsic norms of fairness and empathy. Because of that, behaviourists[2] argue that stimulus control[3] helps illuminate the reinforcement contingencies[4] that signal and perpetrate environmentally harmful behaviour. In other words, contextual factors when manipulated correctly can also increase pro-environmental engagement, even if not increase intrinsic motivation to act. Axsen *et al.* (2013) found that individuals' perceptions change in part through social negotiation of meaning, lifestyle and identity. And neglecting the social influence processes underestimates the potential for shifts in consumer preferences regarding emerging pro-environmental technologies. This statement highlights the necessity for policy makers at all levels of government to construct new public policies that effectively initiate and sustain collective waste prevention behaviour on the individual level, and in a long-term perspective. This challenge requires not only technical aspects (e.g. product design, infrastructure) but also policy legitimacy. In its most basic definition, policy legitimacy refers to the individual's perception of policy goals as morally acceptable in the sense that they build on or can be justified by reference to pro-environmental core values and beliefs established in society (Berglund & Matti 2006). Any attempt to ensure public compliance with a waste prevention policy's requirements will become less successful as the degree of legitimacy for the policy decreases. In their study, Berglund and Matti (2006), suggested that contextual factors: *'are perceived as highly relevant for the promotion of pro-environmental behaviour, however, respondents tend to ascribe far greater importance to the motivational values included in the self-transcendence cluster (altruism) as guiding principles in life than to the opposing values of self-enhancement (egoism)'*. They concluded that this mismatch between the content of Sweden's pro-environmental policy and the general value orientation held by the Swedish population is affecting its performance and obstructing its possibilities for success.

Therefore, an effective waste prevention programme is a joint effort in many areas of scientific knowledge. Policy makers need to consider the citizen-role in policy design. Engineers need to focus on product design and infrastructure availability to easily promote waste prevention behaviour. Sociologists need to comprehend the movements of waste and its definition in our society. Economists need to give our society a sustainable economic system oppose to this current consumption model, and psychologists need to offer effective tools to promote behavioural change. But most of all, all these experts need to communicate in a single language, enhancing the connection between these different scientific fields, so waste prevention policies can be effective in changing human behaviour and, consequently, contributing to a sustainable society.

What relies ahead? The importance of knowledge

According to Gerd Gigerenzer (2013), literacy is 'the precondition for an informed citizenship in a participatory democracy'. As indicated in Chapter 5, information is not necessary knowledge. In fact, one of the biggest challenges individuals have regarding environmental issues is information overload and confusion. Pro-environmental behaviours are often undertaken with less than optimal results because their quantitative dimensions get easily lost. Consider the follow statement: *'between 21% and 40% (by weight) of municipal solid waste in South African cities is organic, increasing to up to 45% if you include paper and cardboard. If the soil component of this waste is included, more than half the waste sent to landfill could be used as a growing media for plants'* (Full Circle 2009).

Can you infer correctly the size of the problem and what do these numbers mean? Is 21 per cent too much waste? And how relevant is South Africa as an example? Most of the waste prevention programmes are based on informational campaigns with numbers and statistical information which are very difficult for individuals to relate to and, more importantly, they do not increase the individual's knowledge of the problem. Irrelevant information on policy campaigns can even cause reasoning difficulties and obstruct the desire to act. In some cases, adding more information (or options) may prevent the agent from making any decision at all (Elster 2007). With more information, which is mostly irrelevant, it is more difficult to affirm that 'this is the best'. And those who need to base their choice on sufficient reasons to act favourably towards environmental protection will abstain from acting. Additionally, irrelevant information can contribute to confirming bias[5] and regression toward the mean[6], in which individuals easily misinterpret actions as causing something that, is happening purely by chance. Yet, when considering how to deal with waste generation issues and enforce waste prevention behaviours, policy makers usually miss a decisive point: helping the population to better understand environmental problems. Gigerenzer (2012) defines risk literacy as the ability to deal with uncertainties in an informed way, and this can be achieved by cultivating statistical thinking. That links with what was discussed in

Chapter 5 and also was also demonstrated by Roczen *et al.* (2013), which suggests that competence formation, knowledge and experience in nature would form a strong base, in a way that the necessity of acting in the sense of conservation is recognised. Experiences in nature contribute greatly to emotional, physical, cognitive, psychological and social aspects of individuals, and consequently, the formation of a pro-environmental self often depends on experiences of nature, especially during childhood (Clayton & Opotow 2003). Strengthening pro-environmental self-identity may be an effective tool to promote waste prevention policies, as individuals with strong pro-environmental self-identity are likely to act in an environmentally friendly way without an external incentive to do so (Van der Werff *et al.* 2013). In their study, Levin and Unsworth (2013) found that children growing up in urban communities in the USA may be receiving cultural input in which they are losing an association between humans and nature when thinking about personal ways to the natural world. This means, that individuals in urban cities are less likely to think about themselves as part of nature compared with those whose culture and rural contexts strongly influence this perception.

Knowledge is not only important to motivate individuals to engage in pro-environmental behaviour. As a researcher in the field of lifecycle analysis, I have encountered many waste experts and policy makers who were unable to correctly infer the impacts of the policies and programmes that were implemented in their companies or cities. There is clearly a gap in the available knowledge and how exactly environmental impact should be measured. Carbon footprint is a popular concept that is mostly misused. Many website calculators and non-scientific reports have been abusing this concept by defining very restrictive boundaries for the measurement of greenhouse gas emissions, aggravated by the confusion of direct and indirect emissions. Take for example the environmental impacts of a notepad. According to its carbon footprint, it comes from its production/delivery, further usage and disposal. However, its impacts also come from its raw materials (e.g. cellulose) extraction, transport and production (e.g. paper) and other stages of its life cycle. Essentially, carbon footprint only traces the greenhouse gas emissions from two levels of the product's life: production/delivery and consumption/disposal. Unfortunately, many waste managers and experts have applied this tool simply because of their lack of knowledge (and understanding) in how to deal with uncertainty and risk. Lifecycle assessment (LCA) is much more than a simple accounting exercise. It is an attempt to quantify the complete environmental impact of a product/service from cradle-to-cradle (McDonough & Braungart 2002). Because of this complexity, managers, NGOs, regulators and even consumers have generally embraced simplistic measurements on a small set of environmental performance criteria across a small number of processes in the supply chain (Faruk *et al.* 2001). And, the consequence of using simple tools to measure environmental impacts is critical. Many cities are implementing kerbside recycling collection schemes without accounting for the indirect emissions from the production of the collection vehicle and its raw materials, fuel extraction, production and transport to the fuel station, the maintenance of the vehicle, and the use of recycled material as a secondary raw material.

Of course, there are more indirect emissions to account for, particularly those originating from the generation of products that would not be produced if there were no secondary raw materials available. Inferring only direct emissions makes it environmentally acceptable to run a kerbside collection two or three times a week. On the other hand, which indirect emissions are worthy of consideration? LCA's increased scientific understanding of the interaction between supply chains, product use, service consumption and the natural environment has often failed to resolve difficult uncertainties. The number of processes and raw materials to account for continues to grow, and efforts to weigh and integrate them are complex and open to controversy. However, these situations could, at least, be alleviated if those making the decisions had the knowledge to infer correctly environmental risks and their impacts. The importance of educating experts and professionals is also highlighted by Konstantinos Katsikopoulos in his discourse about the pragmatic culture. In his words, pragmatic culture focuses 'on the impact of providing people with tools for boosting performance on tasks of practical importance'(Katsikopoulos in press). The pragmatic culture is centred on education which means that people can indeed learn to behave rationally.

Final words

Consider this message: 'Be green, recycle more'. It seems a reasonable message and true in the sense that we should do something with those recyclable materials in our houses. Unfortunately, recycling is not saving the Earth as the message implies. There are just a few environmental benefits of recycling, particularly since it is a slim fraction of the overall waste stream. The problem is mostly due to the fact that recycling schemes divert the focus of environmental concern away from the unsustainability of the current economic system. Householders are usually unanimous and concerned about environmental problems, as well as enthusiastic and active about largely meaningless solutions. Recyclers are mostly extrinsically motivated and recycling gave them the right to keep consuming and discarding. I am not advocating the end of recycling, but the beginning of the real waste prevention era. Most of us do not understand the real impacts of consumption. In 2010, the 27 EU member states produced roughly 219 million tonnes of household waste which additionally generated 672 million tonnes of mining waste, 276 million tonnes of manufacturing waste, 87 million of waste related to energy, and 39 million tonnes from agriculture, forestry and fishing.[7] There is a discrepancy between how much waste a householder produces and the amount of waste that is generated to produce household waste. William McDonough said once that 'what most people see in their waste bins is just the tip of a material iceberg; the product itself contains on average only 5 per cent of the raw materials involved in the manufacturing and delivering processes' (McDonough & Braungart 2002). Waste management technology is still necessary and needs to be improved; however, it will not cure the problem. On the contrary, it tends to legitimate the generation of waste. While recycling can avoid some use of raw materials, waste prevention (i.e. less consumption, ecological product design) is far better. We do not need better ways to treat and to dispose of our waste. We do not need to throw things away, and instead reuse, repair or recycle them or even better, not consume them in the first place. Consumption needs to be responsible. Not only do consumers need to buy less but also demand goods that are more durable, less toxic, able to be reused or recycled, and easily to be returned to the manufacturers. In other words, we need to consume better and manufacturers need to produce more efficient products. Zygmunt Bauman[8] argues we already have – thanks to technology, development, skills, and the efficiency of our work – enough resources to satisfy all human needs. But we don't have enough resources, and we are unlikely ever to have, to satisfy human greed.

Notes

1 For more information see: The Simplicity Collective at http://simplicitycollective. com/; Simplicity Institute at http://simplicityinstitute.org/publications and San Diego Voluntary Simplicity Group at http://www.simplesandiego.org/index.html.
2 Behaviourism is an approach to the study of psychology that concentrates exclusively on observing, measuring and modifying behaviour.
3 Stimulus control is said to occur when an organism behaves in one way in the presence of a given stimulus and another way in its absence.
4 Contingencies of reinforcement describe an antecedent-behavior-consequence link in which the consequence increases the likelihood that a behavior will occur again in the presence of an antecedent.
5 Confirmation bias is the tendency of people to favour information that confirms their beliefs or hypotheses.
6 Regression toward (or to) the mean is the phenomenon that if a variable is extreme on its first measurement, it will tend to be closer to the average on its second measurement—and, paradoxically, if it is extreme on its second measurement, it will tend to have been closer to the average on its first.
7 More information at "Waste statistics" – Statistics Explained (2014/3/4) http://epp. eurostat.ec.europa.eu/statistics_explained/index.php/Waste_statistics.
8 Zygmunt Bauman is Emeritus Professor at the University of Leeds and one of Europe's foremost sociologists. He is the author of Liquid Modernity'(Polity 2000) and many other books on contemporary society.

References

Abbott, A., Nandeibam, S., & O'Shea, L. (2013). Recycling: Social norms and warm-glow revisited. Ecological Economics, 90, 10–18.
Alexander, S., & Ussher, S. (2012). The voluntary simplicity movement: A multi-national survey analysis in theoretical context. Journal of Consumer Culture, 12(1), 66–86.
Axsen, J., Orlebar, C., & Skippon, S. (2013). Social influence and consumer preference formation for pro-environmental technology: The case of a UK workplace electric-vehicle study. Ecological Economics, 95, 96–107.
Bauman, Z. (2013). Consuming life. Hoboken, NJ: John Wiley & Sons.
Berglund, C., & Matti, S. (2006). Citizen and consumer: The dual role of individuals in environmental policy. Environmental politics, 15(4), 550–571.
Clayton, S. D., & Opotow, S. (Eds.). (2003). Identity and the natural environment: The psychological significance of nature. Cambridge, MA: MIT Press.

Elster, J. (2007). *Explaining social behavior: More nuts and bolts for the social sciences.* Cambridge: Cambridge University Press.

Faruk, A. C., Lamming, R. C., Cousins, P. D., & Bowen, F. E. (2001), Analyzing, mapping, and managing environmental impacts along supply chains. *Journal of Industrial Ecology,* 5: 13–36.

Full Circle. (2009). What is waste and why is it a problem? Retrieved from http://www.fullcycle.co.za/index.php/what-is-waste-and-why-is-it-a-problem.html.

Gigerenzer, G. (2012). Risk literacy. In J. Brockman, J. (Ed.) *This will make you smarter* (pp. 259–261). New York: HarperCollins.

Gigerenzer, G. (2013). How I got started teaching physicians and judges risk literacy. *Applied Cognitive Psychology.* Published online: 27 Nov 2013, doi:10.1002/acp.2980

Gregson, N. (2007). *Living with things: Ridding, accommodation, dwelling* (Vol. 2). Canon Pyon, Herts, UK:Sean Kingston.

Kaiser, F. G., Byrka, K., & Hartig, T. (2010). Reviving Campbell's paradigm for attitude research. *Personality and Social Psychology Review: An Official Journal of the Society for Personality and Social Psychology, Inc., 14*(4), 351–67.

Katsikopoulos, K. V. (in press). Bounded rationality: The two cultures. *Journal of Economic Methodology.*

Lejano, R. P., & Fernandez de Castro, F. (2013). Norm, network, and commons: The invisible hand of community. *Environmental Science & Policy, 36,* 73–85.

Levin, W. E., & Unsworth, S. J. (2013). Do humans belong with nature? The influence of personal vs. abstract contexts on human–nature categorization at different stages of development. *Journal of Environmental Psychology, 33,* 9–13.

McDonough, W., & Braungart, M. (2010). *Cradle to cradle: Remaking the way we make things.* Basingstoke: Macmillan.

Otto, S., Kaiser, F. G., & Arnold, O. (in press). The critical challenge of climate change for psychology: Preventing rebound and promoting more individual irrationality. *European Psychologist.*

Roczen, N., Kaiser, F. G., Bogner, F. X., & Wilson, M. (2013). A competence model for environmental education. *Environment and Behavior.* doi: 0013916513492416.

Skinner, B. F., Ferster, C. B., & Ferster, C. B. (1977). *Schedules of reinforcement.* Acton, MA: Copley Publishing Group.

Storch, H. von (2006). Statement to the U.S. House of Representatives Committee on Energy and Commerce, July 19, 2006 Hearing 'Questions Surrounding the 'Hockey Stick' Temperature Studies: Implications for Climate Change Assessments'. Retrieved from http://cstpr.colorado.edu/prometheus/archives/060619_ushouse_energycommercehvs.pdf.

Van der Werff, E., Steg, L., & Keizer, K. (2013). It is a moral issue: The relationship between environmental self-identity, obligation-based intrinsic motivation and pro-environmental behaviour. *Global Environmental Change, 23*(5), 1258–1265.

Index